WISCONSIN WRITERS
Sketches and Studies

WISCONSIN WRITERS

Sketches and Studies

By
WILLIAM A. TITUS

Chicago
1930

Copyrighted, 1930
By
W. A. Titus
Fond du Lac, Wisconsin
All Rights Reserved
Printed in U. S. A.

WISCONSIN WRITERS
Sketches and Studies

PREFACE

WISCONSIN does not claim first place among the states in either the quantity or the quality of its literary productions. Nevertheless, during the comparatively brief period since it became one of the states, many books of exceptional merit have come from the pens of writers whose homes are or were formerly in Wisconsin.

Like the people of this State, its literature is serious and uplifting. In the field of fiction we recall very few books of the sensational type. Freedom of thought and opinion thrives in Wisconsin, but the daring novel, so often approaching the limits of good taste, has rarely found expression among our writers.

This series of "Sketches and Studies" is designed to be an anthology of the work of the best known of Wisconsin's authors. A brief biographical sketch of each writer is followed by a selection from his or her published work. It is hardly possible that the list is complete. New writers are appearing from year to year, and only time can test their final position in the field of literature. For any omission that should have been included, we offer an apology.

W. A. T.

Fond du Lac, Wis.,

INTRODUCTION

IN SENDING this volume out to the reading public, there goes with it the earnest hope that it may tend to make Wisconsin people more familiar with the excellent books that have come from the pens of Wisconsin writers, past and present. With few exceptions the titles mentioned in the following biographical sketches are worthy of a larger consideration at the hands of the general public than has been given them.

One of the pleasing experiences in the compilation of this work has been the helpful suggestions received from the several authors. An extensive personal acquaintance, supplemented by correspondence covering a period of years, has made the writing of the biographical sketches almost a personal matter in many instances. For these courtesies and friendly expressions the writer of this volume here acknowledges his obligation. Of the entire series of authors mentioned in this work, only one has indicated indifference or an unfriendly attitude.

Acknowledgment is also due the several publishers for their co-operation in permitting reprints from works of which they own the copyrights. There have been a few exceptions, and a few reprints have had to be omitted, but this was to be expected in so large a list.

It may be urged that the writers listed in this volume are but a fraction of those residents of our state who have produced books. In explanation it may be said that writers of text books have been omitted as have also the writers of books and magazine articles of merely local or temporary interest. It must be remembered that some excellent writers in Wisconsin are devoting their entire time to newspaper work. It was necessary to keep the present volume within reasonable size, and thus only the more eminent of Wisconsin's writers have been mentioned. It is more than probable that within a few years other writers within our borders shall have attained wide recognition, and new names will have been added to the present roll of literary celebrities.

W. A. T.

September, 1930

Contents

Part I, Writers of Fiction

	PAGE
Hamlin Garland	3
Zona Gale	22
Ray Stannard Baker	32
Honoré Willsie Morrow	48
Frank Hamilton Spearman	60
General Charles King	70
Thornton Wilder	83
Margaret Ashmun	89
Glenway Wescott	99
Lucian Cary	109
Elizabeth Garver Jordan	117
Leslie W. Quirk	132
Robert E. Pinkerton	145
Everett McNeil	153
Charles D. Stewart	159
Charles Tenney Jackson	163
William Henry Bishop	171
Edna Ferber	178
Elizabeth F. Corbett	179
Victor Kutchin	180
Ira A. Kenyon	181
Margery Bodine Latimer	182

Part II, Poets and Song Writers

Ella Wheeler Wilcox	185
James Gates Percival	193

CONTENTS—CONTINUED

	PAGE
William Ellery Leonard	200
Hattie Tyng Griswold	205
Elizabeth Farnsworth Mears	216
Eben E. Rexford	218
S. F. Bennett and Joseph P. Webster	223
William S. Pitts	224
Carrie Jacobs Bond	227
William T. Purdy and Carl Beck	231
W. D. Cornell	233
Carl Sandburg	235
Alice Arnold Crawford	245
Berton Braley	252
William Frederick Kirk	256
Eleanor Sawyer Chase	261
Bernard I. Durward	263

Part III, History, Science and Essays

John Muir	269
Carl Schurz	277
Rasmus B. Anderson	288
Frederic L. Paxson	296
Jenkin Lloyd Jones	309
Increase A. Lapham	315
Eliza R. Scidmore	324
Edward Alsworth Ross	330
Paul Samuel Reinsch	336
Reuben Gold Thwaites	345
Louise Phelps Kellogg	354
Frederick Jackson Turner	359
Milo M. Quaife	367

CONTENTS—CONTINUED

	PAGE
Glenn Frank	372
John R. Commons	376
Richard T. Ely	382
Joseph Schafer	388
Grant Showerman	392
John Nagle	396
Neal Brown	404
Carl Russell Fish	409
Fred L. Holmes	410

Part IV, Humorous Writers

Edgar Wilson Nye	417
George W. Peck	426
Marcus Mills Pomeroy	431
Appendix	432

Part I

WISCONSIN WRITERS OF FICTION

Hamlin Garland

HAMLIN GARLAND occupies an eminent position among Wisconsin writers. For nearly forty years his books have followed each other at short intervals until thirty or more volumes bear testimony to his capacity for work and to his wealth of ideas. His versatility is as remarkable as his energy; he has written fiction, history, biography and poetry, but his fame rests on his inimitable portrayal of pioneer life in rural Wisconsin. William Dean Howells has characterized "A Son of the Middle Border" as "an autobiography that ranks with the greatest in literature."

The test of the work of any writer is its permanency. Hundreds of works of fiction, classed as "best sellers" in their brief day, have appeared and disappeared since Garland began his literary career. The "Middle Border" books will live; they are classics in the realm of the literature of the early settlement of the Middle West.

Hamlin Garland was born on a farm near New Salem, Wisconsin, September 16, 1860. His early life is so well described in *A Son of the Middle Border* that little need be said here of that period. After the Civil War, the family moved to Iowa. Mr. Garland was graduated in 1881 from Cedar Valley Seminary, Osage, Iowa. For a few years he taught school in various places. In 1884 he went to Boston where he was first a student and later an instructor in the Boston School of Oratory. Here he came in contact with Oliver Wendell Holmes, Edward Everett Hale, William Dean Howells and others who were then outstanding figures in literature and the drama. He resumed his residence in New Salem, Wisconsin, in 1893, which has since been his home, although much of his time is spent in New York.

Among his best known books are, *Main Traveled Roads*, 1890, *A Member of the Third House*, 1892, *A Spoil of Office*, 1892, *Prairie Folks*, 1893, *Rose of Dutcher's Coolly*, 1895, *The Eagle's Heart*, 1900, *Her Mountain Lover*, 1901, *The Captain of the Gray Horse Troop*, 1902, *Hesper*, 1903, *The Light of the Star*, 1904, *Victor Olnee's Discipline*, 1911, *and The Forester's Daughter*, 1914.

In 1894 Mr. Garland published a volume of verse under the title of *Prairie Songs*. *Ulysses Grant, His Life and Character*, marked Mr. Garland's first entrance in the field of biography. In the realm of history he has succeeded admirably in his *Book of the American Indian*.

Unlike some writers whose early efforts have been their best, Mr. Garland's work has been a steady development. His three books which, probably more than any of the others, fix his place in literature, *A Son of the Middle Border*, *A Daughter of the Middle Border* and *Trail Makers of the Middle Border*, were written after the author had passed middle age.

From MAIN TRAVELED ROADS, *by Hamlin Garland. Harper & Brothers, Publishers. Reprinted by permission of the author.*

GOD'S RAVENS

CHICAGO has three winds that blow upon it. One comes from the east, and the mind goes out to the cold gray-blue lake. One from the north, and men think of illimitable spaces of pine-lands and maple-clad ridges which lead to the unknown deeps of the arctic woods.

But the third is the west or southwest wind, dry, magnetic, full of smell of unmeasured miles of growing grain in summer, or ripening corn and wheat in autumn. When it comes in winter the air glitters with incredible brilliancy. The snow of the country dazzles and flames in the eyes; deep-blue shadows everywhere stream like stains of ink. Sleigh-bells wrangle from early morning until late at night, and every step is quick and alert. In the city, smoke dims its clarity, but it is welcome.

But its greatest moment of domination is spring. The bitter gray wind of the east has held unchecked rule for days, giving place to its brother the north wind only at intervals, till some day in March the wind of the southwest begins to blow. Then the eaves begin to drip. Here and there a fowl (in a house that is really a prison) begins to sing the song it sang on the farm, and toward noon its song becomes a chant of articulate joy.

Then the poor crawl out of their reeking hovels on the south and west sides to stand in the sun—the blessed sun—and felicitate themselves on being alive. Windows of sick-rooms are opened, the merry small boy goes to school without his tippet, and men lay off their long ulsters for their beaver coats. Caps give place to hats, and men and women pause to chat when they meet each other on the street. The open door is the sign of the great change of wind.

There are imaginative souls who are stirred yet deeper by this wind—men like Robert Bloom, to whom come vague and very sweet reminiscences of farm life when the snow is melting and the dry ground begins to appear. To these people the wind comes from the wide unending spaces of the prairie west. They can smell the strange thrilling odor of newly uncovered sod and moist brown ploughed lands. To them it is like the opening door of a prison.

Robert had crawled down-town and up to his office high in the *Star* block after a month's sickness. He had resolutely pulled a pad of paper under his hand to write, but the window was open and that wind coming in, and he could not write—he could only dream.

His brown hair fell over the thin white hand which propped his head. His face was like ivory with dull yellowish stains in it. His eyes did not see the mountainous roofs humped and piled into vast masses of brick and stone, crossed and riven by streets, and swept by masses of gray-white vapor; they saw a little valley circled by low-wooded bluffs—his native town in Wisconsin.

As his weakness grew his ambition fell away, and his heart turned back to nature and to the things he had known in his youth, to the kindly people of the olden time. It did not occur to him that the spirit of the country might have changed.

Sitting thus, he had a mighty longing come upon him to give up the struggle, to go back to the simplest life with his wife and two boys. Why should he tread in the mill, when every day was taking the life-blood out of his heart?

Slowly his longing took resolution. At last he drew his desk down, and as the lock clicked it seemed like the shutting of a prison gate behind him.

At the elevator door he met a fellow-editor. "Hello, Bloom! Didn't know you were down to-day."

"I'm only trying it. I'm going to take a vacation for a while."

"That's right, man. You look like a ghost."

He hadn't the courage to tell him he never expected to work there again. His step on the way home was firmer than it had been for weeks. In his white face his wife saw some subtle change.

"What is it, Robert?"

"Mate, let's give it up."

"What do you mean?"

"The struggle is too hard. I can't stand it. I'm hungry for the country again. Let's get out of this."

"Where'll we go?"

"Back to my native town—up among the Wisconsin hills and coulies. Go anywhere, so that we escape this pressure—it's killing me. Let's go to Bluff Siding for a year. It will do me good—may bring me back to life. I can do enough special work to pay our grocery bill; and the Merrill place—so Jack tells me—is empty. We can get it for seventy-five dollars for a year. We can pull through some way."

"Very well, Robert."

"I must have rest. All the bounce has gone out of me, Mate," he said, with sad lines in his face. "Any extra work here is out of the question. I can only shamble around—an excuse for a man."

The wife had ceased to smile. Her strenuous cheerfulness could not hold before his tragically drawn and bloodless face.

"I'll go wherever you think best, Robert. It will be just as well for the boys. I suppose there is a school there?"

"Oh yes. At any rate, they can get a year's schooling in nature."

"Well—no matter, Robert; you are the one to be considered." She had the self-sacrificing devotion of the average woman. She fancied herself hopelessly his inferior.

They had dwelt so long on the crumbling edge of poverty that they were hardened to its threat, and yet the failure of Robert's health had been of the sort which terrifies. It was a slow but steady sinking of vital force. It had its ups and downs, but it was a downward trail, always downward. The time for self-deception had passed.

His paper paid him a meagre salary, for his work was prized only by the more thoughtful readers of the *Star*. In addition to his regular work he occasionally hazarded a story for the juvenile magazines of the East. In this way he turned the antics of his growing boys to account, as he often said to his wife.

He had also passed the preliminary stages of literary

success by getting a couple of stories accepted by an Eastern magazine, and he still confidently looked forward to seeing them printed.

His wife, a sturdy, practical little body, did her part in the bitter struggle by keeping their little home one of the most attractive on the West Side, the North Side being altogether too high for them.

In addition, her sorely pressed brain sought out other ways of helping. She wrote out all her husband's stories on the typewriter, and secretly she had tried composing others herself, the results being queer dry little chronicles of the doings of men and women, strung together without a touch of literary grace.

She proposed taking a large house and re-renting rooms, but Robert would not hear to it. "As long as I can crawl about we'll leave that to others."

In the month of preparation which followed he talked a great deal about their venture.

"I want to get there," he said, "just when the leaves are coming out on the trees. I want to see the cherry-trees blossom on the hillsides. The popple-trees always get green first."

At other times he talked about the people. "It will be a rest just to get back among people who aren't ready to tread on your head in order to lift themselves up. I believe a year among those kind, unhurried people will give me all the material I'll need for years. I'll write a series of studies somewhat like Jefferies'—or Barrie's—only, of course, I'll be original. I'll just take his plan of telling about the people I meet and their queer ways, so quaint and good."

"I'm tired of the scramble," he kept breaking out of silence to say. "I don't blame the boys, but it's plain to me they see that my going will let them move up one. Mason cynically voiced the whole thing today: 'I can say, "sorry to see you go, Bloom," because your going doesn't concern me. I'm not in line of succession, but some of the other boys don't feel so. There's no divinity doth hedge an editor; nothing but law prevents the murder of those above by those below.'"

"I don't like Mr. Mason when he talks like that," said the wife.

"Well—I don't." He didn't tell her what Mason said when Robert talked about the good simple life of the people in Bluff Siding:

"Oh, bosh, Bloom! You'll find the struggle of the outside world reflected in your little town. You'll find men and women just as hard and selfish in their small way. It'll be harder to bear, because it will all be so petty and pusillanimous."

It was a lovely day in late April when they took the train out of the great grimy terrible city. It was eight o'clock, but the streets were muddy and wet, a cold east wind blowing off the lake.

With clanging bell the train moved away piercing the ragged gray formless mob of houses and streets (through which railways always run in a city). Men were hurrying to work, and Robert pitied them, poor fellows, condemned to do that thing forever.

In an hour they reached the prairies, already clothed upon faintly with green grass and tender springing wheat. The purple-brown squares reserved for the corn looked deliciously soft and warm to the sick man, and he longed to set his bare feet into it.

His boys were wild with delight. They had the natural love of the earth still in them, and correspondingly cared little for the city. They raced through the cars like colts. They saw everything. Every blossoming plant, every budding tree, was precious to them all.

All day they rode. Toward noon they left the sunny prairie-land of northern Illinois and southern Wisconsin, and entered upon the hill-land of Madison and beyond.

As they went north, the season was less advanced, but spring was in the fresh wind and the warm sunshine.

As evening drew on, the hylas began to peep from the pools, and their chorus deepened as they came on toward Bluff Siding, which seemed very small, very squalid, and uninteresting, but Robert pointed at the circling wine-colored wall of hills and the warm sunset sky.

"We're in luck to find a hotel," said Robert. "They burn down every three months."

They were met by a middle-aged man, and conducted across the road to a hotel, which had been a roller-skating rink in other days, and was not prepossessing. However, they were ushered into the parlor, which resembled the sitting-room of a rather ambitious village home, and there they took seats, while the landlord consulted about rooms.

The wife's heart sank. From the window she could see several of the low houses, and far off just the hills which seemed to make the town so very small, very lonely. She was not given time to shed tears. The children clamored for food, tired and cross.

Robert went out into the office, where he signed his name under the close and silent scrutiny of a half-dozen roughly clad men, who sat leaning against the wall. They were merely working-men to him, but in Mrs. Bloom's eyes they were dangerous people.

The landlord looked at the name as Robert wrote. "Your boxes are all here," he said.

Robert looked up at him in surprise. "What boxes?"

"Your household goods. They came in on No. 9."

Robert recovered himself. He remembered this was a village where everything that goes on—everything—is known.

The stairway rose picturesquely out of the office to the low second story, and up these stairs they tramped to their tiny rooms which were like cells.

"Oh, mamma, ain't it queer?" cried the boys.

"Supper is all ready," the landlord's soft, deep voice announced a few moments later, and the boys responded with whoops of hunger.

They were met by the close scrutiny of every boarder as they entered, and they heard also the muttered comments and explanations.

"Family to take the Merrill house."

"He looks purty well flaxed out, don't he?"

They were agreeably surprised to find everything neat and clean and wholesome. The bread was good and the butter delicious. Their spirits revived.

"That butter tastes like old times," said Robert. "It's fresh. It's really butter."

They made a hearty meal, and the boys, being filled up, grew sleepy. After they were put to bed Robert said, "Now, Mate, let's go see the house."

They walked out arm in arm like lovers. Her sturdy form steadied him, though he would not have acknowledged it. The red flush was not yet gone from the west, and the hills still kept a splendid tone of purple-black. It was very clear, the stars were out, the wind deliciously soft. "Isn't it still?" Robert almost whispered.

They walked on under the budding trees up the hill, till they came at last to the small frame house set under tall maples and locust-trees, just showing a feathery fringe of foliage.

"This is our home," said Robert.

Mate leaned on the gate in silence. Frogs were peeping. The smell of spring was in the air. There was a magnificent repose in the hour, restful, recreating, impressive.

"Oh, it's beautiful, Robert! I know we shall like it."

"We *must* like it," he said.

II

FIRST contact with the people disappointed Robert. In the work of moving in he had to do with people who work at day's work, and the fault was his more than theirs. He forgot that they did not consider their work degrading. They resented his bossing. The drayman grew rebellious.

"Look a-here, my Christian friend, if you'll go 'long in the house and let us alone it'll be a good job. We know what we're about."

This was not pleasant, and he did not perceive the trouble. In the same way he got foul of the carpenter and the man who ploughed his garden. Some way his tone was not right. His voice was cold and distant. He generally found that the men knew better than he what was to be done and how to do it; and sometimes he felt like apologizing, but their attitude had changed till apology was impossible.

He had repelled their friendly advances because he considered them (without meaning to do so) as workmen, and not as neighbors. They reported, therefore, that he was cranky and rode a high horse.

"He thinks he's a little tin god on wheels," the drayman said.

"Oh, he'll get over that," said McLane. "I knew the boy's folks years ago—tiptop folks, too. He ain't well, and that makes him a little crusty."

"That's the trouble—he thinks he's an upper crust," said Jim Cullen, the drayman.

At the end of ten days they were settled, and nothing remained to do but plan a little garden and—get well. The boys, with their unspoiled natures, were able to melt into the ranks of the village-boy life at once, with no more friction than was indicated by a couple of rough-and-tumble fights. They were sturdy fellows, like their mother, and these fights gave them high rank.

Robert got along in a dull, smooth way with his neighbors. He was too formal with them. He met them only at the meat-shop and the post-office. They nodded genially, and said, "Got settled yet?" And he replied, "Quite comfortable, thank you." They felt his coldness. Conversation halted when he came near, and made him feel that he was the subject of their talk. As a matter of fact, he generally was. He was a source of great speculation with them. Some of them had gone so far as to bet he wouldn't live a year. They all seemed grotesque to him, so work-scarred and bent and hairy. Even the men whose names he had known from childhood were queer to him. They seemed shy and distant, too, not like his ideas of them.

To Mate they were almost caricatures. "What makes them look so—so 'way behind the times, Robert?"

"Well, I suppose they are," said Robert. "Life in these coulies goes on rather slower than in Chicago. Then there are a great many Welsh and Germans and Norwegians, living 'way up the coulies, and they're the ones you notice. They're not all so." He could be generous toward them in general; it was in special cases where he failed to know them.

They had been there nearly two weeks without meeting any of them socially, and Robert was beginning to change his opinion about them. "They let us severely alone," he was saying one night to his wife.

"It's very odd. I wonder what I'd better do, Robert? I don't know the etiquette of these small towns. I never lived in one before, you know. Whether I ought to call first—and, good gracious, who'll I call on? I'm in the dark."

"So am I, to tell the truth. I haven't lived in one of these small towns since I was a lad. I have a faint recollection that introductions were absolutely necessary. They have an etiquette which is as binding as that of McAllister's Four Hundred, but what it is I don't know."

"Well, we'll wait."

"The *boys* are perfectly at home," said Robert, with a little emphasis on boys, which was the first indication of his disappointment. The people he had failed to reach.

There came a knock on the door that startled them both. "Come in," said Robert, in a nervous shout.

"Land sakes! did I scare ye? Seem so, way ye yelled," said a high-keyed nasal voice, and a tall woman came in, followed by an equally stalwart man.

"How d'e do, Mrs. Folsom? My wife, Mr. Folsom."

Folsom's voice was lost in the bustle of getting settled, but Mrs. Folsom's voice rose above the clamor. "I was tellin' *him* it was about time we got neighborly. I never let anybody come to town a week without callin' on 'em. It does a body a heap o' good to see a face outside the family once in a while, specially in a new place. How do you like up here on the hill?"

"Very much. The view is so fine."

"Yes, I s'pose it is. Still it ain't my notion. I don't like to climb hills well enough. Still, I've heard of people buildin' just *for* the view. It's all in taste, as the old woman said that kissed the cow."

There was an element of shrewdness and self-analysis in Mrs. Folsom which saved her from being grotesque. She knew she was queer to Mrs. Bloom, but she did not resent it. She was still young in form and face, but her teeth were gone, and, like many of her neighbors, she was too poor to replace them from the dentist's. She wore a decent calico dress and a shawl and hat.

As she talked her eyes took in every article of furniture in the room, and every little piece of fancy-work and bric-a-brac. In fact, she reproduced the pattern of one of the tidies within two days.

Folsom sat dumbly in his chair. Robert, who met him now as a neighbor for the first time, tried to talk with him, but failed, and turned himself gladly to Mrs. Folsom, who delighted him with her vigorous phrases.

"Oh, we're a-movin', though you wouldn't think it. This town is filled with a lot of old skinflints. Close ain't no name for 'em. Jest ask Folsom thar about 'em. He's been buildin' their houses for 'em. Still, I suppose they say the same thing o' me," she added, with a touch of humor which always saved her. She used a man's phrases. "We're always ready to tax some other feller, but we kick like mules when the tax falls on us," she went on. "My land! the fight we've had to git sidewalks in this town!"

"You should be mayor."

"That's what I tell Folsom. Takes a woman to clean things up. Well, I must run along. Thought I'd jest call in and see how you all was. Come down when ye kin."

"Thank you, I will."

After they had gone Robert turned with a smile: "Our first formal call."

"Oh, dear, Robert, what can I do with such people?"

"Go see 'em. I like her. She's shrewd. You'll like her, too."

"But what can I say to such people? Did you hear her say 'we fellers' to me?"

Robert laughed. "That's nothing. She feels as much of a man, or 'feller,' as anyone. Why shouldn't she?"

"But she's so vulgar."

"I admit she isn't elegant, but I think she's a good wife and mother."

"I wonder if they're all like that?"

"Now, Mate, we must try not to offend them. We must try to be one of them."

But this was easier said than done. As he went down to the post-office and stood waiting for his mail like the rest he tried to enter into conversation with them, but mainly they moved away from him. William McTurg nodded at him and said, "How de do?" and McLane asked how he liked his new place, and that was about all.

He couldn't reach them. They suspected him. They had only the estimate of men who had worked for him; and, while they were civil, they plainly didn't need him in the slightest degree, except as a topic of conversation.

He did not improve as he had hoped to do. The spring was wet and cold, the most rainy and depressing the valley had seen in many years. Day after day the rain-clouds sailed in over the northern hills and deluged the flat little town with water, till the frogs sang in every street, till the main street mired down every team that drove into it.

The corn rotted in the earth, but the grass grew tall and yellow-green, the trees glistened through the gray air, and the hills were like green jewels of incalculable worth, when the sun shone, at sweet infrequent intervals.

The cold and damp struck through into the alien's heart. It seemed to prophesy his dark future. He sat at his desk and looked out into the gray rain with gloomy eyes—a prisoner when he had expected to be free.

He had failed in his last venture. He had not gained any power—he was really weaker than ever. The rain had kept him confined to the house. The joy he had anticipated of tracing out all his boyish pleasure haunts was cut off. He had relied, too, upon that as a source of literary power. He could not do much more than walk down to the post-office and back on the pleasantest days. A few people called, but he could not talk to them, and they did not call again.

In the meanwhile his little bank-account was vanishing. The boys were strong and happy; that was his only comfort. And his wife seemed strong, too. She had little time to get lonesome.

He grew morbid. His weakness and insecurity made him jealous of the security and health of others.

He grew almost to hate the people as he saw them coming and going in the mud, or heard their loud hearty voices sounding from the street. He hated their gossip, their dull jokes. The flat little town grew vulgar and low and desolate to him.

Every little thing which had amused him now annoyed him. The cut of their beards worried him. Their voices jarred upon him. Every day or two he broke forth to his wife in long tirades of abuse.

"Oh, I can't stand these people! They don't know anything. They talk every rag of gossip into shreds. 'Taters, fish, hops; hops, fish, and 'taters. They've saved and pinched and toiled till their souls are pinched and ground away. You're right. They are caricatures. They don't read or think about anything in which I'm interested. This life is nerve-destroying. Talk about the health of the village life! it destroys body and soul. It debilitates me. It will warp us both down to the level of these people."

She tried to stop him, but he went on, a flush of fever on his cheek:

"They degrade the nature they have touched. Their squat little town is a caricature like themselves. Everything they touch they belittle. Here they sit while sidewalks rot and teams mire in the streets."

He raged on like one demented—bitter, accusing, rebellious. In such a mood he could not write. In place of inspiring him, the little town and its people seemed to undermine his power and turn his sweetness of spirit into gall and acid. He only bowed to them now as he walked feebly among them, and they excused it by referring to his sickness. They eyed him each time with pitying eyes. "He's failin' fast," they said among themselves.

One day, as he was returning from the post-office, he felt blind for a moment and put his hand to his head. The world of vivid green grew gray, and life receded from him into illimitable distance. He had one dim fading glimpse of a shaggy-bearded face looking down at him, and felt the clutch of an iron-hard strong arm under him, and then he lost hold even on so much consciousness.

He came back slowly, rising out of immeasurable deeps toward a distant light which was like the mouth of a well filled with clouds of misty vapor. Occasionally he saw a brown big hairy face floating in over this lighted horizon, to smile kindly and go away again. Others came with shaggy beards. He heard a cheery tenor voice which he recognized, and then another face, a big brown smiling face; very lovely it looked now to him—almost as lovely as his wife's, which floated in from the other side.

"He's all right now," said the cheery tenor voice from the big bearded face.

"Oh, Mr. McTurg, do you think so?"

"Ye-e-s, sir. He's all right. The fever's left him. Brace up, old man. We need ye yit awhile." Then all was silent again.

The well-mouth cleared away its mist again, and he saw more clearly. Part of the time he knew he was in bed staring at the ceiling. Part of the time the well-mouth remained closed in with clouds.

Gaunt old women put spoons of delicious broth to his lips, and their toothless mouths had kindly lines about them. He heard their high voices sounding faintly.

"Now, Mis' Bloom, jest let Mis' Folsom an' me attend to things out here. We'll get supper for the boys, an' you jest go an' lay down. We'll take care of *him*. Don't worry. Bell's a good hand with sick."

Then the light came again, and he heard a robin singing, and a cat-bird squalled softly, pitifully. He could see the ceiling again. He lay on his back, with his hands on his breast. He felt as if he had been dead. He seemed to feel his body as if it were an alien thing.

"How are you, sir?" called the laughing, thrillingly hearty voice of William McTurg.

He tried to turn his head, but it wouldn't move. He tried to speak, but his dry throat made no noise.

The big man bent over him. "Want 'o change place a little?"

He closed his eyes in answer.

A giant arm ran deftly under his shoulders and turned him as if he were an infant, and a new part of the good old world burst on his sight. The sunshine streamed in the windows through a waving screen of lilac leaves and fell upon the carpet in a priceless flood of radiance.

There sat William McTurg smiling at him. He had no coat on and no hat, and his bushy thick hair rose up from his forehead like thick marsh-grass. He looked to be the embodiment of sunshine and health. Sun and air were in his brown face, and the perfect health of a fine animal was in his huge limbs. He looked at Robert with a smile that brought a strange feeling into his throat. It made him try to speak; at last he whispered.

The great figure bent closer: "What is it?"

"Thank—you."

William laughed a low chuckle. "Don't bother about thanks. Would you like some water?"

A tall figure joined William, awkwardly.

"Hello, Evan!"

"How is he, Bill?"

"He's awake to-day."

"That's good. Anything I can do?"

"No, I guess not. All he needs is somethin' to eat."

"I jest brought a chicken up, an' some jell an' things the women sent. I'll stay with him till twelve, then Folsom will come in."

Thereafter he lay hearing the robins laugh and the orioles whistle, and then the frogs and katydids at night. These men with greasy vests and unkempt beards came in every day. They bathed him, and helped him to and from the bed. They helped to dress him and move him to the window, where he could look out on the blessed green of the grass.

O God, it was so beautiful! It was a lover's joy only to live, to look into these radiant vistas again. A cat-bird was singing in the currant-hedge. A robin was hopping across the lawn. The voices of the children sounded soft and jocund across the road. And the sunshine—"Beloved Christ, Thy sunshine falling upon my feet!" His soul ached with the joy of it, and when his wife came in she found him sobbing like a child.

They seemed never to weary in his service. They lifted him about, and talked to him in loud and hearty voices which roused him like fresh winds from free spaces.

He heard the women busy with things in the kitchen. He often saw them loaded with things to eat passing his window, and often his wife came in and knelt down at his bed.

"Oh, Robert, they're so good! They feed us like God's ravens."

One day, as he sat at the window fully dressed for the fourth or fifth time, William McTurg came up the walk.

"Well, Robert, how are ye to-day?"

"First rate, William," he smiled. "I believe I can walk out a little if you'll help me."

"All right, sir."

And he went forth leaning on William's arm, a piteous wraith of a man.

On every side the golden June sunshine fell, filling the valley from purple brim to purple brim. Down over the hill to the west the light poured, tangled and glowing in the plum and cherry trees, leaving the glistening grass spraying through the elms, and flinging streamers of pink across the shaven green slopes where the cattle fed.

On every side he saw kindly faces and heard hearty voices: "Good day, Robert. Glad to see you out again." It thrilled him to hear them call him by his first name.

His heart swelled till he could hardly breathe. The passion of living came back upon him, shaking, uplifting him. His pallid lips moved. His face was turned to the sky.

"O God, let me live! It is so beautiful! O God, give me

strength again! Keep me in the light of the sun! Let me see the green grass come and go!"

He turned to William with trembling lips, trying to speak:

"Oh, I understand you now. I know you all now."

But William did not understand him.

"There! there!" he said, soothingly. "I guess you're gettin' tired." He led Robert back and put him to bed.

"I'd know but we was a little brash about goin' out," William said to him, as Robert lay there smiling up at him.

"Oh, I'm all right now," the sick man said.

"Matie," the alien cried, when William had gone, "we know our neighbors now, don't we? We never can hate or ridicule them again."

"Yes, Robert. They never will be caricatures again—to me."

Zona Gale

ZONA GALE, to a greater degree than any other well-known writer, belongs to Wisconsin. She was born in Portage, August 26, 1874, and there she has resided to the present time. Miss Gale received her preparatory education in the public schools of her native city and at Wayland Academy in Beaver Dam. She was graduated from the University of Wisconsin in 1895 and four years later was granted her Master's degree by the same institution.

Like many others who have achieved distinction in the field of literature, Miss Gale was first a newspaper and then a magazine writer. A local color is apparent in many of her books, and one who is familiar with the Portage neighborhood can visualize the scenes she so interestingly portrays. Although a writer by profession, Miss Gale has not limited her activities to producing books; she has contributed much to the social and political advancement of her state where she is known as an exponent of right living and of justice for all classes of citizens. For a number of years she has served as a regent of the University of Wisconsin.

It is now more than twenty years since her first book was published. Since that time Miss Gale has given a succession of excellent books to the reading public. Best known among these are: *Romance Island*, 1906; *Friendship Village*, 1908; *Friendship Village Love Stories*, 1909; *Mothers to Men*, 1911; *When I Was a Little Girl*, 1913; *Heart's Kindred*, 1915; *A Daughter of Tomorrow*, 1917; *Birth*, 1918; *Peace in Friendship Village*, 1919;

Miss Lulu Bett, 1920; and a dramatization of *Miss Lulu Bett* which received the Pulitzer prize for that year. She has also written a number of short plays.

Of all her books Miss Gale has said that *Birth* is her favorite, or, as she modestly states it, it is the work with which she is least dissatisfied. Certainly the reader of this excellent character study cannot help but feel that among his acquaintances the Pitts, the Barbaras and the Miss Arrowsmiths are not unfamiliar characters.

Miss Gale was married, June 12, 1928, to William L. Breese, a Portage manufacturer.

From BIRTH, *by Zona Gale, Published by The MacMillan Company, New York, 1924. Reprinted by permission of the publishers.*

(1)

AT four o'clock, Pitt came to Burage alone. He came against the advice of his friend, who remained in town. That they had left at the central police office descriptions of Barbara and the baby and had visited dozens of hotels, were as nothing to Buck.

"I'm going to do more," he said, and stayed. He had no plan, but he was bent on retrieving.

As for Pitt, when he had done all that he could think to do, he wanted to stand on corners and watch the passers.

"She might come past," he said. "Such lots of 'em do."

He did this for two hours. Buck would go away and leave him and return to find him still loitering up and down State Street, searching among the faces. Then Pitt would catch at Buck, and speak to him softly, lest the State Street crowd should hear and know.

"I know why she went, Buck," he would say. "She feels so bad about me paying the mortgage. She wants I should have all the money for the house. I *know* that's why she went. And I've got to find her."

Of his appointment with Strain, Pitt did not once think. Toward three o'clock, he announced his intention of going back to Burage. "If she comes, I've got to be there. I left the key—but she might not just understand. Yes. Yes. I've got to go back."

At Burage, he swung from the train and ran through the streets. On the nail under the vines at his door hung the key.

The exquisite order of the rooms escaped him. To him, everything looked as he had left it. He went in every room, returned to the front porch, sat down and held his head in his hands. So this was what he had done. All this was his own doing.

He reviewed their life together, and blamed himself for everything. Why had he not insisted on selling the house, paying the mortgage, and taking her to the City? Then she could have had some of the things that she wanted—people, little trips to the parks, the Zoo, the store windows. Why had he been so mad? She would have been with him now. Just yesterday—if only he could have thought of this yesterday. It seemed such a little thing, to have thought of this yesterday, instead of to-day; and he had not done it.

He slipped down in his chair and stared across the street. There was Miss Arrowsmith, moving about, knowing nothing of it. If only he could keep it from everyone until Barbara came back. Miss Arrowsmith, how it would grieve her! There she was, looking just as she looked on the day of their wedding. He continued to watch her, fascinated, as if by being there just the same, she could bring back that day.

Miss Arrowsmith rose and came down the veranda steps. Some one was with her—a child. Tenderly she was guiding its steps. She lifted it to its carriage on the walk, and the child laughed out.

At the sound of that laugh, Pitt sprang to his feet, and

stood gaping at those figures. Miss Arrowsmith moved between him and the child, but he could see the hood of the carriage. He ran through the house to his kitchen. No! The carriage was not there. Fool, not to have noticed that. The carriage was not there!

He was across the street, running crazily. As he entered the gate, his child saw him and laughed again, and stretched out his arms. He ran to it. He laid his hands fiercely upon the child, leaned across the carriage to Miss Arrowsmith, and gasped out his question:

"Barbara? Where is she?"

"She left here an hour ago," said Miss Arrowsmith.

"An hour ago? To-day? You mean *to-day*?"

"Certainly, to-day."

"But, my God, where did she go?"

"Down that way. I don't know where. She asked to leave the baby here."

"But where did she come from? Which way did she come?"

"Why, from home. She'd been there at home all day."

"*All day!*" Pitt shouted the words, whirled and looked at his house, then reeled and trembled.

"She must be dead," he thought. "They let her come back—to fetch the baby."

"My friend," said Miss Arrowsmith, "what is the matter?" He told it. The naked briefness of his words was terrible. Meanwhile, the baby rubbed at his hand with the red flannel dog with shoe-button eyes.

"She may be to somebody's house," he said piteously. "Oh, mebbe she's to Mis' Copper's. I'll see." He ran a few steps and turned. "If she comes back while I'm gone, you'll keep her?"

He ran. Miss Arrowsmith stood quiet for a moment. She remembered that Barbara had said good-by, had crimsoned. After a moment, Miss Arrowsmith took the baby, and went to the telephone. The baby leaned and tried to bite the cool nickel of the instrument, and pulled at the cord. No'm, the ticket agent at the station had sold no ticket to Mis' Pitt, but he seen her take the five o'clock train.

Pitt ran from house to house. To Mis' Hellie Copper's, and Barbara had been there for half an hour about noon. To Mis' Miles, and she had talked with her that morning on the street. To Mis' Nick True, and Barbara had given her a dime, missionary money. He raced back to Miss Arrowsmith's, his face pitiful with his hope. She told him her news. He dropped to the step like something broken.

She let him talk, listened to his self-reproaches. Barbara wanted folks, and little trips to the park, and the Zoo, and the store windows. She'd ought to have had them. What a fool he had been. It was too late. Where did people go when they went away like that? Where did Miss Arrowsmith think that he could look for her?

And, oh, my God, if only he had stayed to home that day!

At last, when the baby cried, Miss Arrowsmith went across to his house with him. She wisely did not offer to help him with the child. All this would be something for him to do. She peeped in the refrigerator and the pantry and understood what Barbara had been doing that day. She left him mixing the baby's milk and talking.

Alone, he fed the child, and undressed him. He took the little night things from their accustomed place in the closet. There he saw Barbara's blue work-dress, he gathered it in his arms, buried his face in it, caught the odor of it, and so holding it sank on the edge of the bed and fell to sobbing.

"Barbara!" he called, as if she were somewhere that his lifted voice might reach.

The baby came creeping toward him, his eyes fixed on his father's shoes, but was diverted by the fringe of the rug and lay pulling at it.

(2)

"Barbara: We'll sell and move to the City where you can have it like you said. We both want you back. P."

In the "Personal" column of the Chicago papers this notice appeared, week after week.

"If I take it out," said Pitt, "that might be just the day she'd buy a paper."

Six weeks and no response. On the day when he ordered the notices discontinued at last, Pitt was like a man a part of whom is dying.

"Look at the theatres and little trips that money would have bought her," he said to everyone, over and over again.

He talked with everyone in the village. With Clem Austin who ran the gasoline wood cutter. "Why, Clem," he said, "I never thought of it. I never once thought of it. I give you my word, I didn't." With Peter Meyer, his milkman, "You saw how she was—singing around the kitchen here. That was only a week ago. And now look." With the men in the shops: "Going and coming just like these other women, she was. Don't it seem like she must come in the door there?" It was the surprise of it which he kept on emphasizing, piteously. "I give you my word I never thought of such a thing." And when they sympathized with him and said that it was sad, this business, Pitt would say: "Sure. Sure. I should say."

They were very good to him. Here was grief naked and stunned, and about this they understood. There were not many words. These were not the way of Burage. Food was set inside the screen; or the key was taken from its nail in the vines and the offerings left naïvely in the refrigerator. Once a week in his absence, Mis' Hellie Copper slipped in with broom and duster, and ordered the lonely chaos. This Pitt probably never noticed at all, or ever knew. They tried to invite him to their homes, but he would talk about nothing but Barbara, and his wistful asking for advice in tracing her was more than they could bear. "*You* ain't had any word? I thought maybe—" he would say, when he met Barbara's friends.

One day, wearing his work clothes, he walked into Mis' Hellie Copper's house.

"You know," he said, "that piece Barbara used to hum so much?"

Mis' Hellie did not know. Pitt tried to make her remember. "That one that sort of went up, right from the very beginning?" She could not recall it. Nor could he. "But," he said, "if I could only get a-hold of it, it'd kind of bring her back for me to hum it."

About this tune he asked everyone. No one knew what it could be. At last he rushed to Mayme Carbury, with an air of a man on tip-toe lest something be frightened away. "I got it!" he cried. "You play it off." He sang it to her, with gesticulation, with eager eyes, with utterly unbridled tones. Again and again he did this, and it sounded like nothing at all. No one could play it. He went sorrowfully away.

One day some one stepped to his kitchen door, and Pitt had a crust of bread laid on the grate of the open oven. When he found himself detected:

"Smells like baking day," he said, with a foolish laugh.

Gradually the people began to smile at him. It was sad and all that, but he ought to be more of a man. So, to his grief was added the bitterness of a glance, a shrug, a word aside. His sorrow had its own dignity. But his talk, his ceaseless repetitions, his shy, foolish laughter wore upon his friends. And to his dog-like eyes, forever straying and seeking, they grew cruelly accustomed.

(3)

The one ray of life in this his death was the child. This child was exquisite. He was now a year old, the mind miraculously lighting. He was sturdy, but delicately fashioned. Although he looked normal, solid, rosy, he had all the air of spirit which may shine through a child. And already there came darting through the flesh those arrows of another being dwelling within, speaking in flashes. You touched the child, and you touched a creature unknown to you, but known to a thousand influences transcending you.

The little man Pitt adored. In Barbara's presence the child had been absorbed by her, devoured by her. Pitt had then approached on sufferance. He knew nothing, so to say, of the technique of his baby. He adored from afar, and without comprehension. He never had said: "What are we going to do with the baby?" He had said: "What are you going to do with the baby?" Veils had been between the two. In those few ecstatic intervals during which he had been left alone in the room holding the baby, he had felt suddenly naked. On these occasions, when Barbara returned to the room, she had always found him trying to talk to the child, but acting shamefaced.

And now suddenly the two rushed together. Pitt turned to his child with a passion which was the cry of his own flesh to his own flesh. He clung hungrily to this thing that he could call his. All in him that had been Barbara's went seeking after Barbara and found instead the child. It was the passion of family, of possession. This primitive passion became the driving force of his days. He lived only in the child and in his hope that his wife would come back to them. For Pitt in his essential life, the governments, dreams, ideals, sciences of the world did not exist. In his essential life existed only the powerful, primal race hunger for wife and offspring. This was the flower which Pitt had put forth from his being. It had bloomed upon a twin stalk. When one shoot perished, the other became his sole hold upon the eternal.

At first his work was utterly disregarded and he went nowhere.

"She might come back and go away again, like she done," he would say.

Later he would take the baby in his cart and tramp free of the streets and along the country roads. On these days, he never met a farm wagon or passed a woman working in her dooryard without his piercing scrutiny.

At last, when a job or two clamored to be finished, everybody asked to take the baby. Not offered. Asked. Mis' Nick True, Miss Matt Barber, Mis' Miles,—they all asked. And Mis' Copper swept up time royally with: "Mr. Pitt, any time you go away and can cheat anybody else out of keepin' the baby a spell, just you bring him over to me."

But Miss Arrowsmith simply crossed the street and took possession of the baby. She said to herself that this poor little man must be helped out. In her heart she understood that what she desired was the physical presence of the child, looking in her face. Sitting with the child on her knee, sometimes her senses swam with the wonder of this little being who breathed, turned its eyes, knew simple words, could occasionally speak. On these occasions, she would look about on her sewing basket, her mirror, her flowers, as if these commonplace objects too were motived by unsuspected spirit, like this feeble thing.

"Mr. Pitt," she said one day, "if ever you can think of it and *will* let me have this baby—you know what I want."

Pitt smiled, gratefully, negatively.

"I couldn't, though," he said, his eyes seeking down the street as if some one might at any moment appear. "He's all I've got."

It may have been that to herself she said: "My dear man, you haven't *got* him. This is the great parental delusion." But to Pitt, she merely smiled and understood. He had a torn heart and the business of the baby was to provide balm. The baby did it. Lately, on his father's approach, he had learned to throw up both hands and shout: "Mine! Mine! Mine!" In this gesture Pitt sank as within cherishing arms.

Ray Stannard Baker

※

RAY STANNARD BAKER, biographer, essayist, philosophic writer and novelist, was born at Lansing, Michigan, April 17, 1870. At the age of five years he was brought by his parents to St. Croix Falls, Wisconsin, where he grew to young manhood. He was graduated from the Michigan College of Agriculture in 1889. He then entered the University of Michigan where for a short time he took special work in law and literature.

Mr. Baker began his literary career as a newspaper reporter. From 1892 to 1897 he was on the staff of the Chicago Record where his work brought him in contact with "the other half" of the people, an experience that may account for his sympathy with the more helpless members of society. In addition to his newspaper work, he found time to write short stories which were accepted and published by some of the eastern magazines. These attracted the attention of the editor of McClure's who asked Mr. Baker to come to New York. In 1898 the young writer became editor of McClure's Syndicate; the next year he was made associate editor of McClure's Magazine. This connection continued until 1906 when he joined with a group of brilliant writers to take over the American Magazine. He was one of the editors of that periodical from 1906 to 1915.

Soon after the American Magazine came under its new management, a writer appeared who was as mysterious and elusive as his writings were delightful. Though no one knew him, David Grayson became a household name, and his *Adventures in Friendship*, *Adventures in Content-*

ment, and *Adventures in Understanding* were read by an increasing circle of admirers. The identity of the writer was a carefully guarded secret for ten years; even to this day many well informed readers do not know that David Grayson and Ray Stannard Baker are one and the same person. At first thought it seems difficult to harmonize Ray Stannard Baker, the crusader, the uncompromising opponent of social and economic injustice, with David Grayson, the philosopher of contentment. Yet even in the Graysonian philosophy, one catches glimpses of the Baker type of thought. This extract from The Open Road in "Adventures in Friendship" is indicative; "My Open Road leads not only to beauty, not only to fresh adventures in outer observation. I believe in the Open Road in religion, in education, in politics: there is nothing really settled, fenced in, nor finally decided upon this earth. Nothing that is not questionable. I do not mean that I would immediately tear down well-built fences or do away with established and beaten roads. By no means. The wisdom of past ages is likely to be wiser than any hasty conclusions of mine. I would not invite any other person to follow my road until I had well proven it a better way toward truth than that which time had established. And yet I would have every man tread the Open Road; I would have him upon occasion question the smuggest institution and look askance upon the most ancient habit."

In these charming sketches of rural life, one breathes the invigorating air of the countryside, sees the green meadows and the waving grain and the carpets of wild flowers, and greets the friendly neighbors on the highways. Grayson makes farm life attractive, but never minimizes the hard work that the farm demands.

Among Mr. Baker's earlier books are: *Boy's Book of Inventions*, *Our New Prosperity*, *Following the Color Line*, and *The Spiritual Unrest*.

In the field of biography this versatile writer has

achieved success in his recently published *Woodrow Wilson and The World Settlement*, a work he was especially well qualified to write because of his association with the war-time President at the Paris peace conference.

For a number of years Mr. Baker has resided at Amherst, Mass., but Wisconsin has ever retained an interest in its former son, even as he has shown an appreciation of his boyhood state and its institutions.

From ADVENTURES IN FRIENDSHIP *by David Grayson. Doubleday, Page & Co., Publishers. Reprinted by arrangement with the publishers.*

THE OPEN ROAD

I LOVE sometimes to have a day alone—a riotous day. Sometimes I do not care to see even my best friends: but I give myself up to the full enjoyment of the world around me. I go out of my door in the morning—preferably a sunny morning, though any morning will do well enough —and walk straight out into the world. I take with me the burden of no duty or responsibility. I draw in the fresh air, odour-laden from orchard and wood. I look about me as if everything were new—and behold everything *is* new. My barn, my oaks, my fences—I declare I never saw them before. I have no preconceived impressions, or beliefs, or opinions. My lane fence is the end of the known earth. I am a discoverer of new fields among old ones. I see, feel, hear, smell, taste all these wonderful things for the first time. I have no idea what discoveries I shall make!

So I go down the lane, looking up and about me. I cross the town road and climb the fence on the other side. I brush one shoulder among the bushes as I pass: I feel the solid yet easy pressure of the sod. The long blades of the timothy-grass clasp at my legs and let go with reluctance. I break off a twig here and there and taste the tart or bitter sap. I take off my hat and let the warm sun shine on my head. I am an adventurer upon a new earth.

Is it not marvellous how far afield some of us are willing to travel in pursuit of that beauty which we leave behind us at home? We mistake unfamiliarity for beauty; we darken our perceptions with idle foreignness. For want of that ardent inner curiosity which is the only true foundation for the appreciation of beauty—for beauty is inward, not outward—we find ourselves hastening from land to land, gathering mere curious resemblances which, like unassimilated property, possess no power of fecundation. With what pathetic diligence we collect peaks and passes in Switzerland; how we come laden from England with vain cathedrals!

Beauty? What is it but a new way of approach? For wilderness, for foreignness, I have no need to go a mile: I have only to come up through my thicket or cross my field from my own roadside—and behold, a new heaven and a new earth!

Things grow old and stale, not because they are old, but because we cease to see them. Whole vibrant significant worlds around us disappear within the sombre mists of familiarity. Whichever way we look the roads are dull and barren. There is a tree at our gate we have not seen in years: a flower blooms in our door-yard more wonderful than the shining heights of the Alps!

It has seemed to me sometimes as though I could see men hardening before my eyes, drawing in a feeler here, walling up an opening there. Naming things! Objects fall into categories for them and wear little sure channels in the brain. A mountain is a mountain, a tree a tree to them, a field forever a field. Life solidifies itself in words. And finally how everything wearies them: and that is old age!

Is it not the prime struggle of life to keep the mind plastic? To see and feel and hear things newly? To accept nothing as settled; to defend the eternal right of the questioner? To reject every conclusion of yesterday before the surer observations of to-day?—is not that the best life we know?

And so to the Open Road! Not many miles from my farm there is a tamarack swamp. The soft dark green of it fills the round bowl of a valley. Around it spread rising forests and fields; fences divide it from the known land. Coming across my fields one day, I saw it there. I felt the habit of avoidance. It is a custom, well enough in a practical land, to shun such a spot of perplexity; but on that day I was following the Open Road, and it led me straight to the moist dark stillness of the tamaracks. I cannot here tell all the marvels I found in that place. I trod where human foot had never trod before. Cobwebs barred my passage (the bars to most passages when we come to them are only cobwebs), the earth was soft with the thick swamp mosses, and with many an autumn of fallen dead, brown leaves. I crossed the track of a muskrat, I saw the nest of a hawk—and how, how many other things of the wilderness I must not here relate. And I came out of it renewed and refreshed; I know now the feeling of the pioneer and the discoverer. Peary has no more than I; Stanley tells me nothing I have not experienced!

What more than that is the accomplishment of the great inventor, poet, painter? Such cannot abide habit-hedged wildernesses. They follow the Open Road, they see for themselves, and will not accept the paths or the names of the world. And Sight, kept clear, becomes curiously, Insight. A thousand had seen apples fall before Newton. But Newton was dowered with the spirit of the Open Road!

Sometimes as I walk, seeking to see, hear, feel, everything newly, I devise secret words for the things I see: words that convey to me alone the thought, or impression, or emotion of a particular spot. All this, I know, to some will seem the acme of foolish illusion. Indeed, I am not telling of it because it is practical; there is no cash at the end of it. I am reporting it as an experience in life; those who understand will understand. And thus out of my journeys I have words which bring back to me with indescribable poignancy the particular impression of a time or a place. I prize them more highly than almost any other of my possessions, for they come to me seemingly out of the air, and the remembrance of them enables me to recall or live over a past experience with scarcely diminished emotion.

And one of these words—how it brings to me the very mood of a gray October day! A sleepy west wind blowing. The fields are bare, the corn shocks brown, and the long road looks flat and dull. Away in the marsh I hear a single melancholy crow. A heavy day, namelessly sad! Old sorrows flock to one's memory and old regrets. The creeper is red in the swamp and the grass is brown on the hill. It comes to me that I was a boy once—

So to the flat road and away! And turn at the turning and rise with the hill. Will the mood change: will the day? I see a lone man in the top of a pasture crying "Coo-ee, coo-ee." I do not see at first why he cries and then over the hill come the ewes, a dense gray flock of them, huddling toward me. The yokel behind has a stick in each hand. "Coo-ee, coo-ee," he also cries. And the two men, gathering in, threatening, sidling, advancing slowly, the sheep turning uncertainly this way and that, come at last to the boarded pen.

"That's the idee," remarks the helper.

"A poor lot," says the leader: "such is the farmer's life."

From the roadway they back their frame-decked wagon to the fence and unhook their team. The leader throws off his coat and stands thick and muscular in his blue jeans—a roistering fellow with a red face, thick neck and chapped hands.

"I'll pass 'em up," he says; "that's a man's work. You stand in the wagon and put 'em in."

So he springs into the yard and the sheep huddle close into the corner, here and there raising a timid head, here and there darting aside in a panic.

"Hi there, it's for you," shouts the leader, and thrusts his hands deep in the wool of one of the ewes.

"Come up here, you Southdown with the bare belly," says the man in the wagon.

"That's my old game—wrastling," the leader remarks, struggling with the next ewe. "Stiddy, stiddy, now I got you, up with you, dang you!"

"That's the idee," says the man in the wagon.

So I watch and they pass up the sheep one by one and as I go on down the road I hear the leader's thick voice, "Stiddy, stiddy," and the response of the other, "That's the idee." And so on into the gray day.

My Open Road leads not only to beauty, not only to fresh adventures in outer observation. I believe in the Open Road in religion, in education, in politics: there is nothing really settled, fenced in, nor finally decided upon this earth. Nothing that is not questionable. I do not mean that I would immediately tear down well-built fences or do away with established and beaten roads. By no means. The wisdom of past ages is likely to be wiser than any hasty conclusions of mine. I would not invite any other person to follow my road until I had well proven it a better way toward truth than that which time had established. And yet I would have every man tread the Open Road; I would have him upon occasion question the smuggest institution and look askance upon the most ancient habit. I would have him throw a doubt upon Newton and defy Darwin! I would have him look straight at men and nature with his own eyes. He should acknowledge no common gods unless he proved them gods for himself. The "equality of men" which we worship, is there not a higher inequality? The material progress which we deify: is it real progress? Democracy—is it after all better than monarchy? I would have him question the canons of art, literature, music, morals: so will he continue young and useful!

And yet sometimes I ask myself. What do I travel for? Why all this excitement and eagerness of inquiry? What is it that I go forth to find? Am I better for keeping my roads open than my neighbor is who travels with contentment the paths of ancient habit? I am gnawed by the tooth of unrest—to what end? Often as I travel I ask myself that question and I have never had a convincing answer. I am looking for something I cannot find. My Open Road is open, too, at the end! What is it that drives a man onward, that scourges him with unanswered questions! We only know that we are driven; we do not know who drives. We travel, we inquire, we look, we work—only knowing that these activities satisfy a certain deep and secret demand within us. We have Faith that there is a Reason: and is there not a present joy in following the Open Road:

"And O the joy that is never won,
But follows and follows the journeying sun."

And at the end of the day the Open Road, if we follow it with wisdom as well as fervour, will bring us safely home again. For after all the Open Road must return to the Beaten Path. The Open Road is for adventure; and adventure is not the food of life, but the spice.

Thus I came back this evening from rioting in my fields. As I walked down the lane I heard the soft tinkle of a cowbell, a certain earthly exhalation, as of work, came out of the bare fields, the duties of my daily life crowded upon me bringing a pleasant calmness of spirit, and I said to myself: "Lord be praised for that which is common."

And after I had done my chores I came in, hungry, to my supper.

From ADVENTURES IN CONTENTMENT *by David Grayson, Doubleday, Page and Company, Publishers, New York, 1927. Reprinted by arrangement with the publishers.*

A BOY AND A PREACHER

THIS morning, I went to church with Harriet. I usually have some excuse for not going, but this morning I had them out one by one and they were altogether so shabby that I decided not to use them. So I put on my stiff shirt and Harriet came out in her best black cape with the silk fringes. She looked so immaculate, so ruddy, so cheerfully sober (for Sunday) that I was reconciled to the idea of driving her up to the church. And I am glad I went, for the experience I had.

It was an ideal summer Sunday: sunshiny, clear and still. I believe if I had been some Rip Van Winkle waking after twenty years' sleep I should have known it was Sunday. Away off over the hill somewhere we could hear a lazy farm boy singing at the top of his voice: the higher cadences of his song reached us pleasantly through the still air. The hens sitting near the lane fence, fluffing the dust over their backs, were holding a small and talkative service of their own. As we turned into the main road we saw the Patterson children on their way to church, all the little girls in Sunday ribbons, and all the little boys very uncomfortable in knit stockings.

"It seems a pity to go to church on a day like this," I said to Harriet.

"A pity!" she exclaimed. "Could anything be more appropriate?" Harriet is good because she can't help it. Poor woman!—but I haven't any pity for her.

It sometimes seems to me the more worshipful I feel the less I want to go to church. I don't know why it is, but these forms, simple though they are, trouble me. The moment an emotion, especially a religious emotion, becomes an institution, it somehow loses life. True emotion is rare and costly and that which is awakened from without never rises to the height of that which springs spontaneously from within.

Back of the church stands a long low shed where we tied our horse. A number of other buggies were already there, several women were standing in groups, preening their feathers, a neighbour of ours who has a tremendous bass voice was talking to a friend:

"Yas, oats is showing up well, but wheat is backward."

His voice, which he was evidently trying to subdue for Sunday, boomed through the still air. So we walked among the trees to the door of the church. A smiling elder, in an unaccustomed long coat, bowed and greeted us. As we went in there was an odour of cushions and our footsteps on the wooden floor echoed in the warm emptiness of the church. The Scotch preacher was finding his place in the big Bible; he stood solid and shaggy behind the yellow oak pulpit, a peculiar professional look on his face. In the pulpit the Scotch preacher is too much minister, too little man. He is best down among us with his hand in ours. He is a sort of human solvent. Is there a twisted and hardened heart in the community he beams upon it from his cheerful eye, he speaks out of his great charity, he gives the friendly pressure of his large hand, and that hardened heart dissolves and its frozen hopelessness loses itself in tears. So he goes through life, seeming always to understand. He is not surprised by wickedness nor discouraged by weakness: he is so sure of a greater Strength!

But I must come to my experience, which I am almost tempted to call a resurrection—the resurrection of a boy, long since gone away, and of a tall lank preacher who, in his humility, looked upon himself as a failure. I hardly know how it all came back to me; possibly it was the scent-laden breeze that came in from the woods and through the half-open church window, perhaps it was a line in one of the old songs, perhaps it was the droning voice of the Scotch preacher—somehow, and suddenly, I was a boy again.

—To this day I think of death as a valley: a dark

shadowy valley: the Valley of the Shadow of Death. So persistent are the impressions of boyhood! As I sat in the church I could see, as distinctly as though I were there, the church of my boyhood and the tall dyspeptic preacher looming above the pulpit, the peculiar way the light came through the coarse colour of the windows, the barrenness and stiffness of the great empty room, the raw girders overhead, the prim choir. There was something in that preacher, gaunt, worn, sodden though he appeared: a spark somewhere, a little flame, mostly smothered by the gray dreariness of his surroundings, and yet blazing up at times to some warmth.

As I remember it, our church was a church of failures. They sent us the old gray preachers worn out in other fields. Such a succession of them I remember, each with some peculiarity, some pathos. They were of the old sort, indoctrinated Presbyterians, and they harrowed well our barren field with the tooth of their hard creed. Some thundered the Law, some pleaded Love; but of all of them I remember best the one who thought himself the greatest failure. I think he had tried a hundred churches—a hard life, poorly paid, unappreciated—in a new country. He had once had a family, but one by one they had died. No two were buried in the same cemetery; and finally, before he came to our village, his wife, too, had gone. And he was old, and out of health, and discouraged: seeking some final warmth from his own cold doctrine. How I see him, a trifle bent, in his long worn coat, walking in the country roads: not knowing of a boy who loved him!

He told my father once: I recall his exact words:

"My days have been long, and I have failed. It was not given me to reach men's hearts."

Oh, gray preacher, may I now make amends? Will you forgive me? I was a boy and did not know; a boy whose emotions were hidden under mountains of reserve: who could have stood up to be shot more easily than he could have said: "I love you!"

Of that preacher's sermons I remember not one word, though I must have heard scores of them—only that they were interminably long and dull and that my legs grew weary of sitting and that I was often hungry. It was no doubt the dreadful old doctrine that he preached, thundering the horrors of disobedience, urging an impossible love through fear and a vain belief without reason. All that touched me not at all, save with a sort of wonder at the working of his great Adam's apple and the strange rolling of his cavernous eyes. This he looked upon as the work of God; thus for years he had sought, with self-confessed failure, to touch the souls of his people. How we travel in darkness and the work we do in all seriousness counts for naught, and the thing we toss off in play-time, unconsciously, God uses!

One tow-headed boy sitting there in a front row dreaming dreams, if the sermons touched him not, was yet thrilled to the depths of his being by that tall preacher. Somewhere, I said, he had a spark within him. I think he never knew it: or if he knew it, he regarded it as a wayward impulse that might lead him from his God. It was a spark of poetry: strange flower in such a husk. In times of emotion it bloomed, but in daily life it emitted no fragrance. I have wondered what might have been if some one—some understanding woman—had recognised his gift, or if he himself as a boy had once dared to cut free! We do not know: we do not know the tragedy of our nearest friend!

By some instinct the preacher chose his readings mostly from the Old Testament—those splendid, marching passages, full of oriental imagery. As he read there would creep into his voice a certain resonance that lifted him and his calling suddenly above his gray surroundings.

How vividly I recall his reading of the twenty-third Psalm—a particular reading. I suppose I had heard the passage many times before, but upon this certain morning——

Shall I ever forget? The windows were open, for it was May, and a boy could look out on the hillside and see with longing eyes the inviting grass and trees. A soft wind blew in across the church; it was full of the very essence of spring. I smell it yet. On the pulpit stood a bunch of crocuses crowded into a vase: some Mary's offering. An old man named Johnson who sat near us was already beginning to breathe heavily, preparatory to sinking into his regular Sunday snore. Then those words from the preacher, bringing me suddenly—how shall I express it? —out of some formless void, to intense consciousness—a miracle of creation:

"Yea though I walk through the valley of the shadow of death, I will fear no evil: for thou art with me; thy rod and thy staff they comfort me."

Well, I saw the way to the place of death that morning; far more vividly I saw it than any natural scene I know: and myself walking therein. I shall know it again when I come to pass that way; the tall, dark, rocky cliffs, the shadowy path within, the overhanging dark branches, even the whitened dead bones by the way—and as one of the vivid phantasms of boyhood—cloaked figures I saw, lurking mysteriously in deep recesses, fearsome for their very silence. And yet I with magic rod and staff walking within—boldly, fearing no evil, full of faith, hope, courage, love, invoking images of terror but for the joy of braving them. Ah, tow-headed boy, shall I tread as lightly that dread pathway when I come to it? Shall I, like you, fear no evil!

So that great morning went away. I heard nothing of singing or sermon and came not to myself until my mother, touching my arm, asked me if I had been asleep! And I smiled and thought how little grown people knew —and I looked up at the sad sick face of the old preacher with a new interest and friendliness. I felt, somehow, that he too was a familiar of my secret valley. I should have liked to ask him, but I did not dare. So I followed my mother when she went to speak to him, and when he did not see, I touched his coat.

After that how I watched when he came to the reading. And one great Sunday, he chose a chapter from Ecclesiastes, the one that begins sonorously:

"Remember now thy creator in the days of thy youth."

Surely that gaunt preacher had the true fire in his gray soul. How his voice dwelt and quivered and softened upon the words!

"While the sun, or the light, or the moon, or the stars, be not darkened, nor the clouds return after the rain—"

Thus he brought in the universe to that small church and filled the heart of a boy.

"In the days when the keepers of the house shall tremble, and the strong men shall bow themselves, and the grinders cease because they are few, and those that look out of the windows be darkened.

"And the doors shall be shut in the streets, when the sound of the grinding is low, and he shall rise up at the voice of the bird and all the daughters of music shall be brought low."

Do not think that I understood the meaning of those passages: I am not vain enough to think I know even now —but the *sound* of them, the roll of them, the beautiful words, and above all, the pictures!

Those Daughters of Music, how I lived for days imagining them! They were of the trees and the hills, and they were very beautiful but elusive; one saw them as he heard singing afar off, sweet strains fading often into silences. Daughters of Music! Daughters of Music! And why should they be brought low?

Doors shut in the street—how I *saw* them—a long, long street, silent, full of sunshine, and the doors shut, and no sound anywhere but the low sound of the grinding: and the mill with the wheels drowsily turning and no one there at all save one boy with fluttering heart, tiptoeing in the sunlit doorway.

And the voice of the bird. Not a song but the *voice*. Yes, a bird had a voice. I had known it always, and yet somehow I had not dared to say it. I felt that they would look at me with that questioning, incredulous look which I dreaded beyond belief. They might laugh! But here it was in the Book—the voice of a bird. How my appreciation of that Book increased and what a new confidence it gave me in my own images! I went about for days, listening, listening, listening—and interpreting.

So the words of the preacher and the fire in them:

"And when they shall be afraid of that which is high and fears shall be in the way—"

I knew the fear of that which is high: I had dreamed of it commonly. And I knew also the Fear that stood in the way: him I had seen in a myriad of forms, looming black by darkness in every lane I trod; and yet with what defiance I met and slew him!

And then, more thrilling than all else, the words of the preacher:

"Or ever the silver cord be loosed, or the golden bowl be broken, or the pitcher be broken at the fountain, or the wheel broken at the cistern."

Such pictures: that silver cord, that golden bowl! And why and wherefore?

A thousand ways I turned them in my mind—and always with the sound of the preacher's voice in my ears—the resonance of the words conveying an indescribable fire of inspiration. Vaguely and yet with certainty I knew the preacher spoke out of some unfathomable emotion which I did not understand—which I did not care to understand. Since then I have thought what those words must have meant to him!

Ah, that tall lank preacher, who thought himself a failure: how long I shall remember him and the words he read and the mournful yet resonant cadences of his voice—and the barren church, and the stony religion! Heaven he gave me, unknowing, while he preached an ineffectual hell.

As we rode home Harriet looked into my face.

"You have enjoyed the service," she said softly.

"Yes," I said.

"It *was* a good sermon," she said.

"Was it?" I replied

Honoré Willsie Morrow

☼

HONORÉ BRYANT McCUE, known to present
day readers as Honoré Willsie Morrow, was born
at Ottumwa, Iowa, but came to Madison, Wisconsin while yet a child. Her parents, though poor in material things, were both highly educated. The father, William D. McCue, was employed first, with the Madison Railways Company and later as a clerk in the Federal Court. The family lived for a time in a very modest home on East Johnson Street, but later moved to a small farm house across Lake Monona.

Honoré McCue was educated in the Madison public schools and was graduated from the University of Wisconsin in 1902. She is remembered by her class-mates as a tall brunette, quiet, unobtrusive, a good student, but not especially distinguished for scholastic attainments. A Great Dane dog was her constant companion during her college years; the tall, striking girl and the thoroughbred dog attracting more than usual attention on the campus.

Soon after finishing her course in the university, she married and went with her husband to Arizona where he was employed as a mining engineer. Here she wrote short stories for various magazines and gathered material for some of her later books.

Her first book, *Heart of the Desert*, appeared in 1913. In 1915 *Still Jim* was published and attracted wide attention. About this time she became editor of the *Delineator*, a position she filled with marked success for five years. Her later books are; *The Forbidden Trail*, 1919, *The Enchanted Canyon*, 1921, *Judith of the Godless Valley*,

1922, and *Forever Free*, a popular Lincoln story published in 1927. One of her earlier books, *Lydia of the Pines*, contains a number of scenes and characters inspired by her old Madison home. Two of her latest and most popular books, *With Malice Toward None*, and *The Last Full Measure* deal with the closing months of Lincoln's life. Mrs. Morrow now resides in New York City.

Chapter from FOREVER FREE, *by Honoré Willsie Morrow. Published by William Morrow and Company, New York, 1927. Reprinted by the permission of the publishers, copyright 1927, by Honoré W. Morrow.*

CHAPTER XV

General Scott, to Nicolay's complacent amusement, called on the President, a few days after Baker's funeral, and formally tendered his resignation.

"I am tired, sir," said the old soldier. "I am old, and I suffer continuously from an old hurt. Also, I suffer, Mr. President, from the insubordinate spirit shown me by General McClellan. I might almost say that he heaps contumely upon me."

Lincoln was much touched. "When I consider your years, your infirmities, and your well-earned glories, General, my conscience smites me for the heavy burdens I have imposed upon you, lately. But, my dear General, where was I to turn? There is no one else in these United States in whose military judgment I have such confidence. I can accept your resignation only on one consideration, that you agree that I may come to you at any time for advice."

Scott's downcast face brightened. "Certainly, sir! You do me honor Mr. President. It is with deep regret that I withdraw in such momentous times from the orders of a Chief Executive who has treated me with distinguished kindness and courtesy."

"Even at that, I couldn't keep your pace, General!"

Lincoln smiled. In a moment, he told himself, he'd be pulling his forelock. "And now, sir, before you leave, I wish to tell you that I've actually sent General Fremont his walking papers. I still think well of Fremont's impulses, I only think he is the prey of wicked and designing men, and I think he has absolutely no military capacity. There'll be another scream from the radicals, I suppose, over the dismissal, but that has to be."

"Your decision is wise, sir. It's a pity you have to make these changes, continually, but it is one of the many prices we pay for maintaining no standing army. I hesitate to say it, sir, and would not, if I were not out of office, that I believe that, while Cameron was a wise political choice, he is not well fitted to be Secretary of War."

Lincoln nodded, a little heavily. Cameron was a charming gentleman, and he liked him. But the public suspected him of being swayed by the money interests, and it was true that he lacked the executive ability needed for the present emergency.

"I'm thinking about putting Edwin M. Stanton in his place," he said, watching Scott's face.

The general blinked and coughed. "An able and irascible man, sir, and your very vociferous enemy."

"Shucks! Mighty few who aren't my enemies, General. His integrity is only equalled by his intelligence. And the public has confidence in him. Folk are uneasy, these days, and they have a right to be. Think him over, and I'll come up to talk to you about him soon." He took the old man's hand. "I'll see that you are kept informed of what goes on down here. I'm sorry not to be able to give you full relief but we still need that wise head-piece of yours. So, while officially, I say, Good-by!—unofficially, what's your New Jersey address?"

General Scott smiled, delightedly. "I'll see that you receive it, Mr. President, as soon as Mrs. Scott and I are settled."

And Lincoln noted, with satisfaction not unmixed with a tender sort of sympathy, that the old soldier's limp was less as he left the office than it had been when he came in.

The pressure brought to bear on Lincoln to place McClellan in Scott's position was almost unbelievable. McClellan was an ardent Democrat. Yet Greeley, the Republican, gave Lincoln no rest in his behalf, and the Northern Democrats, with Raymond of the New York *Times* as their mouthpiece, hounded him editorially, while literally thousands of telegrams demanded McClellan as General-in-Chief.

More than all else, his anxiety to unite the uneasy North in a vigorous war spirit moved Lincoln to make the appointment. A sigh of relief and approval went up from the whole country, when he announced McClellan's promotion; a sigh so deep and full, that even the anger of the Abolition forces over Fremont's dismissal, which Lincoln adroitly permitted to become known at the same time, could not seriously impair the President's momentary popularity with all sides.

Lizzie Keckley, about the first of November, reported to Mary that Miss Ford, who had spent a week-end ostensibly with friends in Baltimore, had actually attended a celebration of some sort, at the tavern at Fairfax Court House. The host of this celebration, Jinny had told Lizzie, was a dashing and "powerful smart" Rebel officer, Captain Mosby. The purpose of the celebration was confused in Jinny's mind. She thought that the Battle of Ball's Bluff was the cause. Yet she had heard her mistress propose a toast to General McClellan, the hope of both North and South.

Mary tried to talk this toast over with Lincoln one morning in November, when she caught him alone for a moment at supper. But he was sweating that day under the first news of the intricate problem developing with England, as a result of the Trent affair, and he begged her not to bother him. Mary remarked that she would never mention McClellan's name to him again, but was glad the next moment, as she realized what deep harassment lay in his eyes, that Lincoln probably had not heard her peevish retort.

He had not. Nevertheless, Mary's constant jabbing him with her dislike for McClellan did not leave him unperturbed. Now and again, after she had launched one of her darts at the General, he was conscious of a strange sense of helplessness, a fear that the treachery which lurked in every aspect of the slavery question was too gigantic for his mind to grasp. McClellan's careless contempt toward himself, his frank scorn of the Cabinet members, which was shown most bitterly toward Cameron, made Lincoln uneasy.

The "Anaconda" plan, backed by Scott, the Cabinet, and himself, McClellan ignored. The plan of movement for the armies in Tennessee and Kentucky, as well as those in the States along the Mississippi, which Lincoln had worked out, and which were later to be proved models of military and political skill, McClellan laughed at. Men of real ability were emerging from the chaos in the middle-west, Sherman, Thomas, Hunter, Halleck. Lincoln desired that their talents be put to work at once. They were not.

Again, and yet again, during the early days of November, the President urged his plans on McClellan, but they were ignored. Nothing happened. A black lethargy seemed to hold the army East and West in a nightmare's spell. At last, Lincoln no longer could endure McClellan's silence. One evening toward the middle of November, he gathered up John Hay, led him across the street to Seward's house, gathered up the Secretary of State, and started for McClellan's house on H street.

"Of course," remarked Seward, puffing good humoredly on his usual cigar, "I like to be a good fellow, myself, but why, with all you and I have to do, to say nothing of our young poet, should we wait on McClellan? I've got to get that reply to Lord Russell on the Trent affair into Lord Lyon's hands to-night. You've torn it limb from limb, and time will be needed to put the remnants together, Mr. President!"

Lincoln laughed and flung his arm over Seward's shoulders. "We go to McClellan, Governor, because McClellan is too proud to wait on a couple of old cart horses like you and me."

"McClellan is a brilliant soldier, and I love him," commented Seward, "but he's riding a horse several hands too high, I fear."

"If he's as able as a military man as I guess him to be *un*able as a politician, he'll end the war before he ruins the country,—I hope."

Seward gasped. "And what do you mean by that, Lincoln?"

"Just what I said," replied the President.

There was silence, while the three men tramped thoughtfully along the tree shadowed street, so badly lighted that they were obliged to move slowly. John Hay, who felt keenly McClellan's discourtesies toward Lincoln, broke the silence, and changed the subject.

"Mr. Lincoln, may I ask how you got rid of that committee of Senators, this afternoon? They asked for an hour with you, and they came tumbling out in twenty minutes."

"Senator Trumbull and his gang, eh? They didn't want much! Just said they heard I was going to change the Secretary of War, and that, as the entire Cabinet had lost the confidence of the country, they thought it an opportune moment to change all seven of the Cabinet ministers. I couldn't think of a better answer than to tell them a story. I told it and they left."

"What was the story?" asked Seward.

Lincoln chuckled. "Out on the Sangamon, there was a farmer much troubled by skunks, and his wife insisted he try to get rid of them. So, one moonlight night, he loaded his old shotgun and stationed himself in the yard. Waiting in the house, his wife heard the gun go off and in a few minutes, the farmer came in.

" 'What luck did you have?' said she.

" 'I hid behind the wood,' said he, 'with the shotgun pointed toward the hen roost, and along came, not one skunk, but seven! I took aim, blazed away, and killed one. But he raised such a fearful stink I concluded it was best to let the other six alone!' "

The trio was still chuckling when McClellan's home was reached. The servant told them that the General was attending a wedding. Lincoln declared in favor of waiting, and led the way into the parlor. An hour later, McClellan appeared in the hall, where the three visitors heard the servant apprise him of Lincoln's presence. McClellan brushed by and ascended the stairs. Another quarter of an hour passed. Then the President sent the servant to remind General McClellan of his presence. Much embarrassed, the man returned almost immediately.

"The General has gone to bed, sir, and sends word that he's too tired to see you to-night."

"Good God!" exclaimed Seward, starting to his feet.

Lincoln laid his hand on the Governor's arm and smiled gravely at John Hay. "Come boys, we'll go home," he said.

He did not speak during the return to the Executive Mansion.

* * * *

The following morning shortly after breakfast McClellan's aide appeared with the information that the General-in-Chief would be glad to see the President at his house, where the Secretary of the Navy wished to hold a conference on an expedition against New Orleans.

Lincoln was sitting at his desk, with Willie beside him. He was helping the boy compose a letter to the editor of *The National Republican*, to whom he wanted the youngster to send his poem on Colonel Baker.

When the aide had delivered his message, Lincoln affixed an elaborate title line to Willie's verses before he said shortly:

"Tell McClellan I'm not coming."

The aide raised his eyebrows, saluted and departed. Willie turned to stare up into his father's face.

"What are you mad at McClellan for, Papa day?"

"What makes you think I'm mad, Willie?" asked Lincoln.

"Ho! I always know. Anybody does. And you'd ought to have been mad at him long ago, I guess." The child, with his moving likeness to his father, nodded his head, deliberately.

* * * *

"Yes, what is it, John?" as young Hay came in.

"Brigadier Van Vliet of McClellan's staff, sir, wishes for a few moment's interview."

"It's lesson time for you, Willie, so march," said Lincoln, kissing the child several times, and watching him, with tender, brooding gaze until the door slammed after him. "Show the Brigadier in, John," rising to warm his hands at the fire.

A handsome, upstanding officer clanked into the room and saluted. Lincoln pulled the gray shawl over his shoulders, and deliberately lifted a foot in rumpled wool sock and carpet slipper to the blaze.

"I feel these first fall days more'n I will the real winter, Brigadier," he remarked.

The officer nodded, with a supercilious glance at the shabby legs dangling before the blaze; which glance did not escape the President's eye.

"Mr. President, General McClellan believes that you

did not understand the purport of his previous message. This is the conference which you yourself called with regard to the military and naval plan which you, yourself, sponsor."

"I called last night at General McClellan's house to talk that plan over with him, Brigadier."

"Yes, sir?" The officer's voice was tentative.

"That's all, Brigadier. Fine clear weather we're having! Good fighting weather I'd call it. Virginia roads are in prime condition for marching."

Brigadier Van Vliet flushed, saluted, and turned away. There was no smile on Lincoln's face, as he watched that stiff back disappear into the reception room.

He was deep in conference with Seward and Chase over the floating of a new bond issue, not long before the noon hour, when George Nicolay came in.

"General McClellan is in my office, sir, demanding to see you, at once."

"Tell him I'm busy, George," replied Lincoln.

Chase spoke quickly, "I'm sure Governor Seward and I will both gladly withdraw in favor of the General."

"I'm not so sure, Chase, of that fact," said Seward, placidly turning over a pile of notes.

"The subject of this conference is in my province, sir," Chase threw his handsome head up quickly, "and if I'm willing to end it you have nothing to say."

"Still strong for McClellan, aren't you, Chase!" interpolated Lincoln a little wearily. The friction between Seward and Chase made a consultation with the two extremely wearing. "It won't hurt him to cool his heels for awhile."

"If he cools them!" smiled Seward. Adding as the door burst open, and McClellan strode in, "Which he won't!"

"Mr. Lincoln," demanded the General, "why am I subjected to the sort of treatment you have visited on me this morning?" He stamped up to the table, and paused opposite Lincoln, his gloved hand caught in his yellow sash, the other thrust into the breast of his blue uniform, a picture of the perfect officer.

"You know, McClellan, I didn't have a West Point education," replied the President, "so I'm lacking in a certain polish of manner I could have got there. My wife says she's about given up my manners, in fact, so I'm looking elsewhere for my training. Now you are a West Pointer and a society man, and I've decided to pattern my etiquette after yours for a while."

He paused, watching the young General through half-closed, steel gray eyes. Anger and resentment struggled to free themselves from the tight grip of McClellan's lips. Lincoln brought his bony fist down on the Cabinet table.

"You insulted the high office vested in me, last night, General. Don't repeat the offense, sir." He turned to Nicolay, who had remained standing near the door. "George, send for Welles to come over here. You gentlemen will excuse me, won't you, if I take up another matter now?" looking from Seward to Chase.

Seward, with a twinkle in his fine eyes, replied meekly. "Yes, Mr. President," and rose.

Chase, who was a great admirer of McClellan's obviously was bursting to speak up for his favorite, but something in Lincoln's eye which he never before had observed there, caused the Secretary of the Treasury to gather up his papers and depart in utter silence.

McClellan walked to a window and stood with his back to the room. Lincoln wrote busily for a little while. Then he said urbanely:

"By the way, General, I see you've refused to make good my appointment of Halleck in Fremont's job. Guess you'd better tend to that hadn't you?"

Without turning, McClellan replied, "I've got a better man in view. In the meantime, Hunter will do."

"Halleck," said Lincoln, "is a man of more war experience than yourself. He has had long training in organization. He is an authority on military art and science, as his book proves. Some one has got to get those fellows out West to pulling together,—or their armies will eat their heads off. Scott wanted Halleck to have your job, but I agreed with the public that your youth and general brilliancy were a better bet. The conditions in the West are bad. You need Halleck there."

McClellan whirled round. "You try my patience beyond my strength, Mr. Lincoln."

"Oh, you're a pretty strong fellow, according to my guess!" Lincoln smiled. "Reckon you'd better fix that up with Halleck, George."

McClellan began to walk the floor. "You turn over to me a mob of gutter-snipes and farm boys to make into an army; then you nag me continually, without waiting either for equipment or training, to give battle to the enemy. Next you turn over to me all the armies of the country,—an untrained rabble,—honeycombed by the machinations of politicians, and demand again that I close in on the Rebels, at the same time handicapping me by imposing on me officers in whom I have no confidence. You, sir, utterly ignorant of the most ordinary military facts are doing this!"

"In a kind of a way what you say is true, George. But the fact remains that I'm the head of this government, and it's also a fact that two men can't drive the same horse at the same time."

John Hay opened the door to admit Welles and Cameron. In a moment, the four men were bending over a map, while Lincoln explained the theory of a joint land and naval operation that should open the Mississippi from Cairo to the Gulf. "Tightening up the Anaconda," he called it.

Cameron and Welles were enthusiastically for it. McClellan, with illconcealed contempt, declared the plan to be premature, and that he would not detail a single regiment from the eastern forces for such a movement. There was a long argument, interrupted once or twice by different messengers sent by Mary to urge the President to come to dinner. During the last half hour, Lincoln permitted McClellan to do most of the talking, and it was with a sick feeling of anxiety that he listened. And yet, he thought, McClellan was brilliant, was not to be beaten in his skill as an organizer, and there was not a soldier in the Army of the Potomac who did not adore "little Mac." Once let him overcome his strange inertia, and his compact, loyal fighting unit would be unstoppable. But why that strange inertia? Mary said McClellan was a coward, but he was willing to take his oath that McClellan was a brave man.

Suddenly he rose, and ran his fingers through his hair. "I shall issue an order this afternoon," he said, "directing that preparations for the joint movement be begun at once. And now I'm going to my dinner. By the way, George," pausing with his hand on the door knob, "I shall have some special instructions for Halleck as soon as he takes over his job," and he closed the door firmly behind him.

Frank Hamilton Spearman

☆

FRANK H. SPEARMAN was born in Buffalo, New York in 1859. He came to Wisconsin when a boy and received his early education in the Appleton public schools and later in Lawrence College.

After leaving Appleton Mr. Spearman engaged for some years in the banking business as McCook, Nebraska. McCook was division headquarters for the Burlington Railroad, and most of its people were trainmen or shopmen. Mr. Spearman says that in this environment he had the opportunity to listen to the stories told by the veteran trainmen while they were "held for orders;" and thus absorbed a wealth of railroad lore which he used to advantage when he turned to writing as a profession. He says his first stories were railroad stories because he liked railroad men and railroad life. However this may have influenced him, it is conceded that his railroad narratives have never been equaled by any other author.

Away back on June 14, 1902 there appeared in *The Outlook* a short story by Spearman entitled "As the Despatcher Saw It." Brief as it was, it brought forth the following letter from Thomas Wentworth Higginson to Dr. Lyman Abbott:

June 16, 1902

Dear Dr. Abbott:

Let me thank you for that wonderfully strong page, "As the Despatcher Saw It," in The Outlook for June 14. I once planned a school reader of genuinely strong and simple English, but after I had included Lincoln's Gettysburg address and John Brown's last speech, I stopped because I could find nothing to put with them. I shall set this article for a Number Three. I wish *I* had written it.

Cordially,
Thomas Wentworth Higginson

"As the Despatcher Saw It" was later interpolated in Spearman's book, *The Daughter of a Magnate* which, throughout, is filled with stirring scenes from railroad life. Other well known books by this charming writer are: *The Nerve of Foley* which appeared in 1900; *Held for Orders*, 1901; *Doctor Bryson*, 1902; *Whispering Smith*, 1906; *Robert Kimberly*, 1911; and *The Mountain Divide*, 1912. None of these books were written while the author was a resident of Wisconsin, but it is worthy of note that the foundation for his future work was laid in the schools of this State. Mr. Spearman now resides at Hollywood, California.

From THE NERVE OF FOLEY AND OTHER RAILROAD STORIES, *by Frank H. Spearman. Harper & Brothers, Publishers, New York, 1902. Reprinted by permission of the author and of the publishers.*

SECOND SEVENTY-SEVEN

IT IS a bad grade yet. But before the new work was done on the river division, Beverly Hill was a terror to trainmen.

On rainy Sundays old switchmen in the Zanesville yards still tell in their shanties of the night the Blackwood bridge went out and Cameron's stock-train got away on the hill, with the Denver flyer caught at the foot like a rat in a trap.

Ben Buckley was only a big boy then, braking on

freights; I was dispatching under Alex Campbell on the West End. Ben was a tall, loose-jointed fellow, but gentle as a kitten; legs as long as pinch bars, yet none too long, running for the Beverly switch that night. His great chum in those days was Andy Cameron. Andy was the youngest engineer on the line. The first time I ever saw them together, Andy, short and chubby as a duck, was dancing around, half dressed, on the roof of the bath-house, trying to get away from Ben, who had the fire-hose below, playing on him with a two-inch stream of ice-water. They were up to some sort of a prank all the time.

June was usually a rush month with us. From the coast we caught the new crop Japan teas and the fall importations of China silks. California still sent her fruits, and Colorado was beginning cattle shipments. From Wyoming came sheep, and from Oregon steers; and all these not merely in carloads, but in solid trains. At times we were swamped. The overland traffic alone was enough to keep us busy; on top of it came a great movement of grain from Nebraska that summer, and to crown our troubles a rate war sprang up. Every man, woman, and child east of the Mississippi appeared to have but one object in life—that was to get to California, and to go over our road. The passenger traffic burdened our resources to the last degree.

I was putting on new men every day then. We start them braking on freights; usually they work for years at that before they get a train. But when a train-dispatcher is short on crews he must have them, and can only press the best material within reach. Ben Buckley had not been braking three months when I called him up one day and asked him if he wanted a train.

"Yes, sir, I'd like one first rate. But you know I haven't been braking very long, Mr. Reed," said he, frankly.

"How long have you been in the train service?"

I spoke brusquely, though I knew, without even looking at my service-card just how long it was.

"Three months, Mr. Reed."

It was right to a day.

"I'll probably have to send you out on 77 this afternoon." I saw him stiffen like a ramrod. "You know we're pretty short," I continued.

"Yes, sir."

"But do you know enough to keep your head on your shoulders and your train on your orders?"

Ben laughed a little. "I think I do. Will there be two sections to-day?"

"They're loading eighteen cars of stock at Ogalalla; if we get any hogs off the Beaver there will be two big sections. I shall mark you up for the first one anyway, and send you out right behind the flyer. Get your badge and your punch from Carpenter—and whatever you do, Buckley, don't get rattled."

"No, sir; thank you, Mr. Reed."

But his "thank you" was so pleasant I couldn't altogether ignore it; I compromised with a cough. Perfect courtesy, even in the hands of the awkwardest boy that ever wore his trousers short, is a surprisingly handy thing to disarm gruff people with. Ben was undeniably awkward; his legs were too long, and his trousers decidedly out of touch with his feet; but I turned away with the conviction that in spite of his gawkiness there was something to the boy. That night proved it.

When the flyer pulled in from the West in the afternoon it carried two extra sleepers. In all, eight Pullmans, and every one of them loaded to the ventilators. While the train was changing engines and crews, the excursionists swarmed out of the hot cars to walk up and down the platform. They were from New York, and had a band with them—as jolly a crowd as we ever hauled—and I noticed many boys and girls sprinkled among the grown folks.

As the heavy train pulled slowly out the band played,

the women waved handkerchiefs, and the boys shouted themselves hoarse—it was like a holiday, everybody seemed so happy. All I hoped, as I saw the smoke of the engine turn to dust on the horizon, was that I could get them over my division and their lives safely off my hands. For a week we had had heavy rains, and the bridges and track gave us worry.

Half an hour after the flyer left, 77, the fast stock-freight, wound like a great snake around the bluff, after it. Ben Buckley, tall and straight as a pine, stood on the caboose. It was his first train, and he looked as if he felt it.

In the evening I got reports of heavy rains east of us, and after 77 reported "out" of Turner Junction and pulled over the divide towards Beverly, it was storming hard all along the line. By the time they reached the hill Ben had his men out setting brakes—tough work on that kind of a night; but when the big engine struck the bluff the heavy train was well in hand, and it rolled down the long grade as gently as a curtain.

Ben was none too careful, for half-way down the hill they exploded torpedoes. Through the driving storm the tail lights of the flyer were presently seen. As they pulled carefully ahead, Ben made his way through the mud and rain to the head end and found the passenger-train stalled. Just before them was Blackwood Creek, bank full, and the Bridge swinging over the swollen stream like a grape-vine.

At the foot of Beverly Hill there is a siding—a long siding, once used as a sort of cut-off to the upper Zanesville yards. This side track parallels the main track for half a mile, and on this siding Ben, as soon as he saw the situation, drew in with his train so that it lay beside the passenger-train and left the main line clear behind. It then became his duty to guard the track to the rear, where the second section of the stock-train would soon be due.

It was pouring rain and as dark as a pocket. He started

his hind-end brakeman back on the run with red lights and torpedoes to warn the second section well up the hill. Then walking across from his caboose, he got under the lee of the hind Pullman sleeper to watch for the expected headlight.

The storm increased in violence. It was not the rain driving in torrents, not the lightning blazing, nor the deafening crashes of thunder, that worried him, but the wind—it blew a gale. In the glare of the lightning he could see the oaks which crowned the bluffs whip like willows in the storm. It swept quartering down the Beverly cut as if it would tear the ties from under the steel. Suddenly he saw, far up in the black sky, a star blazing; it was the head-light of Second Seventy-Seven.

A whistle cut the wind; then another. It was the signal for brakes; the second section was coming down the steep grade. He wondered how far back his man had got with the bombs. Even as he wondered he saw a yellow flash below the head-light; it was the first torpedo. The second section was already well down the top of the hill. Could they hold it to the bottom?

Like an answer came shorter and sharper the whistle for brakes. Ben thought he knew who was on that engine; thought he knew that whistle—for engineers whistle as differently as they talk. He still hoped and believed—knowing who was on the engine—that the brakes would hold the heavy load; but he feared—

A man running up in the rain passed him. Ben shouted and held up his lantern; it was the head brakeman.

"Who's pulling Second Seventy-Seven?" he cried.

"Andy Cameron."

"How many air cars has he got?"

"Six or eight," shouted Ben. "It's the wind Daley—the wind. Andy can hold her if anybody can. But the wind; did you ever see such a blow?"

Even while he spoke the cry for brakes came a third time on the storm.

A frightened Pullman porter opened the rear door of the sleeper. Five hundred people lay in the excursion train, unconscious of this avalanche rolling down upon them.

The conductor of the flyer ran up to Ben in a panic.

"Buckley, they'll telescope us."

"Can you pull ahead any?"

"The bridge is out."

"Get out your passengers," said Ben's brakemen.

"There's no time," cried the passenger conductor, wildly, running off. He was panic stricken. The porter tried to speak. He took hold of the brakeman's arm, but his voice died in his throat; fear paralyzed him. Down the wind came Cameron's whistle clamoring now in alarm. It meant the worst, and Ben knew it. The stock-train was running away.

There were plenty of things to do if there was only time; but there was hardly time to think. The passenger crew were running about like men distracted, trying to get the sleeping travellers out. Ben knew they could not possibly reach a tenth of them. In the thought of what it meant, an inspiration came like a flash.

He seized his brakeman by the shoulder. For two weeks the man carried the marks of his hand.

"Daley!" he cried in a voice like a pistol crack, "get those two stockmen out of our caboose. Quick man! I'm going to throw Cameron into the cattle."

It was a chance—single, desperate, but yet a chance— the only chance that offered to save the helpless passengers in his charge.

If he could reach the siding switch ahead of the runaway train, he could throw the deadly catapult on the siding and into his own train, and so save the unconscious travellers. Before the words were out of his mouth he started up the track at topmost speed.

The angry wind staggered him. It blew out his lantern,

but he flung it away, for he could throw the switch in the dark. A sharp gust tore half his raincoat from his back; ripping off the rest, he ran on. When the wind took his breath he turned his back and fought for another. Blinding sheets of rain poured on him; water streaming down the track caught his feet; a slivered tie tripped him, and, falling headlong, the sharp ballast cut his wrists and knees like broken glass. In desperate haste he dashed ahead again; the head-light loomed before him like a mountain of flame. There was light enough now through the sheets of rain that swept down on him, and there ahead, the train almost on it, was the switch.

Could he make it?

A cry from the sleeping children rose in his heart. Another breath, an instant floundering, a slipping leap, and he had it. He pushed the key into the lock, threw the switch and snapped it, and, to make deadly sure, braced himself against the target-rod. Then he looked.

No whistling now; it was past that. He knew the fireman would have jumped. Cameron too? No, not Andy, not if the pit yawned in front of his pilot.

He saw streams of fire flying from many wheels—he felt the glare of a dazzling light—and with a rattling crash the ponies shot into the switch. The bar in his hands rattled as if it would jump from the socket, and, lurching frightfully, the monster took the siding. A flare of lightning lit the cab as it shot past, and he saw Cameron leaning from the cab window, with face of stone, his eyes riveted on the gigantic drivers that threw a sheet of fire from the sanded rails.

"Jump!" screamed Ben, useless as he knew it was. What voice could live in that hell of noise? What man escape from that cab now?

One, two, three, four cars pounded over the split rails in half as many seconds. Ben, running dizzily for life to the right, heard above the roar of the storm and screech of the sliding wheels a ripping, tearing crash, the harsh scrape of escaping steam, the hoarse cries of the wounded cattle. And through the dreadful dark and the fury of the babel the wind howled in a gale and the heavens poured a flood.

Trembling with excitement and exhaustion, Ben staggered down the main track. A man with a lantern ran against him; it was the brakeman who had been back with the torpedoes; he was crying hysterically.

They stumbled over a body. Seizing the lantern, Ben turned the prostrate man over and wiped the mud from his face. Then he held the lantern close, and gave a great cry. It was Andy Cameron—unconscious, true, but soon very much alive, and no worse than badly bruised. How the good God who watches over plucky engineers had thrown him out from the horrible wreckage only He knew. But there Andy lay; and with a lighter heart Ben headed a wrecking crew to begin the task of searching for any who might by fatal chance have been caught in the crash.

And while the trainmen of the freights worked at the wreck the passenger-train was backed slowly—so slowly and so smoothly—up over the switch and past, over the hill and past, and so to Turner Junction, and around by Oxford to Zanesville.

When the sun rose the earth glowed in the freshness of its June shower-bath. The flyer, now many miles from Beverly Hill, was speeding in toward Omaha, and mothers waking their little ones in the berths told them how close death had passed while they slept. The little girls did not quite understand it, though they tried very hard, and were very grateful to That Man whom they never saw and whom they would never see. But the little boys—never mind the little boys—they understood it, to the youngest urchin on the train, and fifty times their papas had to tell them how far Ben ran and how fast to save their lives. And one little boy—I wish I knew his name—

went with his papa to the depot-master at Omaha when the flyer stopped, and gave him his toy watch, and asked him please to give it to That Man who had saved his mamma's life by running so far in the rain, and please to tell him how much obliged he was—if he would be so kind.

So the little toy watch came to our superintendent, and so to me; and I, sitting at Cameron's bed-side, talking the wreck over with Ben, gave it to him; and the big fellow looked as pleased as if it had been a jewelled chronometer; indeed that was the only medal Ben got.

The truth is we had no gold medals to distribute out on the West End in those days. We gave Ben the best we had, and that was a passenger run. But he is a great fellow among the railroad men. And on stormy nights switchmen in the Zanesville yards, smoking in their shanties, still tell of that night, that storm, and how Ben Buckley threw Second Seventy-Seven at the foot of Beverly Hill.

General Charles King

✯

GENERAL CHARLES KING, soldier and novelist, is the most prolific writer that Wisconsin has produced. Except for the time spent at West Point and in the military service of his country, General King has lived nearly the whole of his long life in this state, and Wisconsin is justly proud of him. The King family has long occupied a conspicuous place in American annals. Four generations in direct descent are mentioned in Americana. General Rufus King, father of the Wisconsin author, was a general in the Civil War and United States Minister to Rome. Charles King, the grandfather, was for many years president of Columbia College. Rufus King, great-grandfather of General Charles King was one of the signers of the Federal Constitution, a United States Senator, and Minister to Great Britain. Such is the ancestral background of the subject of this sketch.

Charles King was born in Albany, N. Y., October 12, 1844. The family came to Milwaukee in 1845; thus the boy's earliest recollections were of Wisconsin. When fourteen years of age he was sent to New York for his education. After a preparatory course of study he entered Columbia College of which his grandfather was president. The college work was not entirely agreeable to the young student. His preference was for a military career, but his mother and other relatives objected. His wishes finally prevailed and in 1862 he was appointed to West Point by President Lincoln from which institution he was graduated in 1866. Then came military service in New Orleans during the early post-war period. There followed

GENERAL CHARLES KING

for a number of years assignments to various frontier army posts, where frequent Indian uprisings enlivened the monotony. It was in this environment that General King accumulated the material that was later incorporated in his stories of army life. In 1879 King, then a captain, was retired from the regular army becauses of severe wounds received in Indian warfare in Arizona. Prior to this time he had taken an active part in the Sioux-Cheyenne campaign of 1876 and in the Nez Perces outbreak in 1877. In 1880 he was appointed instructor in military tactics in the University of Wisconsin where he soon brought the student cadets to a high degree of efficiency. Later he became inspector in the Wisconsin National Guard where for over thirty years he was known and admired by every member of that organization. He was made brigadier general of volunteers during the Philippine Insurrection. There he led his brigade in the battle of Santa Ana, his gallantry in this action gaining for him special commendation.

General King is unexcelled as a writer of army stories. His long years of military service in the untamed West gave him unusual opportunities for gathering first-hand the material which he skillfully incorporated in his tales. He has said in explanation of his literary ventures that he sometimes used his pen as the only effective weapon to keep the wolf from his door. In any event he found a demand for his books, and, after his retirement from the regular army in 1879, they came from the press in rapid succession. *The Colonel's Daughter*, *Marian's Faith*, *Warrior Gap*, *A Garrison Tangle*, *Trumpeter Fred*, *An Army Wife*, *A Wounded Name*, *Fort Frayne*, *A War Time Wooing*, and *Between the Lines* are a few of the sixty volumes that have been written by General King. His *The Real Ulysses S. Grant* is a biographical work of merit.

These stories are virile and interesting. They were written at a time when there was still a frontier; when the western characters were real rather than of the modern staged type.

FORT FRAYNE, *by Captain Charles King, U. S. A. F. Tennyson Neely, Publisher, Chicago and New York, 1895. Used by permission of the author.*

THE snow was falling in a dense white mist, powdering beards and broad-brimmed campaign hats and silvering the dusty black of the fur caps of the men. Objects fifty feet away were invisible, and all sounds muffled by the soft, fleecy blanket that everywhere covered the earth. Silently, yet with soldierly alertness, the officers hastened to look quickly over their troops. Silently the veteran colonel turned once more to the front and rode a few yards out beyond the head of the column and sat there on his horse, a white mantled statue, peering intently through the slowly falling flakes.

"We move the moment Bat gets back," murmured the adjutant to Captain Leale. "He crawled out to locate the herds and pick our way. There are some cross gullies beyond that ridge and down near the village. Bat says he feels sure most of the warriors are miles away to the east, but—there are enough and to spare right here."

"Is Kill Eagle still to be given a chance to surrender?" asked Leale. "That was the understanding at one time, wasn't it?"

"That was it—yes, and Bat was to hail as soon as we deployed within striking distance. Unless some scouts or the ponies find us out, we can creep up under this snow cloud to within a few yards, and they'll be none the wiser. The colonel hoped that the show of force would be ample and that the old scoundrel would throw up the sponge right here, but—I don't know," he added doubtfully. "if only the women and children weren't in that village, it would be simple enough. We could pitch in and double

them up before they knew what struck them. As it is—"
and here the young officer broke off with a wave of the
hand that meant volumes of doubt. Then he turned and
looked eastward again to where, silent and statuesque
still, Colonel Farrar was seated on old Roderick.

The same thought seemed to occur to both officers at
the same instant. Ormsby, once more testing the lock of
his revolver and narrowly observing his new comrades,
remarked it at the time and spoke of it often thereafter.

"Can't you make him keep well back?" asked Leale.

"Won't you remind the chief he oughtn't to be in the
front?" asked the adjutant.

And then each shook his head, as though realizing the
impossibility of getting their old war horse of a colonel
to take a position where he would be less exposed to the
fire of the Indian marksmen.

"*You* might give him a tip, Ormsby," said the adjutant, in the cheery confidence the comradeship a few days'
campaigning engenders. "You are his guest, not his subordinate. Tell him what the Seventh thinks the colonel
should do," he added, with an attempt at jocularity that
somehow failed to provoke a smile.

But Ormsby in turn shook his head. "I haven't known
your colonel a week," said he, "but I've learned to know
him well, and when he means to go in, all you've got to
do is to go, too. That's what I've mapped out for myself,
and doubtless so, too, have these gentlemen," he continued, indicating the two ranchmen, now eagerly fingering their Winchesters and getting ready for business. The
elder of the two it was who answered:

"No man who has been through what we have, and seen
the sights and heard the sounds of their raids on the
ranches down the Fork, would do less than thank God
for a chance of meeting those brutes on anything like
equal terms. My poor brother lies there, hacked and
scalped and mutilated; his wife and daughter, I believe,

are somewhere among those foul tepees now, unless God has been merciful and let them die day before yesterday. We fought as long as there was a show, and we got away in the dark. These poor women wouldn't leave their dead."

A tear was trickling down his cheek as he finished speaking, but his lips and jaws were firm set. "You gentlemen," he continued, "are going into this thing just from sense of duty, but think what it is to me and to young Crawford here. His old father and mother were just butchered, by God!—butchered—and the worst of it is that if that damned hound Graice had stood by him ten minutes he might have got them safely away. They were too old to make any time, and it was no use. That fellow's a white-livered pup, and if ever I come upon him again I'll tell him what I think of him."

"I wish you had seen that fellow, Ormsby," said Leale, in a low tone. "The more I think of it, the more I am sure he had some reason for fearing to meet our party here. They tell me he seemed excited and worried the moment he heard we were the Twelfth Cavalry. I only saw his back as he rode away, but I've seen that man before somewhere. He rode like a trooper, and it's ten to one he's a deserter."

"He's a deserter this day if he never was before," said Ormsby in reply. "I judge we need every man, do we not?"

"Looks like it," was the brief reply. "All right, gentlemen?" he continued, turning with courteous manner to the two younger officers, his first and second lieutenants, who came striding up through the snow. Leale was famous in the cavalry for his subalterns. He had the reputation of never speaking hastily or harshly, and of getting more out of his men than any other captain in the regiment.

"All right, sir!" was the prompt reply. "Every man in

my platoon boiling over with ginger," added the younger, his blue eyes flashing though his cheeks were pale and his lips twitching with pent-up excitement.

"I see the guidon is being unfurled, Cramer," said the captain, quietly. "Perhaps Sergeant West wants to land it first in the village, but tell him to handle his revolver instead, if we charge," and touching his fur cap, the officer turned back. "The colonel has said nothing about the plan of attack. We may be going to charge right in, for all I know. Ha! Ormsby, there comes the word!"

Looming up through the snow a young German trooper rode rapidly back toward the little group, and, reining in his horse a few yards away, true to the etiquette of the craft, threw his carbine over his shoulder and started to dismount before addressing officers afoot, but Leale checked him. "Never mind dismounting, orderly. What's the message?"

"The colonel's compliments, sir, and he would wish to see Captain Leale a minute, and the command will mount and move slowly forward."

Instantly the group dissolved, each officer turning quickly to his horse and swinging into saddle. No trumpet signal was given. "Mount," said Leale, in the same quiet, conversational tone. "Mount," repeated the first sergeant, halted alongside the leading set of fours, and, all in a few seconds, the burly forms of the riders shot up in the eddying fleece, and every horse, far back as the eye could penetrate the mist, was suddenly topped by an armed rider. Then, first thing, the fur-gloved right hands went up to the shoulder and drew over the little brown carbines and drove the muzzle through its socket. Then, in the same soldierly silence the horsemen edged in toward the center of each set, and there sat, boot to boot, erect and ready. One or two spirited young horses began to paw the snow in their impatience, and to snort excitedly. The adjutant trotted briskly back along the column in order to see that all four troops were similarly ready, cautioned the rearward troop leaders to keep well closed on the head of the column and signaled "Forward," while Leale disappeared in the snow clouds ahead.

Not knowing what else to do, Ormsby ranged alongside the senior lieutenant of Leale's troop, as in perfect silence the column bore steadily on. A few seconds brought them in sight of the colonel's form again, and he waved his hand cheerily as though to say, "All right, lads, come on." Then, sitting Roderick as squarely as ever, the gray-mustached commander took the lead, a swarthy half-breed Sioux scout riding on one side, the grave, soldierly Leale on the other. The adjutant, the chief trumpeter, sergeant major, and orderlies fell in behind, and the crack battalion of the old Twelfth rode noiselessly in to take position for the attack.

For perhaps a hundred yards they followed the windings of the ravine in which they had been concealed, had concealment been necessary. Then, turning abruptly to his left as he passed a projecting shoulder, Little Bat looked back and motioned to the colonel, "This way." And then the leading horsemen began to ascend a gentle and almost imperceptible slope, for the snow was sifting down so thick and fast that the surface was invisible thirty feet ahead.

"We might ride square in among them at this rate," muttered the sergeant-major to his friend, the chief trumpeter, "and never know it until we stumbled into the tepees."

"How far ahead is it?" asked the latter.

"A mile, they say. We'd be deployed by this time if it were less."

Less than five minutes of gradual ascent, and the crest of the divide was reached, and, one after another, every horseman realized that he was then on the downward slope of the eastern side. Somewhere ahead, somewhere between this ridge and its nearest neighbor, lay the hostile village, all unconscious of foeman's coming, looking for disturbers as yet only from the eastern side. Old cavalrymen used to declare their horses could smell an Indian village before the sharpest eyes could "sight" it, and the packers swore the statement was true, "if it were only made of the mule."

"The colonel knows. He hasn't forgotten, you bet," was the comment, as again the orderly rode swiftly rearward with orders for the pack train to halt just west of the crest, and then every man seemed to know that the village couldn't be far ahead, and some hands went nervously to the holster flaps, others loosened the carbines in their leather sockets, and men took furtive peeps at one another's faces along the shadowy column, and then at their officers riding so confident and erect along the left flank. And still no man could see more than the depth of three sets of fours ahead. "Ain't we going to dismount and go afoot?" muttered a young recruit to his neighbor. "I thought that was the way we always did."

"Of course; when one could see to shoot and would be seen himself anywhere within five miles," was the disdainful answer. "What'd be the good of dismounting here?"

And now in places the horses plunged deeper into the snow and tossed up drifting clouds of feathery spray as the column crossed some shallow ruts in the eastward face, and then once more, snakelike, it began to twist and turn, following the track of those invisible guides, and then it seemed to take to evil courses and go spluttering down into sharp, steep-banked coulees, and scrambling out again on the other side, and still the sure-footed horses tripped nimbly on, and then, presently, his eyes a-twinkle, the adjutant came riding back.

"Just half a mile ahead, Billy," he murmured to the lieutenant riding in Leale's place at the head of the first troop. "Form left front into line and halt. I'll post the other troop."

Quickly the young officer reined out of column to the left about. "Keep straight to your front, leading four," he cautioned. Then barely raising his voice and dropping for the time the conventional commands of the drill book, he rode back along the column, saying "Left front into line," until all the rearward fours were obliquing; then back to the front he trotted, halted the leading set, each of the others in succession reining in and generally aligning itself, all without a sound that could be audible ten yards away. Almost at the same time the second troop headed diagonally off to the left and presently rode up into line with the first, while the third and fourth were halted in similar formation at troop distance in rear. "By all that's glorious, we're going in mounted!" was the word that seemed to thrill down along the line. "Then we're not going to wait—not going to give him a chance to surrender."

Another moment and the word was, "Hush! silence there!" for dimly seen through the drifts, the colonel with his little party of attendants, came riding to the front of the line. Long, long afterward they remembered that clear-cut, soldierly, high-bred face, with its aquiline nose, keen, kindly, deep-set eyes, the gray-white mustache, snow-white now, as was his close-cropped hair.

"Men," said he in the firm tones they had known so long and well, "fully half the band are some miles away, but Kill Eagle, with over a hundred warriors, is right here in our front; so, too, are his women and children; so, too, worse luck, are some of our own unhappy captives. You all know the first thing those Indians would do, were we to attack as usual, would be to murder those poor white women. This snowstorm is in our favor. We can creep right in upon them before we charge. The ponies are down in the valley to the south. Let the first line dash straight through the village and stampede the herd, then rally and return. Let the second follow at a hundred yards and surround the tepees at the eastward end—what white women are with them are there. The Indian men, as a rule, will make a dash in the direction of the ponies. Shoot them down wherever you can, but mark my words now, be careful of the women and children. I had intended summoning Kill Eagle to surrender, but we did not begin to know he had so many warriors close at hand, and did not know about the captives. Bat has seen, and that is enough. There is no other way to settle it. It's the one chance of rescuing those poor creatures. Now keep together. Watch your officers' commands and signals and spare the squaws and papooses. Be ready in two minutes."

And then every man took a long breath, while the colonel rode through to say similar words to the second line. Then, returning, he placed himself just in the rear of the center of the first squadron, the second line noiselessly advancing and closing up on the leaders, and then he seemed to think of another point.

"Ask Mr. Ormsby if he will ride with me," said he to the adjutant. "Now, Leale, forward at a walk. Follow Bat. It's all level ahead of you. You'll sight the village in three or four minutes."

The tall, stalwart captain touched his hat, took off his "broadbrim," shaking away a load of snow, and spurred out a little to the front. There, looking back to both his right and left, he gave the signal forward, and with almost a single impulse, the long dark rank of horsemen, open at the center in an interval of some half a dozen yards, without other sound than the slight rattle of accoutrements and the muffled rumble of five hundred hoofs, moved steadily forward. A moment the colonel sat and watched them, smiled a cordial greeting to Ormsby, who, pistol in hand, came trotting over with the adjutant, then signaling to the second line, he too gave his horse the rein, and at a steady walk followed close to the center of Leale's command. In his hand at the moment he held a little pocket compass, and smiled as he noted the line of direction.

"Almost due southeast at this instant," said he. "We ought to bag our game and be well across the Mini Pusa with them in less than an hour."

Unconsciously the pace was quickening. Foremost of all, well out in front of the center, rode the half-breed Indian guide, bending low over his pony's neck, his black, beady eyes peering ahead. Well out to the right and left were other scouts, eager and alert, like Bat himself. Then, squarely in the center, on his big, powerful bay, rode Leale, commander of the foremost line, and Ormsby's soldierly heart throbbed with admiration as he marked, just before Leale was hidden from view, his spirited, confident bearing, and noted how the eyes of all the line seemed fixed on their gallant leader. And now some of the horses began to dance and tug at the bit and plunge, and others to take a jog trot, for the Indian scouts were at the lope, and their gesticulations became every moment more vehement, and then Bat was seen, though visible only to the first line, to grab his revolver, and Leale's gauntleted hand almost instantly sought the holster, and out came the ready Colt, its muzzle raised in the air. Out in quick and ready imitation leaped a hundred more, and instinctively the jog changed to a lively trot, and the dull, thudding hoofs upon the snow-muffled earth rose louder and more insistent, and Ormsby, riding at the colonel's left, gripped tighter his revolver and set his teeth, yet felt his heart was hammering loud, and then dimmer and dimmer grew the first line as it led away, and still the colonel's firm hand kept Roderick dancing impatiently at the slower gait and then, just as it seemed as though the line would be swallowed up in snow and disappear from view, quick and sudden, two muffled shots were heard from somewhere just in front, the first syllable perhaps of some stentorian shout of warning, and then one magnificent burst of cheers and a rush of charging men, and a crash and a crackle and sputter of shots, and then fierce rallying cries and piercing screams of women and of terrified little ones, and like some huge human wave the first line of the Twelfth rode on and over and through the startled camp, and bore like a whirlwind, yelling down upon the pony herds beyond.

And now comes the turn of the second line. Seeking shelter from the snowstorm, warriors, women and children were for the most part within the tepees, as the line crashed in. Some few were with the miserable captives, but at the first sound of danger every warrior had seized his rifle and rushed for the open air. Some few, throwing themselves upon their faces, fired wild shots at the foremost troopers as they came bounding through, but as a rule only a few opposed their passage, so sudden was the shock.

Then came the realization that the herds were being driven, and that not an instant must be lost in mounting such ponies as were still tethered about the villages, and darting away in a wide circle, away from the troops, yet concentrating again beyond them and regaining the lead. And so, where the first line met an apparently sleeping village, the second comes cheering, charging, firing, thundering through a swarming mob of yelling braves and screaming squaws. Farrar, foremost in the charge, with the civilian guardsman close at his side, shouts warning to the women, even as he empties his pistol at the howling men. Close at his back come Amory and his sorrel troop, cheering like mad, battering over Indians too slow to jump aside, and driving their hissing lead at every warrior in their path. And still the colonel shouts, "This way!" and Ormsby, Amory, and the adjutant ride at his heels, and the sorrels especially follow his lead, and dashing through a labyrinth of lodges, they rein up cheering about two grimy tepees at which Bat is excitedly pointing and the ranchmen both are shouting the names of loved relatives and listening eagerly for answer; and thrilling voices within are crying, "Here! Here!" and stalwart men, springing from the saddle, are rushing in, pistol in hand, and tearing aside the flimsy barriers that hide the rescued captives from the eyes of their deliverers, and the other troop, reinforced again by strong squads from Leale's rallied line, are dashing to and fro through the village, firing at the Indians who are scurrying away. Just as Amory and the adjutant charge at a little knot of scowling redskins whose rifles are blazing at them at not a dozen yards' distance, just as the good old colonel, afoot now, is clasping the hand of some poor woman whose last hope was gone but a moment before, and even while listening to her frantic blessings, finds time to shout again to his half maddened men, "Don't hurt the women, lads! Look out for the children!" a hag-like, blanketed fury of a Brulé squaw springs from behind the shelter of a pile of robes, levels her revolver, and, pulling trigger at the instant, leaps screaming down into the creek bottom, leaving Farrar sinking slowly into the snow.

An hour later, with strong skirmish lines out on every side of the captured village, with a score of Indian warriors sent to their last account and the others scattered over the face of the earth, the little battalion of the Twelfth is wondering if, after all, the fight were worth the winning, for here in their midst, his head on Leale's arm, his fading sight fixed on the tear-dimmed eyes of his faithful comrade, here lies their beloved old colonel, his last messages murmured in that listening ear: "Leale —old friend—find—find that poor girl—my—my son robbed and ruined and deserted—and be the friend to her —you've been to me—and mine. God bless—"

And this—while the regiment, obeying its stern duty, goes on in pursuit—this is the news Jack Ormsby has to break to the loving, breaking hearts at Frayne.

Thornton Wilder

☼

THORNTON WILDER was born, April 17, 1897, in Madison, Wisconsin, where his father, Amos Parker Wilder, was connected with the *Wisconsin State Journal* from 1894 to 1911. Amos P. Wilder was consul general at Hong Kong, China from 1906 to 1909, and at Shanghai from 1909 to 1914. Thus it happened that Thornton Wilder spent a portion of his childhood years in an Oriental atmosphere. He was graduated from Yale College in 1920; then spent two years in the American Academy in Rome. Wilder's first story, *The Cabala*, attracted little attention at the time. After this early literary venture he taught school for a while. Later he spent some time studying and writing at the Princeton Graduate College. During this period Mr. Wilder wrote a play, *The Trumpet Shall Sound*, which was produced with moderate success in New York. There was nothing in either of these productions to mark the young writer as a future literary genius. Then in the latter part of 1927 appeared his *Bridge of San Luis Rey*, which received the Pulitzer prize as the best work of fiction produced during that year. It won instant popularity and made the writer famous. This was followed by the *Woman of Andros*, also a pronounced success. With his active life still before him, much may be expected from the young author in the years to come. Mr. Wilder now resides in New York City.

THE BRIDGE OF SAN LUIS REY *by Thornton Wilder. Albert & Charles Boni, Publishers, New York, 1928. Reprinted by permission of the author and publishers.*

PART ONE: PERHAPS AN ACCIDENT

On Friday noon, July the twentieth, 1714, the finest bridge in all Peru broke and precipitated five travellers into the gulf below. This bridge was on the high-road between Lima and Cuzco and hundreds of persons passed over it every day. It had been woven of osier by the Incas more than a century before and visitors to the city were always led out to see it. It was a mere ladder of thin slats swung out over the gorge, with handrails of dried vine. Horses and coaches and chairs had to go down hundreds of feet below and pass over the narrow torrent on rafts, but no one, not even the Viceroy, not even the Archbishop of Lima, had descended with the baggage rather than cross by the famous bridge of San Luis Rey. St. Louis of France himself protected it, by his name and by the little mud church on the further side. The bridge seemed to be among the things that last forever; it was unthinkable that it should break. The moment a Peruvian heard of the accident he signed himself and made a mental calculation as to how recently he had crossed by it and how soon he had intended crossing by it again. People wandered about in a trance-like state, muttering; they had the hallucination of seeing themselves falling into a gulf.

There was a great service in the Cathedral. The bodies of the victims were approximately collected and approximately separated from one another, and there was great searching of hearts in the beautiful city of Lima. Servant girls returned bracelets which they had stolen from their mistresses, and usurers harangued their wives angrily, in defense of usury. Yet it was rather strange that this event should have so impressed the Limeans, for in that country those catastrophes which lawyers shockingly call the "acts of God" were more than usually frequent. Tidal waves were continually washing away cities; earthquakes arrived every week and towers fell upon good men and women all the time. Diseases were forever flitting in and out of the provinces and old age carried away some of the most admirable citizens. That is why it was so surprising that the Peruvians should have been especially touched by the rent in the bridge of San Luis Rey.

Every one was deeply impressed, but only one person did anything about it, and that was Brother Juniper. By a series of coincidences so extraordinary that one almost suspects the presence of some Intention, this little redhaired Franciscan from Northern Italy happened to be in Peru converting the Indians and happened to witness the accident.

It was a very hot noon, that fatal noon, and coming around the shoulder of a hill Brother Juniper stopped to wipe his forehead and to gaze upon the screen of snowy peaks in the distance, then into the gorge below him filled with the dark plumage of green trees and green birds and traversed by its ladder of osier. Joy was in him; things were not going badly. He had opened several little abandoned churches and the Indians were crawling in to early Mass and groaning at the moment of miracle as though their hearts would break. Perhaps it was the pure air from the snows before him; perhaps it was the memory that brushed him for a moment of the poem that bade him raise his eyes to the helpful hills. At all events he felt at peace. Then his glance fell upon the bridge, and at that moment a twanging noise filled the air, as when the string of some musical instrument snaps in a disused room, and he saw the bridge divide and fling five gesticulating ants into the valley below.

Anyone else would have said to himself with secret joy: "Within ten minutes myself . . . !" But it was another thought that visited Brother Juniper: "Why did this happen to *those* five?" If there were any plan in the universe at all, if there were any pattern in a human life, surely it could be discovered mysteriously latent in those lives so suddenly cut off. Either we live by accident and die by accident, or we live by plan and die by plan. And on that instant Brother Juniper made the resolve to inquire into the secret lives of those five persons, that moment falling through the air, and to surprise the reason of their taking off.

* * * *

It seemed to Brother Juniper that it was high time for theology to take its place among the exact sciences and he had long intended putting it there. What he had lacked hitherto was a laboratory. Oh, there had never been any lack of specimens; any number of his charges had met calamity,—spiders had stung them; their lungs had been touched; their houses had burned down and things had happened to their children from which one averts the mind. But these occasions of human woe had never been quite fit for scientific investigation. They had lacked what our good savants were later to call *proper control*. The accident had been dependent upon human error, for example, or had contained elements of probability. But this collapse of the bridge of San Luis Rey was a sheer Act of God. It afforded a perfect laboratory. Here at last one could surprise His intentions in a pure state.

You and I can see that coming from anyone but Brother Juniper this plan would be the flower of a perfect skepticism. It resembled the effort of those presumptuous souls who wanted to walk on the pavements of Heaven and built the Tower of Babel to get there. But to our Franciscan there was no element of doubt in the experiment. He knew the answer. He merely wanted to prove it, historically, mathematically, to his converts,—poor obstinate converts, so slow to believe that their pains were inserted into their lives for their own good. People were always asking for good sound proofs; doubt springs eternal in the human breast, even in countries where the Inquisition can read your very thoughts in your eyes.

This was not the first time that Brother Juniper had tried to resort to such methods. Often on the long trips he had to make (scurrying from parish to parish, his robe tucked up about his knees, for haste) he would fall to dreaming of experiments that justify the ways of God to man. For instance, a complete record of the Prayers for Rain and their results. Often he had stood on the steps of one of his little churches, his flock kneeling before him on the baked street. Often he had stretched his arms to the sky and declaimed the splendid ritual. Not often, but several times, he had felt the virtue enter him and seen the little cloud forming on the horizon. But there were many times when weeks went by . . . but why think of them? It was not himself he was trying to convince that rain and drought were wisely apportioned.

Thus it was that the determination rose within him at the moment of the accident. It prompted him to busy himself for six years, knocking at all the doors in Lima, asking thousands of questions, filling scores of notebooks, in his effort at establishing the fact that each of the five lost lives was a perfect whole. Everyone knew that he was working on some sort of memorial of the accident and everyone was very helpful and misleading. A few even knew the principal aim of his activity and there were patrons in high places.

The result of all this diligence was an enormous book, which as we shall see later, was publicly burned on a beautiful Spring morning in the great square. But there was a secret copy and after a great many years and without much notice it found its way to the library of the University of San Marco. There it lies between two great wooden covers collecting dust in a cupboard. It deals with one after another of the victims of the accident, cataloguing thousands of little facts and anecdotes and testimonies, and concluding with a dignified passage describing why God had settled upon that person and upon that day for His demonstration of wisdom. Yet for all his diligence Brother Juniper never knew the central passion of Dona Maria's life; nor of Uncle Pio's, not even of Esteban's. And I, who claim to know so much more, isn't it possible that even I have missed the very spring within the spring?

Some say that we shall never know and that to the gods we are like flies that the boys kill on a summer day, and some say, on the contrary, that the very sparrows do not lose a feather that has not been brushed away by the finger of God.

Margaret Ashmun

☼

THE RURAL communities of Wisconsin have produced a number of men and women who, in their several lines of endeavor, have given their native state cause for honest pride in their achievements. In the absence of present-day amusements, they made books their companions and became serious-minded. It is more than likely that the restricted environment was a blessing in disguise to these aspiring young people.

Margaret Ashmun, educator and writer, was born in Rural, Waupaca County, Wisconsin. Her birthplace is all that the name implies, and a search for Rural on most maps of Wisconsin would probably end in disappointment. As a guide to the visitor, it may be said that Rural is near the southern end of the beautiful Chain of Lakes that has made the vicinity of Waupaca famous. One of Miss Ashmun's books, *The Lake*, has its scenes laid among these lakes. She has stated that this is one of her productions with which she is most satisfied.

Miss Ashmun received her early education in the public schools of her county, in the Stevens Point Normal School, and in the University of Wisconsin; from which last named institution she was graduated in 1904. She taught English at the University from 1907 to 1912, during which time she received her Master's degree. Prior to this time, Miss Ashmun had taught school in Montana where she found inspiration for a number of her later stories. In 1912 she removed to New York to engage seriously in literary work. Her earlier publications were largely text-books. Among her later works are: *Stephen's*

Last Chance, 1918; *Marion Frear's Summer*, 1920; *Isabel Carlton in the West*, 1920; *Topless Towers*, 1921; *Support*, 1922; *Including Mother*, 1922; *The Lake*, 1924; *No School Tomorrow*, 1925; and *School Keeps Today*, 1926.

From THE LAKE *by Margaret Ashmun. Published by The Macmillan Company, New York, 1924. Reprinted by permission of the author and the publishers. All rights reserved.*

THE next evening, immediately after supper, Alexander McLean drove over in his buckboard. He came over frequently—two or three times a week. There was nothing to keep him home, he said; and he had to find company among the neighbours. Alec and Willard had been friends ever since the Faradays had come to this region. In fact it was in an indirect way through the influence of Alec that the Faradays had come. About the time that Averil and Willard were married, in Western New York State, and Willard was trying to make up his mind whether to settle down there, or migrate farther west, his uncle had a letter from a young man named McLean, who had gone out to Wisconsin the year before. He had painted an attractive picture of his prosperity, and said that a farm near him was for sale, and he hoped that someone from home would come out. "Why don't you try it, Will?" the uncle had said. "I'll help you a little, and your father can give you a boost, and you can buy the place all right, with a mortgage on it."

* * * * *

Time was going on swiftly now, and summer had emerged into autumn. Bert was in school again—but there were always Saturdays. Potato digging was nearly over; corn husking was coming. Willard and Alec had worked hard on their respective farms. Crops and prices were promising.

One Saturday Willard was taking a load of potatoes to Prattsville, the county seat, nine miles away. He started early, and would be back before nightfall. In the middle of the forenoon, Alexander McLean called up on the telephone. He wanted to speak to Bert. He never talked to Averil over the telephone, except in the most perfunctory and guarded way, and seldom at that; because all the country lines were "party" lines, and everybody listened in to hear what everybody else was saying.

"Oh, say, Bert," said Alexander, his voice full and suave on the wire, "why can't you and I have an outing together? It's a great day, but there's no telling how long such weather will last. Want to go?"

"Yes, yes, of course I do." Bert was always awkward at the telephone. "But where—what—"

"We'll go out in the woods. I'll meet you at the log house at three o'clock. Ask your mother if that's all right."

Bert left the receiver swinging, and went to the kitchen door to tell his mother. She looked disturbed. "I'd like it awful well," urged Hubert.

"Tell him you can go, then," she said unwillingly. "Did he say anything about taking a lunch?"

Bert shook his head. "I guess we'll be back for supper. He didn't say."

"Well," Averil had consented, though with apprehension. Bert scuttled back to the telephone.

That afternoon he started out early, so that he might be sure not to keep Uncle Alec waiting. He was resolved not to stop at the Hunts', lest he should be overpersuaded and lured into delay. There were always so many things to talk about. The old man, Mr. Gleason, was raking dry maple leaves in the long front yard. His shoulders were hunched a little, but he wielded the rake with quick strong motions. "Hello," he called out happily to Bert. He looked clean and well cared for, and his blue eyes were beaming with satisfaction. Even Bert could not help seeing how happy the old man was to be at Libbie Hunt's.

Bert called back "Hello!" and remarked on the size of the pile of leaves in the driveway.

"Got yours all raked yet?" asked Mr. Gleason, proud of his work.

"Not all. I'm leaving some till to-morrow."

"Oh, that's Sunday. Better rake 'em to-day," said the old man. He felt proud to be so active, so forehanded, so virtuous in his regard for the Sabbath. Bert backed away from the fence. "Caddie's pulling the carrots," the old man told him.

"I got to go on. I got to meet somebody," said Bert. He felt important, meeting Uncle Alec in that way. The old man nodded, snatching at the leaves with his wooden rake, and rustling them into a pile.

Bert was early, after all, and had to wait a long time for Alec at the log house, a deserted cabin set where a grass-grown road branched off from the highway.

But after a while, there was Alec striding along in corduroys and flannel shirt, with a gun over his shoulder. He walked as if getting over the ground were a process of nature, involuntary and unnoticed, like breathing. "Hey, there!" he called, laughing. "Been waiting long?"

"Not so awful," answered Bert. "But I guess I was early."

"Guess you were. I'm just on time." Alec pulled out his watch. He wore a short wool jacket, and a soft felt hat, shapeless with age, but he seemed to Bert impressively well dressed. "We'll go along the Chain," he said. "You don't get over there very often."

"No," said Bert.

"Well, we'll see what's over there," smiled Alec.

They walked down the grassy road, between neglected fields. In ten minutes, the lustred surface of a lake appeared. It was the first of the Chain. Bert had been there before, a good many times if they were all counted; but not so often that the lake did not seem new to him on this autumn afternoon. The warm sun beat down upon him, but the cool wind took away the sting of the heat. White clouds billowed along the sky. Across the lake a tamarack swamp showed misty blue.

They turned in along the edge of the marsh, where twisted gentians stood up stiffly, and iris pods were dry and slitting. On a harder knoll a hickory tree showed its dark round fruit. The squirrel instinct of the boy would hardly let him pass.

Up a small rise in the road they went, and then were on a flat wooded space which stretched away toward the Big Lake. Here the trees were mostly maples and butternuts and bass-woods, whose leaves turned to pure gold at the touch of frost. Looking up through the laced branches and the yellow leaves already thinned, Hubert could see the sky, bluer than it had been before.

Under foot were the fallen leaves and the jewel-colours of red and coral and orange mushrooms. Here and there a vine, blood-red, climbed a tree and hung along the boughs, dripping its sanguinary foliage far down.

"This is the finest time of the year," said Alec. "Can you see how wonderful it is lad?"

"Uh-huh, I guess so," answered Bert, gruffly, because he felt so shy about things that were beautiful.

Alec seemed to understand. "It's the kind of thing that there's no use in talking about," he said. Bert looked up at him, and his face was still and brooding. The boy dared not interrupt the man's thoughts with speech. They went on, bound for nowhere in particular, treading the gold carpet of the woods. Sometimes Hubert scuffled in the leaves, to see the sun glint upon them through the boughs.

After a while a faint sound came to his ears, above the flittering of the foliage in the wind, and above the screaming of jays and the tapping of nut-hatches on the boles.

Hubert heard it again. "What is that?" he asked breathlessly.

Alec stopped and listened. "It's a partridge," he said, his face alert. "It's over that way. Let's go as still as we can."

They crept along under the branches, stopping frequently to crouch and listen. They came at last to an open place where in times past two or three trees had been brought down by wind or lightning. Here the drumming was loud and insistent. "Ssh," whispered Alec. He held his gun in his hand. "See her, Bert?" he said.

At first Bert could not make out anything except a huge fallen tree trunk with broken branches. But in a minute he could see something moving and then the regular beating of wings, from which came the muffled sound of drumming. "She's almost the colour of the log," whispered Bert.

Alec raised his gun to his shoulder. Hubert held his breath. But a pang shot through him which was almost like the lead which was in a moment to pierce the sentient creature beating out the last of life before him. "Oh-h!" he gasped. Was it too late? He had wanted to say, "Oh, don't!" but he had not been able to speak.

Alec, without hearing him, had already lowered his gun. "Shall we let her live, Bert?" he said thickly. "I can't kill a thing like that, out here in the open, enjoying the sun and the air and the woods as much as we do. Hadn't we better let her go on living?"

Hubert gave a cry of relief. "You bet," he said, louder than he intended. "I was awful scared you was going to kill her!"

The bird, hearing the voices, stopped the beating of its wings, and stood transfixed; then in a flurry of feathers was off on wing, floating silently away like a shadow into the thicker woods. "I hope she'll make the most of her chance," muttered Alec. "The next fellow's heart may not be so soft!"

Hubert rejoiced openly, in exclamations which had no definite wording.

Alec looked sheepish but pleased. "I'm glad you feel the way I do, kid," he said. "I'm not much for killing things. But it wouldn't do to tell anyone what ninnies we are."

"No," agreed Bert. There was no use in telling people everything you knew. He had found that fact out before this.

They turned back toward the lake, and walked along exuberantly. Each was exulting at having given its life to this creature of the woods. "Swell hunters, we are," laughed Alec. "Ain't we the Hiawathas? Oh, well," he added, "I guess we can do as we like when we're off on an excursion all by ourselves." There was a suggestion of intimacy in his tone, an affectionate welding of the two that made Bert take delight in this companionship. "I brought sandwiches," said the man, as they drew near the lake. He reached into the sagging pocket of his jacket. "Folks are always hungry in the woods."

Hubert felt suddenly hungry, though he had not thought about the matter before. They were now on the bank of the lake, which lay below an abrupt slope of thirty feet. The banks were slippery with brown pine needles, and the warm scent of pine was in the air, the pitchy smell which is the sweetest aroma of the woods. "Gee! Ain't it great?" said Bert sniffing.

They sat down on a log, and Alec unrolled the paper parcel which contained the snack. There were thick sandwiches of meat and cheese. As he ate, Hubert sent pine cones spinning down the slippery banks, or shied pebbles out upon the water. "This lake is different from ours," he said.

"It's a great deal higher," said Alec. "It lies on higher ground. Did you know that?"

"No, I never knew about it," answered Bert, accepting another sandwich.

"Your lake is down on a different level," Alec explained. "If these on this Chain should have a channel cut through, the water would rush in and cover all your father's land—and then where'd you be?" He laughed, taking another big bite of bread and meat.

Bert looked startled. The idea was a strange one. "You mean, the water would run right out over our land?"

"Yeah," replied McLean. "That's just what I mean. You see, there's only a little bit of a place that separates them, separates the Chain from your lake, I mean. It could be cut through."

Bert pondered, staring at the blue water below him. "How do you know it would drown our land?" he asked incredulously.

"I can see for myself," returned Alec. "I know the place where the lakes come the nearest together. You see, your house and the land around it, and most of your father's farm are not very high above the water."

"I know that," Hubert conceded, still holding his sandwich in his hand.

"Your lake is fed by springs, and not by rivers, and it hasn't any outlet," said McLean. "It's all right if it's let alone. That house has stood there for sixty or seventy years, I guess; but if the water should come through from the other side, it would be a bad day for all concerned." Hubert looked so alarmed that Alec began laughing again at the sight of the boy's face. "You needn't be scared," he hastened to say. "It won't ever happen. I just thought you'd like to hear about it."

"Funny I never heard about it before," grumbled Bert.

"Hardly anybody knows it, I guess," answered Alec. "What people don't know won't hurt 'em."

They ate, chatting of other things. Alec had a way of speaking to the boy as if they were equals. Hubert liked such treatment, which was different from that which he received from anyone else. Alec took out his pipe and tobacco, and sat with a blue haze around his head, his hat pushed back, his cheeks red, his hair showing brown under the rim of his hat. He was like a big friendly boy; but it would take only an instant to change him to a stern and gloomy man.

They sat for a long time; or at least Alec did. Hubert was up and down, running to watch a squirrel circling an oak tree, with bitter cries of indignation at this human invasion; or listening to bird calls; or marvelling at the coarse laughter of a pair of loons swimming and diving in the lake.

The man and the boy had another tramp into the woods before they started for home. Alec looked at his watch. "Getting late," he said. "I'm a free man. I don't have to account for myself; but it's different with you." He did not seem to be joking.

"I guess I'm all right," Bert made sturdy answer. He did not want to act scared, nor to whine about things; but he had thought all at once of what his father would say if he were late. Why should his father care if he were out with Uncle Alec? He might know that Alec would not let anything happen to him. Perhaps he wouldn't be angry. Perhaps it would be all right. Even if it should be a trifle unpleasant, he was glad he had had this afternoon. He could stand a lot to pay for it. But he cringed, too, when he thought of Willard Faraday's face distorted by anger.

They were now at a considerable distance from the road. They trudged along in the dulling splendour of the golden forest. When they came to the road, Alec said, "I wonder if I'd better go home with you, Bert?"

"Oh, I guess not," answered the boy quickly. "You've got quite a ways to go, an' there's no use in bothering with me."

McLean stood considering. "I don't want to muddle

things," he said. "I guess, on the whole, it would be better if I didn't go." He let his gaze fall upon the boy with an anxious affectionate look. "I believe it's better this way." His face cleared. He stood watching as the boy went down the road, and disappeared behind the hazel bushes. With a long sigh, he turned, shouldered his unused gun, and walked away toward home.

Glenway Wescott

☼

GLENWAY WESCOTT, one of the youngest of Wisconsin's writers, was born in 1901 at Kewaskum, Wisconsin where his father, B. P. Wescott, was a farmer, an occupation that had been followed continuously by his ancestors since the time of Roger Williams in Rhode Island. B. P. Wescott now resides in Ripon, Wisconsin where he is manager of the Farmer's Exchange.

Glenway Wescott attended the public schools of West Bend and was graduated from the Waukesha High School, after which he entered the University of Chicago. There he was known as a browsing student with scant patience for some of the required subjects. When he had spent a little more than a year in the university, ill health forced him to leave school. He lived in Santa Fe, New Mexico for a time until improved health permitted him to return to Chicago. There he set himself in earnest to a literary career. A desire to visit Europe was made possible of realization when he succeeded in selling his articles to several of the eastern magazines. For some time past Mr. Wescott has resided in Ville Franche, a small fishing village near Nice in southern France. He says that his foreign residence is only temporary, and that he looks forward to the time when he can establish himself in his native country.

Mr. Wescott wrote his first book, *The Apple of the Eye*, when he was only seventeen years of age. Twice he rewrote and revised it before it was published serially (under another title) in the *Dial*. This work contained little more than a promise for future efforts. Some of his well-wishers regretted its publication and pronounced it vulgar as well as mediocre. His next book, *The Grandmothers*, was well received and showed a marked development on the part of the young writer. His latest book, *Good-Bye Wisconsin*, is, as were its predecessors, a narrative dealing with his native state. It has been called the Wisconsin "Main Street." As Mr. Wescott has announced that he is now done with Wisconsin scenes and characters, his next literary production will be awaited with interest.

GOOD-BYE WISCONSIN, *by Glenway Wescott, Harper and Brothers, Publishers. New York and London, 1928. Reprinted by permission of the author and of the publishers.*

HOMEWARD bound at last, north from Milwaukee on Christmas Eve. The red-towered station looks very German. But the stern, tattered, tall twilight is American; little by little it will change the German faces; and all that in the near future we can hope for, or fear, is resemblance. There used to be a saintly Scotchwoman in the waiting room to keep country girls from getting into trouble. In the train-shed the crowd surges against a high picket fence, sways in one piece like a boxcarful of cattle: a mixed population, returning to maternal arms, infant arms, arms in love. As the train moves north a blizzard comes south.

My life of the rest of the year being left behind, being buried beneath new impressions, trampled underfoot by resurrected ones, passing through and out of my head, bit by bit. . . . The stiff carnations ofthe Mediterranean are in bloom. Never live in Paris: everyone there has done some harm to everyone else; the heart must be kept in fashion, there was the influence of Henry James, so it is no longer elegant to quarrel; they go on dining together, a malicious intimacy with a lump in its throat. In mid-Atlantic, a short rainbow alongside of the ship with both feet in the sea. Never live in New York either: a town in which "it is essential to wear one's heart on one's sleeve as one's tongue in one's cheek." New York is halfway between the south of France and Wisconsin, always halfway between any two such places; that is its importance. . . .

The train jerks, because the cars are of steel, I suppose. Oranges and green plush. The heat of a Turkish bath into which, through opened doors, through double windowpanes, the awful wind penetrates; nature and a comfort-loving race between them have made this the worst climate in the world. Somewhere up ahead everyone's Christmas tree, squat and dazzling.

A wild-looking youngster asks if anyone has seen his wife and baby. An old man watches over a girl as lovely as a film star. She wears in her hat a tied ostrich plume which looks as if long tresses of hair had grown on a stem; no other woman in the car is unfashionably dressed. She is a half-wit, and keeps eating sandwiches with the impressive ferocity of a monkey, clutching them with both hands. Here and there, students on their way home from college. Middle-class young men in France are less fine physically. Heads almost uniformly well-proportioned; the relaxed look that experts in dissimulation have when they are alone. Either they are blush-pink or they have that translucent dead-leaf skin, without yellowness, without whiteness, which seems peculiar to America and is said to be increasingly common, a result of American air, of the way of life and the climate. The mad girl has it, too.

Throbbing on the rails, the train begins running downhill, which means, I remembered from childhood, that we have passed a town called Marblehead. That name and the mature schoolboys make me think of Greece—many-headed, marble-headed. France is its heir, eldest son in this generation of nations. I am jealous of every national glory. Not that I expect my country to become a poets' colony, a sculptors', architects', and moralists' colony. There were all sorts of Greeks. . . . Heads of all complexions, even in the sculptured stone: ruddy and ivory and the very vivid brown—as if red rose-leaves had been tanned and made into a leather—which some of my friends, visiting the Mediterranean beaches, find objectionable and others do their best to acquire.

I have to change trains. The snowstorm is over, or we have passed through it. I share a corner of what is called a milk-train with a lot of baggage and two young workmen. One seems unhealthy: large hands bright with chemicals. The other has that look of sheepish melancholy which I frivolously associate with socialism. They engage in conversation about their jobs and each other's relatives which they know by name; their fathers are farmers; the yellow-handed one works in a tannery in Fond du Lac, the other is an ironworker in a Milwaukee foundry. They speak a mixture of several kinds of English— Swedish, German, Polish, Irish—immigrants' children of the second generation having inherited accents from all their parents at once, all the accents. They keep looking at my cigarette-lighter, my gloves, my tight black cap, a Basque *beret*.

The tanner: "Where d'ya work in Mulwauky?"

"I came up from Chicago."

"Yuh got some folks here?"

"My father and mother live in Claron. He was a farmer until he moved to town."

A pause without embarrassment on their parts. The ironworker: "Wha' d'ya work at'n Chicago?"

"I don't work in Chicago. I've been in New York." I see myself retreating right around the world. . . .

So I offer them cigarettes; they look at the mark; and out of timidity I open Thomas Mann's *Hochstapler Krull*.

If this were Europe I could have told them that I was a writer, which would have been the end of it. One day years ago when I was wearing a rather pretentious black cape, I tipped a porter in a Munich railway station. "Thank you kindly, Herr poet," he said.

The train is making up for lost time. I know, I say to myself, what the country is like beyond the syncopated noise, the shaken light-bulbs, outside the sooty windows in the dark. The state with a beautiful name—glaciers once having made of it their pasture—is an anthology, a collection of all the kinds of landscape, perfect examples side by side. Ranges of hills strung from the great lake to the Mississippi River in long, lustrous necklaces, one above another from the northern throat of the state until well below its waist. Peacock lakes of bronze weeds and vivid water, with steep shores; four or five of them to be seen at a time from certain hilltops. Fertility and wilderness in rapid succession along powdery highways: classic meadows where cattle seem to walk and eat in their sleep, sandy slopes full of foxes, ledges where there are still rattlesnakes. Sad forests full of springs; the springs have a feverish breath. There are metallic plants which burn your hands if you touch them. All summer the horizon trembles, hypnotically flickering over the full grain, the taffeta corn, and the labor in them of dark, overclothed men, singing women, awe-stricken children. These say nothing; their motionless jaws give an account of their self-pity, dignity, and endurance. Sheet-lightning at night, and they sleep in the grass, in hammocks, on folded blankets on the floor—the beds are too hot. They get up and work with strange, ardent motions and the obstinacies of ghosts in the heat; there is wealth in it. In the sky mocking marble palaces, an Eldorado of sterile cloud. Not sterile—for down fall large black-and-blue rains, tied with electric ribbons; they never seem to be doing much good, but the crops are saved. . . .

Thus, neglecting the masterpiece which I keep in my hand to prevent the workmen from asking questions but not uninfluenced by its mood of shameless, summary confession—in which the true nature of Herr Krull is almost obscured by the bright light shed on every detail—I think of the land outside the train window as one of perpetual summer. Then the door swings open; the blown cold pounds on the nape of my neck; in spite of the coal-gas, the tobacco, the oranges, the opium-sweetnesss of warm bodies, I imagine that I can smell snow.

For in reality this is a sort of winter resort for storms from the North Pole; now all the half-tropic vegetation, the flesh and the fruitfulness, stripped and lying quite still, are theirs. You seem to be on a lofty plateau, and you can see with your own eyes that the world is convex. The villages are almost as lonely as the farms. It is like Russia with vodka prohibited and no stationary peasantry —strictly speaking, with none at all. The soul hibernates in the cold body; your feet ache for months at a time. I remember, at church, in my childhood, prayers that were visible, white and tenuous and moustaches covered with frost through which the slow, discouraging hymn made its way. A good many men got drunk a great deal of the time in spite of everything. Once a month the new moon sets out like the crooked knife of a fairy story in search of a heart to bury itself in. This is the dying-season for old men and women. When the moon is full, over the crusted snow, men go rabbit-hunting.

The train stops at a junction and makes its presence known; with another lowing, female sound, another train replies. I have a vague remembrance of that junction, those two deep voices. I ask, and am told that we are coming into Claron.

Out of the dark run forward my young father, my small mother. Across the town in an automobile, no distance at all; home, the new house, a home in town. On the small square of property close-pressed by other houses, collies with no more herds to tend; the color of pheasants with ruffled plumage, under the arc-light, against the snowbanks. Up the icy steps; a tumult in the doorway; energetic kisses which smell good, smell of health and warm wool; my brother, my sisters. Their courtesy a little affected but with burning eyes, breaking down repeatedly in the stress of the exuberance which they have in common, the stress of joy or disappointment, pride, contention, yearning. This is the wild fountain of friendliness. Sometimes it occurs to me that I ought to play the Ancient Mariner, but I am evidently always to be wedding guest.

There are chocolates and fruit; I remember the annual basket of grapes which my father used to bring from the state fair when we were children, a wooden basket with a wire handle and pale, elongated California grapes—each of us ate his share grape by grape, there were so few. The floors are waxed; carpets like everyone else's have taken the place of the rag rugs accumulated by my grandmothers. That fruitful, severe farmhouse of childhood, it seemed to have an immortal soul and now seems to have borne a physical resemblance to my mother—a house so cold at this time of the year that every vessel which held water had a lip of crystal. Here there is a bathroom. Progress, I think sleepily. The king is dead, long live the king; deprivation is dead. . . . I rejoice, but regret some of his poetry. Fortunately, progress has not gone far enough here to deprive me of a cold bed, of the drug of zero weather, the barbaric luxury of frost, in my nostrils all night long.

Early in the morning I go out to look at the town. It is like any other not too new or too large or too small in the state—or perhaps in any state not too far east or west. Main Street down the middle—beef-red brick and faded clapboards; it is lamentably impressive. The new banks, I must admit, are of lighter brick and adorned with brief, reasonably Roman pillars. The churches have an athiestic look and must have been very cheap to build. Dry-goods stores remarkably full of luxury; drug stores which sell everything (at a glance everything seems made of paper) the most expensive cameras and the cheapest books; a windowful of superb apples. Apples are wealth in midwinter; in fact it is all wealth, though it resembles the meanest poverty. Branching off Main Street at right angles, up small hills and down gentle slopes, the other streets: short but spacious avenues, noble trees over the snow-banks, lawns under them. Actually it is one lawn, there being no hedges or fences or walls (during the burning summers, no privacy). The houses are variations on one house, a sort of palatial cottage; principally wood, you can see into most of them and through some, and they do not seem to rest solidly on the ground; the difference between them and a tent is precisely that between moving every generation and moving every month. . . .

Where the houses leave off lugubrious poetry begins: never-painted landscape, chiaroscuro of twigs and snow. Framed by a puerile architecture, a patchwork of advertisements, a frieze of restless and almost beautiful men and women. The country, there it lies, a fitful and mysterious source—nothing more. The source of the sunrises, the bad weather, and the food, and of certain books already a little out of date. For the country, in the old sense of the word, has ceased to exist. Wisconsin farmers are no longer rustics; they have become provincials. The former ardent, hungry, tongue-tied life with its mingling of Greek tragedy and idyll has come to an end. Labor for the men, labor-pains for the women, elementary passions like gusts of storm moving unembarrassed in empty hearts, strong minds empty from birth until death of everything but the images of fowls in the rain, lonesome barns in the yellow sunshine—all over and done with. Now, by telephones, the radio, and automobiles, the farms have been turned into a sort of spacious, uncrystallized suburb around towns like Claron; and between the town and the suburb the contact is close. Now hired men, for example, have the privilege of being in love with Miss Garbo, whose troubling face I find on a bright poster.

Here are the humble looking churches, half of whose faithful are farmers; many variations, both in appearance and in doctrine, on one church. I attend an elaborate pageant of the Nativity. All of the congregation's tapestries and many of its best bedsheets; rented crowns and curtains, silly angels painted on a backdrop of sky; footlights and spotlights worthy of an assembly of radio fans. A gaunt little girl in gilt and muslin represents the Angel of History; she plays theatrically, has a very modern body and a cropped honey-colored head, and even her solemnity suggests profane shows in the East. Other all too Western muses. An adolescent chokes on his words, as indeed the original shepherd probably did. One of the Wise Men has forgotten to take off his horn-rimmed spectacles. The Babe in the manger is electricity, which is moving and seems true. It is all moving and true. But as the collection-boxes on long handles are passed, rather too plaintive an appeal for generosity is made; one would suppose that there were niggardly church-goers. And a kindly deacon improvises this prayer:

"Dear Father, we thank Thee that we live in a day when men are given to enjoy many things that they never had before. Especially women—I think women's lives have been made easy and lifted out of the darkness, thanks to the right interpretation of Thy Scriptures. And dear Father, we hear at present a great deal of talk against Thy church. It has its limitations, we know, but it has done a wonderful work for mankind. And what have they found to take its place? Until another institution comes along which can do that work better, let us be faithful to it. Bless us in the name of the Son who, as we have seen, was born unto us this day. Amen." I realize that it is not blasphemous, for it is only rhetorically addressed to God, not meant to be heard in heaven but overheard in this town. Thus the religion of Calvin, holding its own in society at all costs, is helping itself cease to be a religion at all, the little churches becoming—oh, let us say, clubs.

There is a denominational college. I imagine the president of a poor school as a solicitor, a beggar of bequests, moving with anxious sociability from deathbed to deathbed, an advertiser by word of mouth, a human form-letter, praising his institution and arousing pity for it at the same time. Scandal—an indecorous dance or sometimes any dance at all, an instructor whose opinions on any subject are foolhardy or whose private life is subject to any remark—may occasion an unpleasant talk with some elderly person who has already been generous, relatively generous, or even cause a will to be revised. He has another source of revenue to keep flowing: the tuition fees, which are high. The young people are lawless, effervescent with strong ideas, insidiously persuasive; if his puritanism is tyrannical or the curriculum behind the times, friendly fathers, impatient brothers, will let them go elsewhere or try to have him removed. It is an unhappy position; he must be nobly patient and politic. . . . At all events, the college reflects some such mournful reasonableness, timeserving, and trembling.

Lucian Cary

☼

LUCIAN CARY, who was born in Hamlin, Kansas, January 1, 1886, is a member of a family well-known in Wisconsin. His father, C. P. Cary, was for many years Superintendent of Public Instruction in Wisconsin, and is a lecturer and writer of note. Lucian Cary was graduated from the University of Wisconsin in 1906, and then did post-graduate work at the University of Chicago during 1907-8. From 1908 to 1910, he taught English in Wabash College, Crawfordsville, Indiana. Mr. Cary was on the staff of the Chicago Tribune from 1910 to 1912, when he became literary editor of the Chicago Evening Post for two years. In 1916 and 1917 he was connected with Collier's Weekly. Most of his excellent literary work has been in the form of magazine articles. His most popular story, *The Duke Steps Out*, was published in 1928.

From THE DUKE STEPS OUT *by Lucian Cary. 1928. Reprinted by joint permission of the author and of the publishers, Doubleday, Doran & Co., Garden City, N. J. All rights reserved.*

THE DUKE received, a day or two later, his notice from the dean of women to appear at her office. He read it through twice, and called up Pauline and read it to her.

"It's happened," Pauline said.

"You think she's heard about the party?"

"Of course. Though she has no business to summon you. She's supposed to report anything she hears about a man to the dean of men. She's so incorrigibly curious that she probably couldn't bear to do that. She wants to question you herself first. You'd better come over here at teatime and we'll frame up the story. I'll ask Susie to be here too. She's got the low-down on Florence Atwater and she knows how to handle her."

When the Duke arrived at Pauline's house after his daily work-out at Cranesville, he found her alone. She gave him tea, as usual, and refrained from saying "I told you so." Instead, she announced that she had decided the best thing the Duke could do when he met Miss Atwater was to make a flat denial of everything.

"One good thumping lie that you can stick to might do the trick," Pauline explained. "Then there's no danger of getting mixed up in your story."

"You mean to tell her that there wasn't any party at all?"

"Precisely. You see the chances are ninety-nine to one that she's merely heard some gossip. She hasn't anything tangible to go on. She will be a little flabbergasted if you tell her that the gossip is entirely without foundation. She may think you're lying. But after all, what's she going to do? How's she going to prove anything on you? She isn't a prosecuting attorney, with a staff of policemen and detectives at her elbow."

"But look here, Pauline, the whole town knows that I had a theatre party."

"Naturally," Pauline said. "There's no use denying that part. But if you nicked the rules a bit in doing that, you didn't break them to smithereens. It'll be regarded as one of those minor things for which you should be warned but not punished. After all, you know, the university doesn't want scandals. All the sensible people on the discipline committee would rather wink at something they suspect than dig in and find out exactly what happened. Because if they do find out that somebody's been naughty, they've practically got to act, and they don't want to act. It gives the place a bad name with parents."

"In that case," the Duke said, "I wonder that Miss Atwater bothers to have me up on the carpet. If she's heard something why doesn't she forget it?"

* * * * *

The Benham had been washed and polished until it was spotless and shining and Barney had been forced into a chauffeur's livery. The Duke had been tempted by the idea of wearing a cutaway and a silk hat and spats. He never had worn the cutaway. But he decided that it would be laying it on a bit thick. He had chosen instead a sack coat and waistcoat of Oxford gray worsted, and a pair of tweed trousers in a fine check that the tailor had especially recommended to go with that jacket, and a bowler hat. The eyeglasses were a nuisance, especially as he was carrying a stick, but he thought Susie Corbin was right in recommending them, and they would be something to occupy his hands with in an embarrassing moment.

He was secretly encouraged by the flurry he created in the dean's outer office. And when he was shown into Miss Atwater's presence he was almost at ease.

Miss Atwater was a large woman with a tendency to breathlessness, and the executive manner. As dean of women, she was father, mother and Beatrice Fairfax to more than three thousand coeds and she took her responsibilities seriously. She was sometimes discouraged that the girls who came to her for advice were so invariably troubled because they were not popular, whereas those others, the popular ones, never came to her for advice at all and seemed never to be troubled about anything, unless it was the fact that the vast continuous house party which they considered the university to be was periodically interrupted by examinations which you had to pass. But Miss Atwater was naturally of an optimistic disposition. She felt that she was doing a useful work in the world.

"I've heard a great deal about you, Mr. Van Blarcom," she said to the Duke.

"Indeed?" the Duke said, adjusting his eyeglasses.

"Yes," Miss Atwater continued, "your name has come up a good many times in the last few months, and once, at a meeting of the faculty discipline committee, it was suggested that we ought to investigate the persistent rumor that you were not a bona-fide student—that you had been sent here to make a first-hand study of a Middle Western university. My answer was that so long as you conformed to our requirements there was no reason to investigate you."

"That was most awfully kind of you," the Duke said.

"The truth is I thought the gossip about you absurd. I didn't believe you were somebody important visiting us incognito. But now that I've seen you, I should not be surprised if there is something in it. You don't look like a college boy."

"I don't do it awfully well, do I?" the Duke said. Miss Atwater smiled and the Duke smiled back.

"Then the rumor about you isn't wholly without foundation?"

The Duke twirled his eyeglasses, frowning at them. After a moment he looked up at Miss Atwater.

"No," he said, "it isn't wholly without foundation. I am trying to understand college life from a somewhat—a somewhat alien point of view. I wish I felt at liberty to discuss the circumstances of my being here. But I don't. I can only assure you that my purposes are not a—a—inimical to the university."

"I'm not going to press you about the circumstances," Miss Atwater said. "They are not important from my point of view. But unfortunately I have just had a most disturbing report about you. I am informed that you recently gave the wildest party that has ever been given in Grandison—a party at which chorus girls from a musical show mingled with college women and college men, a party at which liquor was served, a party that lasted till dawn."

"It is true that I gave a party, Miss Atwater. But it didn't last till dawn. There were no chorus girls. Principals from the theater do not ordinarily mingle with chorus girls socially, any more than officers mingle socially with privates in the army. And there was no liquor—nothing but champagne."

"From our Middle Western point of view, Mr. Van Blarcom, champagne is liquor."

"Really?" the Duke said.

"What would you call it?"

"Why," the Duke said, "I'd call it a mild wine. I went to a great deal of trouble to get it because I was anxious to give a good party, and yet I was unwilling that anybody should become intoxicated. I can assure you that nobody did get intoxicated either."

"Suppose," Miss Atwater said, "you tell me exactly what happened."

"I'll be glad to," the Duke said. He proceeded to give Miss Atwater a complete account of his party, beginning with his anxiety to return the hospitality he had enjoyed since he came to Grandison and his pleasure in learning that his old friend Norah McCune was to appear at the local theater; and explaining how he made up a list of guests by asking each of the students whom he had met repeatedly to bring several friends, so that the party had ultimately numbered about forty, counting Norah McCune and the principals from her company and two professors and their wives. When he had finished, Miss Atwater laughed heartily.

"I don't see what's so funny," the Duke said.

"Why," Miss Atwater said, "the superb innocence with which you have violated all the rules by which we set most store at Minnewaska is funny. I can understand perfectly that you thought in giving your guests champagne you were protecting them from the evils of drink. But to us the idea is humorous."

"My dear Miss Atwater," the Duke said, "it may be humorous, but I can assure you it is also intensely practical."

"Mr. Van Blarcom," she said, "your frankness is disarming. It is plain your intentions were of the best. And if there is any way to settle the matter without a wholesale expulsion I shall take it." She gave him a warm, motherly smile.

"You see," she continued, "the problem you have created has never come up before. Ordinarily students do not have the facilities for giving parties—at least mixed parties—except through some organization. If a club or a fraternity wishes to give a party, the party must be registered in advance either at my office or that of the dean of men. Whoever is in charge must fill out a card, which we furnish, stating when and where the party is to be given and who the chaperons are. The chaperons must be officially approved. We hold the chaperons responsible for seeing that the party breaks up at the appointed hour. Except at prom time a party must stop at one o'clock. And the general rule is that university women must be at home by eleven o'clock unless they have special permission."

"I did hear something about that when I first came," the Duke said. "I was told that was the rule. But I must say it doesn't seem to be rigidly enforced."

"We can't enforce it rigidly, Mr. Van Blarcom. We should need a hundred proctors to enforce it. Nevertheless, it is the rule and I believe that most of the women in the university obey it most of the time."

The Duke twirled his eyeglasses thoughtfully. He believed that the day was saved, but he wanted to be sure.

"Miss Atwater," he said, "is there anything I can do to

straighten out this affair? I mean that I can't bear the idea that I have got a lot of young people into trouble. Would it do any good if I were to withdraw from the university?"

"No," Miss Atwater said, "there is nothing you can do. These young people are supposed to look out for themselves. They are supposed to know whether a party is registered or not, and to stay away if it isn't. I suppose it would be too much to expect them to stay away from a party at which they had a chance to meet Norah McCune. Nevertheless, the university women are responsible to me for being there. And the faculty people who were there have no excuse at all."

"Don't you suppose that the whole trouble is this?" the Duke asked: "Though I am technically a student at the university, still, as you say, I am not a typical college boy. None of my guests thought of me as a student, amenable to student rules and student discipline, but rather as a town resident. After all, I'm not living in a fraternity house or a dormitory, but in an establishment of my own."

Miss Atwater nodded. "Yes," she said, "that's true. And it does seem a pity that fifteen or twenty students should be expelled from college for a comparatively harmless episode. I am inclined to take the matter under advisement, and if I do, it will probably remain there indefinitely."

"You could really do that?"

"I can and I shall—on one condition. You must promise me that you won't give any more parties without registering them in advance and getting permission like anybody else."

"I shall be very glad to promise you that, Miss Atwater."

"I shall count on you."

The Duke rose to go, but she stopped him with a gesture. "One moment, Mr. Van Blarcom," she said. "Would you mind telling me what you think about the younger generation? Do you find that she is as bad as she's said to be?"

"I don't know what to think," the Duke replied. "My first impression was unfavorable. But if I were to judge by what I've actually seen in the few weeks I've been here, I'd have very little to base an indictment on."

"That's just what I think," Miss Atwater said.

When the Duke had bowed himself out he told Barney to drive to the Gardiners', but on the way down Green Street he saw Susie Corbin walking alone. She had probably had tea with Pauline and was on her way home to dinner at the Gamma Delta house. The Duke had Barney stop the car and jumped out and caught up with her. She looked at him with that same amused smile he had observed the day before.

"I've just come from Miss Atwater's office," the Duke said, "and it's all right."

"You high-hatted her out of it?"

"I did what we agreed I should do."

"I'm glad it worked," Susie Corbin said. "I'd hate to be fired a month before graduation. And it might have been serious to Pauline and Jack and the Widdecombs if Miss Atwater had gone through with an investigation."

"I'm rather proud of myself," the Duke said. "I may have appeared a little more innocent than I am, but I didn't lie to her."

Elizabeth Garver Jordan

☼

ALTHOUGH most of her literary work has been done in New York City, Miss Elizabeth Garver Jordan is a native of Wisconsin. She was born in Milwaukee, May 9, 1867, and there grew to womanhood. Her education was received in the convent of Notre Dame in her native city. After her graduation she was on the editorial staff of the New York World for ten years. Miss Jordan was editor of Harper's Bazaar from 1900 to 1913, when she became literary adviser to Harper and Brothers. She has been an industrious writer as the long list of her books testifies. Some of her shorter stories in *Tales of Destiny*, and *Tales of the City Room*, strike a responsive chord in the reader because of their fidelity to the details of everyday life. Among her best known works are: *Tales of the City Room*, 1898; *Tales of the Cloister*, 1901; *Tales of Destiny*, 1902; *May Iverson, Her Book*, 1904; *Many Kingdoms*, 1908; *May Iverson Tackles Life*, 1913; *May Iverson's Career*, 1914; *Lovers' Knots*, 1916; *Wings of Youth*, 1918; *Girl in the Mirror*, 1919; *The Blue Circle*, 1922; *Black Butterflies*, 1926; and *Miss Blake's Husband*, 1926.

From THE BLUE CIRCLE *by Elizabeth Garver Jordan. The Century Co. Publishers, New York. 1922. Reprinted by permission of the publishers.*

IT WAS late in the afternoon, and the autumnal twilight fell while he stood there, hesitating. In the dim windows of the house, set so far back among the oaks and maples that many of its outlines were lost to the observer in the road, lights began to twinkle, like smiles in tired eyes. There was something very soothing in the sight. It suggested rest. With a long sigh, Renshaw replaced his hat, casually dusted his shoes on the grass of the roadside, and picked up the traveling-bag. He had decided to remain and work for David Campbell.

He made his way up the avenue, sagging a little under the weight of the case, and, gratefully dropping the latter on the broad veranda with which an architect unbound by tradition had embellished the front of the Colonial dwelling, he again hesitated, with his finger on the button of the electric bell. To press that button meant to re-enter life. If he pressed it, and some one came, he would be committed to an interview, to explanations, to the carrying out of a plan—the first plan he had formed in two years. It had been very hard to make that plan—it would be nothing short of grilling to carry it through. Yet there was only one alternative—and this alternative his sick soul sometimes approached, sometimes rejected, but always abysmally abhorred. The memory of it now steadied his nerves. He pressed the button.

As he did so he picked up the suit-case, in confiding expectation of immediate entrance. But there was a delay; four, five, at least six minutes passed without response. Apparently the Campbell servants were not especially well trained. Or, as this was the tea hour, possibly there were other guests and the butler was busy. The reflection that there might be other guests sent Renshaw back across the veranda; but, even as his instinctive retreat began, it was checked by the sound of approaching footsteps. The door opened, and a man servant stood outlined against the light of the inner hall. He was tall, straight, neat, round-faced, and vacuous. Though he was still in the thirties, he appeared to have reached the summit of his ambitions. He exuded complacency as he stared past the caller's profile with exactly the degree of human detachment that is the highest ideal of his kind.

"Is Mr. Campbell at home?" Renshaw was fumbling for his card.

"I will inquire, sir."

"If you please." Renshaw handed him the card and crossed the threshold into the hall. The servant hesitated a fraction of a second, while his glance touched and slipped past the traveling-bag. He closed the door, leaving the case where it lay.

"If you will sit here a moment, sir—"

His manner was entirely correct, yet it subtly conveyed to Renshaw the impression that the man had not accepted him, that, though he had crossed the actual threshold of Tawno Ker, he was still waiting on its door-step. He nodded and seated himself on a carved settle that stood at the right of the entrance. The servant disappeared through a door opening into a room on the same side of the hall. Almost immediately he returned, the subtle atmosphere of his disapproval slightly intensified.

"Mr. Campbell is not at home, sir," he formally reported.

Renshaw nodded. "Of course he isn't. I forgot to send in my letter of introduction with my card. Stupid of me."

He drew the letter from his pocket and handed it over. "Give him that," he directed. A certain pride in him, that rallied in any association with other human beings, led to an automatic correctness of speech and manner that was the result of early years of habit. His attitude toward the butler was exactly what it should have been, though every instinct in him rejoiced in the respite he was offered and urged immediate flight.

Again a faint hesitation obscured the perfection of the butler's manner, as a light mist momentarily dims a view. For an instant his eyes met the caller's and the two wills clashed. Renshaw's head jerked forward in the nod that once had been a command. The servant slowly turned away with the letter, and then, quickening his steps, again disappeared through the door at the right of the hall. This time his absence was longer. Five minutes passed before Renshaw was conscious of his unobtrusive return.

"Mr. Campbell will see you, sir," he reported.

Renshaw rose, nodding toward the right-hand door.

"In that room?"

"Yes, sir."

"All right. Bring my bag into the house, please, and leave it here in the hall."

The man obeyed, and Renshaw walked into the big room where the master of the house awaited him. It was a comfortable room, even a beautiful one. Its walls were lined with books with special, much-handled bindings. Its deep chairs were the sort one sank into with an inner sigh of comfort. Its rugs were dim-toned and exquisite examples of the ancient art of the Orient from which they came. At its far end logs blazed in a huge bricked fireplace, and in front of the fire an old man sat alone.

Renshaw, walking toward him across the long room, had time to realize that he was a very old man indeed, and so small and thin that he seemed almost lost in the recesses of his big chair. He had time also to trace a resemblance that immediately struck him. In repose David Campbell looked surprisingly like Leo the Thirteenth. A narrow chaplet of white hair outlined the shape of his fine head. The skin of his delicate, ascetic face was colorless; but as the visitor came close to him he turned up to the young man the sudden gaze of a pair of eyes so blue and keen that the latter was almost startled. Simultaneously he held out a shrunken hand, and as he spoke the resemblance to the great Italian faded, leaving in the big chair merely a quaint little old gentleman, wholly American, with a charming manner and a worldly smile.

"You will forgive me for not getting up, Mr. Renshaw," he said, in a voice that seemed much younger than its owner. "I'm not moving about in a very sprightly fashion these days, but I am glad to see any one who comes to me from my friend Doctor Stanley. Will you draw that chair a little closer and sit down facing me, please? I don't hear quite so well as I used to."

Renshaw released the hand he had been holding as its owner spoke, and obeyed his instructions. He felt a sentiment for the old man, sudden and to him surprising. It was more than interest. It was almost liking. Possibly it was merely a response to the unusual degree of personal magnetism that Campbell undoubtedly possessed. He settled comfortably into the soft depths of his chair, and fixed his dark eyes on the face of his host with an emotion that was almost satisfaction. This plan of his seemed to be a good one. He did not speak, however, and under his steady but oddly detached gaze Campbell grew restless. Mechanically the old man unfolded the letter of introduction he had been holding in his left hand, and cleared his throat.

"This letter," he began, "is dated to-day. You have just come from town and from Doctor Stanley?"

"Yes, sir."

"He hasn't been here to see me for a fortnight," Campbell grumbled. "Of course I know he's busy, but he might find time for his patient, if not for his old friend. Stanley and I were young together, you know."

"Yes, sir. He told me that."

The familiar lassitude was attacking Renshaw's will, like a creeping paralysis. He had got this far, and apparently the effort had exhausted him. The thought of the impending interview filled him with a kind of horror. If only Campbell would take the situation in hand and settle everything! But Campbell did nothing of the sort, because Campbell had as yet no notion of what the situation was.

"Stanley's got the advantage of me by about eight years," Campbell was saying. "And he's kept himself in fine condition—the lucky old dog!"

He waited, but his visitor said nothing. The host decided that this was a young man who had no intention of wasting time in generalities. That being so, they would come at once to the point—whatever the point was. He leaned back and smiled at his caller. It was his most engaging smile, gracious and whimsical—a smile that illumined his delicate old face like a light from within. Under its charm the set lips of the visitor slightly relaxed, but he did not return the smile. With Renshaw, smiling was a lost art.

"Doctor Stanley tells me you have a proposition to make to me—a rather unusual and startling one," the host began comfortably. "He asks me to give it the most careful consideration."

"Yes, sir."

This was a difficult young man—although an extremely good-looking one. Campbell lost the details of line and color that would have charmed women. What he took in, with an unconscious sigh of envy, was the chap's splendid physique. Six feet at least, he told himself, and superbly made. The fellow was young, too, probably not much more than thirty, and, despite his odd lack of response, obviously a thoroughbred. David Campbell liked thoroughbreds, being a thoroughbred himself. Again he waited for the younger man to speak, and the beautiful old room seemed to wait, too,—taking on a deeper silence in the long pause. Renshaw's somber gaze had fixed itself on a door behind the host, but not more than eight feet away. He was trying to lash his will to the task before him; but again it shied, and, as he looked, his ears caught a sound that gave him a legitimate excuse for delay. The sound was like the rustle of stiff linen garments. Some one was on the other side of the door. His attention caught and held, he waited, expecting to see the door open. Campbell, hearing nothing, bit his lip. This *was* a difficult fellow!

"I am ready to listen to your proposition," he said, more concisely than he had yet spoken.

"Thank you." Renshaw replied almost absently, his eyes, with a quickening expression, still on the door he was facing. "But what I have to say is confidential. If you will permit me—"

He was on his feet as he spoke, and in three strides had reached the door and opened it. As he did so he experienced a sense of chagrin. The door led into a side corridor, wide and empty. No one was there, though it was possible that he had caught the flutter of a white garment disappearing around a corner. He returned to his chair, looking and feeling rather sheepish. In a way, however, the little incident had steadied him by diverting his mind from himself. His host was regarding him with courteous surprise.

"I want to be sure we are not overheard," Renshaw explained as he sat down again. "You see, my proposition is so unusual—"

Campbell nodded. "You may feel quite safe," he said. "No one in the house could have any reason for listening to us, even if we had any one here who—ah—did that kind of thing."

Again he wished this young man would come to the point; and now, as if in response to the telepathic command, the caller did so, taking the moment as if it were a hurdle.

"The truth is, sir," he blurted out, "I—have come here to ask you to buy me!"

Campbell leaned forward.

"I beg your pardon," he said apologetically, "but I shall have to ask you to speak very distinctly. Of late my hearing—"

"I have come here, Mr. Campbell," Renshaw repeated, slowly and clearly, "to ask you to buy me!"

The old man, who was still bending toward him with

a look of almost strained attention, relaxed in his chair and smiled. It was a courteous smile, but a weary one, the smile of a man constrained by good breeding to accept a dull jest. He shook his head.

"And now," he invited, "let us get to the point."

"That *is* the point." Renshaw spoke with an apathetic flatness of tone. He was struggling with a tremendous temptation to get up and get out; to drop the whole business; to take the other way—which, for the moment at least, seemed the easier way.

"Will you—ah—elucidate?"

Campbell was watching him closely. In his heart he half believed he was dealing with a madman; and yet surely Dick Stanley, his old friend and physician, would not have sent him a madman to deal with. However, what explanation save madness could there be of this amazing request, unless there were some sort of practical joke involved?—and, whatever else this fellow looked like, he did not suggest a practical joker. With a slight prickling of his scalp, the old man played for time. Possibly some one would come in. Yes, of course; it was the hour Jenks brought the tea. He stretched his hand toward an electric button on a table near him, but Renshaw stopped him with a gesture. He had read his host's thoughts.

"It sounds rather weird, I know," he said apologetically, "but Doctor Stanley warned you it was unusual. He knows all about my plan and highly approves of it."

"Dick approves of my—my buying you?" Campbell was puzzled, unconvinced, annoyed, and still a bit apprehensive.

"Yes, sir. And if you don't mind postponing for a moment the interruption of tea, I should like to explain."

The other's waiting hand dropped.

"I wish you would," he said almost fretfully. "And of course we will wait for tea," he forced himself to add.

"Mr. Campbell, I don't expect you to take in the thing all at once, but the facts are these." Renshaw had begun almost glibly, because he had rehearsed his opening speech. Now he stopped, as if uncertain how to proceed.

"Yes?" prompted his hearer. Renshaw drew a deep breath.

"Two years ago," he said, "I had an unusual experience—a terrible shock. I will not trouble you with the details; in fact, I could not discuss them. The result is what I am talking about. The experience knocked me out completely for a year. The second year I was able to crawl around, in leading-strings, as it were. Now I am well, or almost well—but there is still one thing I can't face. Stanley tells me it's my last obsession, and that it will pass as soon as I get into a normal way of living. However that may be, it has got me now."

He brought out the last words between set teeth.

"What is it?" Campbell asked the question very gently.

"A fear of the responsibility for my own life and self-support, a fear that amounts to a nightmare."

"What? I beg your pardon, but I am never quite sure I am hearing things correctly," the old man interrupted.

"A horror of the responsibility for my self-support," Renshaw almost fiercely repeated. "I can't endure it. If I have to face it in the half-baked state I am in now, I shall never get well. I know that. If, on the other hand, some one else will be responsible for me a year longer, I am beginning to believe that, with the start I've got, I can be cured. But—I've got to be owned and supported by another. I've got to be a bondman. I've got to be as irresponsible and dependent as a slave, doing as I'm told and absolutely assured of a living."

David Campbell shook his head. He was still puzzled, but he felt he was beginning to understand. The poor chap needed humoring.

"My dear fellow," he began soothingly, "surely there are sanatoriums where you can have every care—"

"I've been in them; I have had every care. That's just the point. I am ready for the next step. The doctors have turned me out. They say I am well but don't know it. They say I will never know it as long as I remain in institutions. I must live a normal life. I must work. And I can work."

He was rushing on now because he was afraid that if he stopped he would lose all the impetus he had gained.

"I can work like a steam-engine if you put me at it. They all admit that. And it's good, stiff, intelligent work, too. There's nothing the matter with my brain, Mr. Campbell; don't imagine that there is. There never has been, even when things were at their worst." He dropped his head into his hands. "But there will be," he ended, with an irrepressible groan, "unless, for just a little while longer, some one else is responsible for my support. So Doctor Stanley sent me to you. He said he was sure I could be of great use to you—that you needed some one—"

David Campbell leaned back again in his chair, joined the fingers of his thin hands together, and looked past them into the fire.

"Useful? Yes, perhaps," he murmured, "if you had merely come to me for a situation. But this proposition— It's all very unsettling." He broke off. "Why wouldn't it do to accept a situation on salary?" he asked abruptly.

"Because if I did that I should live in terror of losing my job. No; I've got to fix things in another way. I've got to find a man who will take me on in such a binding fashion that he simply can't get rid of me."

"Humph!" Campbell stared into the flames. The caller watched him.

"What can you do?" the old man asked at last.

"Anything!" The word came from the caller's lips like a bullet.

Campbell shook his head. "Anything is nothing," he pointed out with sudden austerity. "What can you do, really, that is worth a salary?"

The young man flushed.

"I can keep accounts," he said doggedly. "I can act as secretary and general utility man, and guard your health. That's what Doctor Stanley especially wanted me to do," he remembered to add. "Look after you and see that you look after yourself. He said there were conditions just at present that were rather trying to you. He thought there ought to be a younger man here with you."

Campbell nodded. For the first time, he was impressed as well as interested. Startling as Renshaw's proposition had been, there must be something in it worth considering, or Stanley would not have advocated it in the strong letter he had written. Also, the reference to his health appealed to him.

"If it were merely a matter of engaging your services—" he murmured discontentedly.

The other interrupted him.

"It's not that," he pointed out. "I could not consider for a moment the mere offer of a situation. Please remember the vital detail that I am asking you to *buy* me. For the next year I want to be your property as absolutely as if I were a bought slave. Also, try to remember that my obsession does not impair my ability in any way. Doctor Stanley guarantees that. I can be very useful to you if I am certain of my future for a year—if, in a phrase, my future is off my mind."

Campbell, his eyes still on the fire, again reflected. One point increasingly impressed him. Possibly this extraordinary young man could prolong his life. Stanley seemed to think so. At the thought his keen eyes took on a new expression. Deep in the heart of this worn-out human mechanism, and unsuspected by any one but his physician, burned an almost abnormal passion to live on.

"All this," he said slowly, "is the most impossible thing I've ever listened to."

The visitor's glance dropped.

"I suppose so," he dully conceded. "I realize how it must sound to any one else. But Doctor Stanley understood, and he hoped you would. It is just a form of nerve obsession, you see, sir," he patiently repeated, "a fear of life and of the future. If I merely had a job I should live in a panic. Whereas, if I were actually *bought* for a year, I'd be off my own mind; don't you see?"

"And on mine," Campbell dryly commented. "Yes, I see."

Again the young man flushed.

"It isn't as if I were useless," he muttered. "You will find that I can work like a horse. I'll do anything I'm told."

"Anything?" Campbell spoke with sudden meaning.

"Anything," the caller replied without hesitation.

The keen blue eyes of his host remained on his face.

"In fiction or the drama," he murmured thoughtfully, "the hero would qualify that remark. He would grandiloquently protect his honor."

"We are not in fiction or the drama," Renshaw wearily reminded him. "And I am discussing this matter with you, sir, not with some one casually selected. I will put my honor into your hands as absolutely as my life."

The old man nodded.

"I see that you are at least in earnest," he conceded.

"It's a matter of life or death with me, Mr. Campbell."

Campbell hesitated.

"I might ask you to do some odd things," he hinted—"things you would not understand at first. The situation here just now is a trifle—ah—abnormal. And I might not be able to explain for a few weeks certain matters not clear to a newcomer."

"I rather expect that, from a remark or two that Doctor Stanley dropped."

"And you are sure the kind of responsibility that attends working for another—perhaps more or less in the dark—would not worry you?" the old man asked curiously.

"Not a bit. You see, some one else is responsible for me, and I am certain of a bed, a roof over my head, and enough food to fill my stomach. I am"—his head dropped under the humiliation of the admission—"at the end of my resources."

"Your family—" Campbell began, after a moment's silence.

"So far as I know, I have not a relative in the world. But Doctor Stanley knows who my people were."

"Humph!" The word sounded ungracious; it was merely thoughtful.

"Doctor Stanley told me you really needed a secretary," Renshaw went on. "He thought there was no doubt you would give me a job, but he was not sure you would buy me."

Campbell grimaced. "Oh, he wasn't—wasn't he? Confound him!"

The last words broke from his lips before he could check them. He tried to drown them in a cough, but the visitor heard. For the third time he flushed, this time deeply and unbecomingly. Simultaneously, as if moved by a spring, he rose.

"Mr. Campbell," he said formally, "I hope you will forgive me for troubling you. I realize what an unpardonable nuisance I have been and how wild my scheme must have sounded to you. A doctor, of course, would understand. Very few laymen could. I am grateful for the time you have given me, and I will not take any more of it. Good night."

He held out his hand, and the somber veil on his face

lifted a trifle. After all this would settle things and he would not have to plan again! "Good night," he repeated, and, dropping the hand the other man had mechanically extended, turned to go.

"Wait a minute. Don't be in such a hurry!"

Campbell's voice was almost peevish. He struggled up from his chair, slowly and with much difficulty, till he stood facing his caller. His slight figure was unexpectedly tall, but his brilliant eyes were far below the somber level of his visitor's. He looked at the latter with a new expression in them. He had liked this young man's valedictory.

"Wait a minute," he repeated in a different tone. "Do I understand you to say that Stanley actually approves of this mad notion of yours?"

"Yes, sir. He thinks I would be very useful to you. He repeated that again and again. I think so too," Renshaw sedately added.

"How much salary do you want? I mean,—" Campbell corrected himself before the other could speak, but dropped his serious tone, "—what price are you asking for this—ah—purchase you suggest?"

"Anything you choose. Fix the price yourself, and pay it in monthly installments if you like, or at the end of the year."

Renshaw spoke indifferently, and the dark veil that had temporarily lifted from his face again settled there. So it wasn't over, after all, he was reflecting.

"Three hundred dollars, payable in twelve monthly installments of twenty-five dollars each?"

Campbell watched him closely as he spoke, but the caller's expression did not change.

"Anything you choose," repeated the latter. "The only important detail is that you make yourself responsible for my support for a year—as absolutely responsible," he repeated, "as if I were your property."

"We will say twenty-four hundred dollars," the old man amended without explanation. "Will that do?"

"Yes, sir."

The voice and manner of the visitor were as unresponsive as before.

"When do you want to begin?"

"Now—this minute."

"Oh! Then you came prepared to stay?"

"Yes, sir."

Campbell digested this in silence. "Would you like a contract?" he asked at last.

"No, sir. A contract of this sort would not be legal, of course. Besides, it is unnecessary. We will consider this a gentleman's agreement."

"Very well." Campbell held out his hand. "Now if you have no deep-rooted objections to tea, we will drink some," he added as he slowly settled back into the big chair. "And I, for one, am ready for it! Buying a man, if you will permit me to say so, is rather an exhausting business."

He rang the bell as he spoke, and the complacent personality of the servant who had admitted Renshaw promptly injected itself into the room.

"Jenks," said his master, "bring tea, and tell Miss Campbell when it is here. And by the way, Jenks—" He stopped the man on his way to the door, and turned to Renshaw. "Did you bring any luggage?"

"A bag. It is in the hall."

Campbell spoke to the butler:

"Take it up to the north room. Mr. Renshaw, who is my new secretary, will use that room—unless, after he has tried it, he prefers another."

Jenks left the room. He had not spoken, and he did not glance at Renshaw; but to the young man every line of his erect figure conveyed an august disapproval.

Leslie W. Quirk

☼

LESLIE W. QUIRK, writer of juvenile books, was born at Alta, Iowa, May 12, 1882. He spent two years at the University of Wisconsin, after which he became publisher and editor of *The Editor Magazine*, 1903-1908. Mr. Quirk has written many short stories for the popular magazines, and a number of books for boys. The list includes: *How to Write a Short Story*, 1903; *Baby Elton, Quarterback*, 1904; *Midget Blake*, 1906; *Freshman Dorn, Pitcher*, 1911; *Freshman Friends*, 1913; *The Fourth Down*, 1912; *The Freshman Eight*, 1913; *Playing the Game*, 1914; *The Third Strike*, 1914; *Boy Scouts of Black Eagle Patrol*, 1915; *Iceboat Number One*, 1916; *Boy Scouts on a Crusade*, 1917; *Boy Scouts of Lakeville High*, 1920, and others. Mr. Quirk might be termed the writer laureate for the boy scouts. It has been said that his books are more fully appreciated in other parts of the country than they are in Wisconsin. Mr. Quirk was with the American Expeditionary Forces in France from 1917 to 1919. His home is in Madison, Wisconsin.

From FRESHMAN DORN, PITCHER, *by Leslie W. Quirk. Published by The Century Company, New York, 1911. By permission of the publishers.*

CHAPTER IV

THE FUMBLED PUNT

SATURDAY dawned clear, but windy and cold. By two o'clock, the stands were well filled, although the game was not scheduled to begin for another half hour. When Cree's squad trotted out upon the great field with its whitewashed lines, Dorn heard the deep rumble and roar of the college yell. Active young men with canes and pennants rushed wildly up and down, and led the cheering through great megaphones. Dorn felt very small and insignificant in the midst of the circus-like tiers of seats that soared skyward on all sides. Somehow or other, the feeling grew that he was to be offered as a sacrifice to some herd of angry, bellowing wild animals.

A few minutes later, the visitors emerged. The cheers this time were weak, owing to lack of numbers, but the little band of enthusiasts up in the north stand did its best. Beloit always played good football, and this year there were rumors of a full-back, Wright by name, who could drop-kick goals from the field at any angle and apparently from any distance.

While Cree put his eleven players through brisk signal practice, Dorn crouched on the sidelines covered with a cardinal blanket, like some war-bedecked Indian chief, and watched the tall, rangy full-back of the visitors send the ball whirling, end over end, squarely between the goal posts, just clearing the crossbar. Evidently, he had not been greatly overrated, and Dorn began to feel uneasy as he watched the ease with which, time after time, the pigskin was pounded skillfully for scoring points.

Presently, somebody tossed a coin, and Cree won. He elected to begin the game against the wind, probably to have the advantage later should the score be close. Dorn found himself trembling as the men lined up for the kick-off. He had seen them do it—had been one of them himself—in a hundred practice games; but, somehow or other, this was entirely different.

The visiting full-back arranged a little mound of dirt in the middle of the field, adjusted the ball with exasperating deliberateness, and stepped back. Dorn heard an official ask: "Are you ready, Beloit?" And then the same question was asked of his own team. Wright raised his arms suddenly, looking, to Dorn, for all the world like a guide-post at a street corner, ran a few steps, and swung the toe of his yellow shoe against the ball.

It was a terrific kick, almost to the home goal line, although the wind carried it to one side. But there was a player waiting for it, and Dorn, torn between loyalty to the team and repugnance toward the man who waited with open arms, saw that Wrenn was to have first chance to win fame.

Wrenn saw it, too. To-day he was alert and eager, ready to sacrifice everything to show his prowess. His catch was admirable, and he swung in behind the quickly formed interference with perfect skill. Down the field they charged, five strong at the outset, like a great battering-ram, bowling aside tacklers and dropping off themselves, one by one, till at the fifty-five-yard line Wrenn was running alone, with only three or four Beloit players between him and a touchdown.

Not for an instant did he hesitate. The first tackler was dodged, and the second shoved away with the open hand. The third dived and caught him low, and, although Dorn could see that the runner was greatly shaken by the impact, Wrenn kept on, fighting for ground, until the very motion of his legs shook off the tackler. Once more he was free.

Fifteen yards from the goal line the last player launched himself. Possibly trying to profit by his fellow player's error, he caught Wrenn very high, almost at the waist. This merely slowed the runner, and when little Phillips, who had been racing just behind, reached him, he propped the runner as best he could, and the two of them literally bore the tackler across the line with them for the first touchdown.

Dorn watched breathlessly till Phillips had kicked the

goal before he relaxed. Then he discovered that the tremendous buzzing in his ears was the cheering of the crowd. The score was 6–0, and Wrenn had made one of the most sensational one-hundred-yard runs on record. Dorn dug a little hole in the soft turf with his noseguard, chuckling softly to himself, as if he were directly responsible for the play; and when Wrenn passed him to take his position on the next kick-off the freshman called out a word of praise that set the other's heart thumping.

But one touchdown is not always a victory. Five minutes later, after a series of scrimmages that failed to net the required distances for either side, an exchange of kicks, aided by the wonderful Wright and the wind advantage, gave Beloit the ball on the twenty-yard line of the home team's goal. The big full-back grinned confidently, stepped well back of the stone-wall line, and drop-kicked a neat goal.

The score was now 6–3.

After that, Cree evidently thought it time to try end runs and trick plays. At any rate, Phillips changed the style of play entirely. It proved effective in so far as preventing other scoring on Beloit's part, but it failed to accomplish any great offensive work. When the field judge announced that there were only five minutes to play, the ball was nearly in the center of the field. Dorn saw Phillips look up with dismay at the announcement, and suddenly change signals.

Wrenn took the ball on a straight line plunge, and gained five yards. Again the same play netted three. Still a third time it was used for a material advance. Phillips had evidently detected a weak place in Beloit's line, or else Wrenn was playing like a demon. Certainly he was distinguishing himself, Dorn admitted; and a great part of the boy's anger gave way to satisfaction. Even if he were not playing, as was his right, his proxy bade fair to win the game.

And then, on a third down, with only inches to go, it was Wrenn's own line that gave way before the play was fairly started, and two of the big visiting players were upon the runner, who was thrown for a loss near the thirty-yard line. When they piled off, the boy himself lay white and motionless.

Dorn sprang to his feet, and tore off the red blanket. His cheeks crimsoned, and his eyes brightened with the possibilities. If Wrenn were hurt, his chance had come.

Trainers and doctors ran out to the boy. It seemed he had been playing beyond his natural strength and speed, and a slight accident had brought about a collapse. When he opened his eyes, he was weak and trembling, although not seriously hurt in any way.

Dorn was stamping nervously up and down the side lines, when Cree touched his shoulder.

"Don't do that," said the coach sharply. "You'll have to go in, and if you can't calm yourself you'll make some blunder. Get out there now, and work for the team and for the college."

Nobody spoke to him as he ran up. Some, indeed, looked away. The crowd, knowing only of Wrenn's great work, had no cheers for the untried freshman. Phillips merely motioned him to play well back on defense, to be ready for a punt. It was Beloit's ball.

Forty yards back of the crouching players, Dorn waited. He plucked a blade of grass, he shifted his position without reason, he tried in every way to stop the tremendous pump-pump of his heart. But it was all too wonderful. Following disappointment after disappointment, he was at last playing on the Varsity team. Surely a little nervousness was not a thing at which to wonder.

He watched Wright spring suddenly far back of the line, and hold out his arms. Even from where he stood, he could see the big full-back's hands open suddenly, and, an instant later, close on the ball. Almost before he could shift his weight, ready to run forward or backward, the pigskin came hurling through the air, end foremost, like a screw cutting its way through the atmosphere.

Dorn knew he must catch it. Here, on the very first play, was a chance to duplicate Wrenn's famous run; and the boy braced himself, trying to be cool and unmoved in the face of this magnificent opportunity.

The punt was almost perfect. The ball soared up and up till the freshman saw it only as a speck, not unlike other bits of grass and dirt carried along by the high wind. At the apex of its flight it seemed to hesitate. Dorn found himself wondering if it were to drop suddenly or to continue soaring like a balloon. Already the Beloit ends were tearing down the field, almost upon him. The crowd had hushed, waiting for another brilliant play, and the very silence seemed to unnerve the boy. He ran a little forward and then retraced his steps. He circled to the left and then to the right. Would it ever come down?

When the whirling pigskin finally neared the ground again, Dorn was ten feet to one side, having misjudged its flight. There was still time to get under it, however; and he sprinted desperately, holding out his hands, as if he were to catch a baseball. Coach Cree's old advice flashed through his mind: "Always catch the ball against the body, ignoring the tacklers till you have it, and slightly raising one knee to prevent its slipping to the ground." It had seemed laughably simple, and it had proved simple in practice when he waited for a punt; but now, too far to one side, with tacklers charging and thousands watching critically, a great fear welled up in his heart and added to his nervousness. He must catch it, skillfully if possible; but, at all hazards, he must catch it.

The ball struck his outstretched hands, but its whirling, twisting motion tore it loose. In an instant, it was on the ground; in another, it had bounded into the hands of one of the opposing ends, who was still running at full speed.

For perhaps ten seconds Dorn stood stock-still, quite unconscious of what had taken place. A sharp, strident yell of exultation bore down from the north stands; from the others, beginning near the goal, came a murmur, growing constantly in volume, till it swept around the entire field. In it was disappointment, despair, anger. Back of him, just over his goal line, Phillips was piling slowly off the runner, who had scored a touchdown. Not until Dorn heard a sharp whistle, followed by the announcement of time, did his brain become clear.

Mechanically, he lined up with the others, and watched with growing pangs of pain as Wright made the goal. The first half was ended, and the visitors had scored in each quarter, with a final advantage of 9–6. And Dorn had been responsible for six of those nine points against his team.

In the dressing room between halves, there were many uninvited callers, come to praise and to condemn, and to offer asinine suggestions as to how Coach Cree should instruct the team for the balance of the game.

The coach himself did not appear for several minutes. When he did come, he had lost none of his emotionless temperament. But there was a queer look in his eyes, and a sharp discourtesy, as he bundled everybody out but the players, that suggested some unusual advice. When it came, nobody was more surprised than Dorn.

"Boys," he said—Cree always called them boys when his heart was full—"boys, one of us made a bad error, just now, and you're all blaming him. Thursday, one of our players was hurt, and made an ugly accusation. I think all of you will understand that Dorn, here, was playing under an enormous handicap. He is naturally nervous, and to-day he was doubly so; first, because his initial play was critical; and, second, because he was keeping a secret and was unjustly accused of Thursday's accident. Now, there's no time for details; but I want each man of you to know that Dorn had nothing whatever to do with the breaking of Clifford's leg. Wrenn has confessed that he did it, but that his guilt is cowardice in not telling us about it at the time rather than deliberate assault. It was an accident, we are all agreed, and absolutely unavoidable. I may add that, because of his father's business reverses, Wrenn is obliged to leave college at once."

He paused a minute, and Dorn stepped to his side.

"Fellows," he said earnestly, "he's proved his loyalty to the old school by what he did out there on the gridiron. Up in the grandstand his father and mother have followed his every move—as fathers and mothers always do. I mean, he's the right sort at heart, and I wish you would all shake his hand before he goes. I intend to."

Quarter-back Phillips came over to the big freshman and pumped his arm with unnecessary vigor.

"Why, of course," he answered for the team. "And I'm sorry, old man, that we suspected you. Aren't we, fellows?"

"We are," chorused the others, roaring it a little too loudly and a little too sincerely to leave any suspicion of previous drill.

"Exactly," nodded Cree. "Now, that's all, except that Dorn is fresh and that he is to take Wrenn's place in those line smashes. And the man who doesn't help push or pull or steady him won't stick on this team. Understand?" He thrust out his chin aggressively, and narrowed his eyes, only to break into a good-natured smile as one or two said, "Aw Cree!" protestingly, for doubting them; and the others stopped rubbing bruised legs and arms, and straightened their shoulders, as if a new honor had been thrust upon them.

CHAPTER V

The Game

WHEN the fifteen minutes were ended, and the teams lined up again, Dorn was a new man. He was smilingly confident and sure of himself, glad to be playing, not alone for his own reputation, but to help such chaps as Cree and the others. The talk had been a tonic to all.

The Beloit man who caught the kick-off was downed almost in his tracks. It seemed to take the other team a minute or two to brace, and the visitors ran the ball to the fifty-yard line before Wright was forced to kick. This time, Dorn caught the ball without the suspicion of a fumble, and had dodged a tackler and gained twenty-five yeards before he was downed. Then began a series of merciless line bucking, with the freshman taking the ball at least every other time. Down the field swept the perfect machine, one or two or three or five yards at a time, apparently sure of a touchdown. Already the crowd was cheering him, and on every play imploring Phillips to give Dorn the pigskin. Victory seemed only a matter of minutes.

And then, as has happened so often in games when a score is imminent, there came a fumble. The other half-back, on a crossfire buck, missed the ball, and, although little Phillips recovered it, the loss was too great to make up on the next and last down, and Wright punted far back up the field.

Back fifty yards the attack began all over. Precious time had been lost, but it was still early in the quarter and the besiegers were not discouraged. On their own ten-yard line, Beloit braced for a minute. Rogers failed to gain; Dorn made only three yards, although he fought desperately for more. As he clambered up from the scrimmage, he wondered what Phillips would try to do, and decided that perhaps a try for a goal from the field would be made, despite the wide angle. But Phillips knew his players. Crouching low, he called shrilly:

"Six—four—nine."

The signal was ten, being merely the addition of the first two numbers, and gave the ball to Dorn for a line plunge.

The freshman was perfectly cool now. His great chance had come. Lowering his shoulders, he sprang forward on the exact psychological instant, and was upon the line with the ball under his arm before his opponents were quite ready.

Somebody grabbed him, but he shook the man off as he would a child. Two, three, four forms loomed ahead. Just back of them, five yards away, was a blurred line of white on the ground. Setting his teeth and putting his head down, the boy lunged forward, swaying, half falling, but always fighting for inches as nobody else had ever done on that historic field.

Slowly he felt them yield. Back of him, with all the might and brawn and doubled strength of the possible touchdown, Phillips and Rogers and the others pushed and pulled and yelled encouragement. Just when it seemed he must come to a full stop, the men in front faltered for a second, and he dived to one side, swinging practically the whole group as on a pivot, and falling, face downward, where the whitewash mark splashed the grass, with outstretched arms planting the ball over the goal line for the precious five points.

It was almost impossible for the spectators to distinguish who had made the touchdown, and they cheered the team in general and each player in particular. Even when Phillips failed to kick goal from the difficult angle, each told his neighbor that it was a good try, and, anyhow, the boys did not need the extra point; for were they not already leading, with the score 11–9 in their favor?

And was not the Varsity with that freshman, Dorn, in the line-up, clearly proving its ability to score almost at will?

But football is a game of chance. Five minutes later, little Phillips was hurt, not seriously, but enough to demand a substitute. Blake took his place, and, although his playing was accurate enough, he lacked the generalship of Phillips. He was a star pitcher on the college nine, and it was upon the diamond rather than upon the gridiron that he excelled. Now his poor campaigning finally culminated when he attempted to gain seven yards on the last down in his own territory and lost the ball to Beloit. Close on this catastrophe came a still greater one when the visitors made twenty yards on a trick play.

The ball was now on the twenty-five-yard line, and Beloit took quick advantage to try for another field goal. It was nip and tuck this time, but Wright, by a skillful dodge, found time to get off his drop-kick after his own line had parted, and his unerring toe booted the ball with fatal accuracy. The visitors led, by the score of 12—11.

There was still the last quarter to play, and Blake, at the suggestion of Rogers, began once more the bombardment of the line. After they had gained twenty yards, Beloit met the attack by putting in a substitute tackle, a great, powerful, fresh fellow who braced the others wonderfully, and who effectively stopped the gains.

When the five-minutes-to-play announcement was made, the ball was in the middle of the field. Dorn gained only a scant yard, Rogers did no better in his attempts, and Blake made ready for a punt. Then Dorn, the freshman, the substitute half-back, did something that, a week before, would have won for him only derision. He suggested the play; he practically took control, and asked to be given the ball.

"Try the fake kick," he told Blake, "and give me the ball."

The little quarter, sorely worried over his own blunders, was quick to shift the responsibility. He nodded, rattled off the signals, and suddenly crouched behind the center.

To outguess your opponents in football is quite as effective as in baseball. Every Beloit man expected a kick, and Dorn had the ball and was skirting the end before the trick was exposed. The other half-back bowled over the end tackler, and, except for three others, the runner had a clear field.

It was the first time Dorn had been clear with the ball. The goal posts looked miles ahead. The tacklers seemed irresistible. An impulse to give it up because it was impossible came over him; but he shook it off quickly.

He was surprised to find himself as cool and clear-headed as ever he was in practice. The first tackler was pushed aside with ridiculous ease, but the second was surer of himself. He caught the boy a little high after a clean dive through the air; and Dorn realized that his chance to get clear was slight, although almost at the same moment he saw a possible escape. As the man caught him, Dorn turned suddenly, keeping the man in the air, and whirled completely around. The tackler fought desperately, but the momentum made him lose his grip; he shot off to one side as the "snapper" in a crack-the-whip game might do.

Not only had he failed to stop the runner; but Dorn had thrown him straight at the other tackler, who went down like a pin on a bowling alley. With a triumphant little squeak of joy, that sounded ridiculously like a giggle, the freshman ran on, straight between the goal posts, and planted the ball behind the line for a touchdown.

Then, for the first time in his life, he heard thousands of spectators go fairly insane over his playing. The cheering rumbled up and down like thunder, and megaphones asked what was the matter with Dorn, and students and gray-haired men with hats awry, and young ladies, who had been taught to speak only in refined tones, yelled back uproariously that he was all right. And over in one stand they fitted to a well-known tune a refrain about

>Freshman Dorn! Freshman Dorn!
>Finest chap was ever born.

And, at last, to cap the climax, Cree allowed him to try for the goal, now that Phillips was out, and he sent the ball squarely over the bar, clear into the bleachers behind. A minute later, the whistle blew, and the game was over. His team had won by the score of 17–12, and he had proved his worth.

Everybody wanted to shake his hand. Presently, he found Cree was gripping it firmly, and saying gruffly: "Good work, boy; good work," which was superlative praise from the coach.

But his greatest thanks came outside, after he had dressed, when Wrenn introduced his father and mother, and then took him aside and whispered:

"Thank you, old man, for their sake. And now I don't mind telling you, when I see what a fool I was from first to last, that out there, in business, this lesson is going to make at least one chap work out a regeneration because of the help he will get from his belief in the loyalty and big-heartedness of fellows like you."

"Oh!" said Freshman Dorn, very much embarrassed, and yet very much elated over his victory, "oh, I didn't do anything much!"

Robert E. Pinkerton

※

ROBERT E. PINKERTON, another native son of Wisconsin, was born at Arena, March 12, 1882. After completing his preparatory education, he entered the University of Wisconsin where he continued as a student for two years. Thereafter Mr. Pinkerton was a newspaper writer until 1910 when he engaged in literature as a profession. Among the books he has written are: *The Canoe*, 1914; *Penitentiary Post*, 1920; *The Long Traverse*, 1920; *The Test of Donald Norton*, 1924; *White Water*, 1925; and *The Fourth Norwood*, 1925. Mr. Pinkerton writes entertainingly of the far North, of the Hudson Bay region where everything is subordinated to the fur trade. He now resides in San Francisco.

From THE TEST OF DONALD NORTON, *by Robert E. Pinkerton. The Reilly & Lee Company, Publishers, Chicago, 1924. Reprinted by permission of the publishers.*

CHAPTER XXVI

AT THE END OF THE TRAIL

WHEN Donald reached Fort Bruce with Millington he placed him in charge of the Mounted Police, who had returned, and then went to the Keewatin headquarters down the shore. He did not go near the Layard home but Evelyn drove down as soon as she heard he had returned.

"Donald," she began at once, "this can't go on any

longer. Janet is breaking her heart. I know I sent you away once. I have never forgiven myself but I want you to forgive me and I want you to forget your groundless fears."

He turned quickly away and stood at a window with his back to her. Even in those first days of disillusionment he had never held her action against her, recognizing in it the instinctive recoil of a mother from what she felt to be disaster, but now he saw the Evelyn he had always known.

"It is very wonderful of you to come here and say that," he said.

In that moment he was tempted to break forth with his momentous news. Every instinct save that of caution prompted it, though the last two years had destroyed his faith in many things.

That first night after Millington had told his story, Donald had thought only of hurrying back to Fort Bruce and Janet. He had started with that idea but as the miles slipped behind he began to see the possibilities of the situation.

At first he had believed, wholly and without suspicion, and then reflection showed how flimsy was the thread by which his whole future was suspended—Millington's second-hand story, a story as incredible as it was diabolical, and the little gold ring which he carried in his pocket.

In those first moments his mind had swept back through his life and had gathered many bits of circumstantial evidence that supported Nee-tah-wee-gan's actions and her confession. He remembered particularly the manner in which the Indian woman had received the account of his fasting dream, her abject fear when he had spoken of fire, how she had exhibited unmistakable signs of terror upon learning that he was to be manager at Fort James.

But later when he had sifted all these facts, had built up the case as his heart wished it to be, he realized that it all hung on one thing, on one man's action. Whatever he, Donald, might hope or believe, the matter of his birth would never become an established fact until Corrigal had stamped it with the seal of his own faith. As soon as Donald grasped this he determined that he would not tell the story to anyone until he had talked with Corrigal. He wanted to go to Janet at once. He wondered if he could keep away from her while at Fort Bruce, and yet he saw the cruelty of such an action if Corrigal repudiated Millington's tale.

Even now, when Evelyn Layard had come to him with her double plea, he was tempted more strongly than ever to tell. He felt that he must, that something within him would burst if he did not relieve the pressure, but as he turned toward her he determined to adhere to his original plan.

"It was wonderful of you to come," he repeated. "I— I don't know what to say. I must go to Fort James immediately, but I'm coming back this winter and when I do I will talk to you about it."

"But why wait?" Evelyn pleaded.

Again he faltered and then he saw that everything, all he had dreamed of, all that Janet wished, depended on one thing, on the reactions of one man. The need of settling it as quickly as possible became more overwhelmingly imperative than ever.

"Please don't ask," he begged. "There is a reason. I can't tell it now. I left in a hurry. Things are in a mess. I must get right back."

"But Donald! You're in no condition to travel. You're worn out."

"I'll get a chance to rest in the spring," he said with a smile.

Hope had flared again, irrepressible hope, youth's indomitable faith and desire, and Evelyn, seeing the evidences of it, was puzzled.

"Has Corrigal given in?" she demanded. "Will he take you back?"

"Yes," he admitted.

"And you will be with the Hudson's Bay again?"

"Next summer."

"Then why—?"

Evelyn did not finish the sentence. An inspiration had come, one born of the suppressed emotion evident in Donald's manner and of a woman's intuition.

"I don't understand," she faltered. "I only know you are wrong. But you will promise to come to me when you return to Fort Bruce?"

"Yes, I promise."

She went at once to the door and opened it.

"Good-by. I'll be waiting Donald."

He heard the tinkle of sled bells as she was driven away to the Hudson's Bay but when he was alone he did not go to bed as he should have done, nor did he even sit down. Many hours before dawn the next morning he would be on the trail, eastward bound, facing three hundred and fifty miles of toil and cold and darkness, of aching muscles and frost-scorched lungs. He was in need of rest and yet something drove him to striding back and forth the length of his office.

His thoughts were at the end of that trail, in the living room of the Hudson's Bay at Fort James, in the presence of a cold, sorrow-hardened man, a man whose inner nature he had glimpsed on two occasions and to whose racked soul he must penetrate again.

So preoccupied was he the sound of sled bells did not impress themselves until the door was thrown open and Janet entered.

"Donald!" she cried. "Mother said you wished to see me, that you were worn out, unable to—"

He had successfully conquered the temptation to see her even when he had been swayed by Evelyn's pleading, and now the integrity and strength which had carried him through a similar meeting in that same room rose instinctively to wage the same old fight.

Yet words would not come. It was as if he faced an opponent with the gloves and could not raise his hands. He was helpless in her presence, aware only that she was there, that some power over which he had no control was driving him forward.

In a last desperate effort he tried to turn his eyes from that eager face, from all that he read in it. He saw that she had come with the confident expectation that he had abandoned his former stand. He knew she believed the end of their disheartening trail had been reached and he could not bear to tell her of the hazard still remaining.

Then the light in her eyes died. She drew back against the door, her hand searching behind her for the latch.

"I am sorry," she whispered. "I see it now. Mother thought—she did not know—understand. She believed—"

Her hand found the latch and she turned quickly.

"Janet!" Donald cried.

With a bound he was across the room and whirling her toward him. He lifted her chin and looked down into a face blank with despair.

"Janet! Janet!" he exclaimed. "Nothing matters. Nothing! Nothing! I've been a fool, a stubborn, selfish fool!"

His arms went around her but even before he had drawn her close he felt the quick, passionate straining of her body as she swayed against him. She lifted her face—a face so radiant he was dazzled—and as they clung together he knew that nothing could ever separate them, that whether white or smeared with red he had not the right to deny her even a brief happiness.

For an instant he was tempted to tell Millington's story but as he lifted her head and looked into her eyes, now glowing through tears, he understood that nothing could add to that moment, that nothing counted with Janet but he himself, that the question of his parentage weighed so little in her mind that the mere introduction of the subject would only mar her ecstasy.

Then there came to him a complete realization of how marvelous a thing the love of a woman could be. It had risen above race, had scorned the teachings of precedent and the counsel of wisdom. It had dared custom, defied opinion, braved all the future might hold.

"Janet," he whispered brokenly, "you are the most glorious being in the world. I didn't know it, but from that day you looked through the picket fence at me at Kenogami I have loved you. And I always will, always."

She drew away and looked at him.

"There never was a fence, dearest, except in your own mind. And no matter what comes, Donald, always think first that I love you."

"But you give me so much and I—"

"You give me all that I wish, and you always can. There are only three things in the world, you and I and our love for each other, and the three, dearest—don't you see? They are inseparable, and always will be, no matter what happens, for we have the power to make them so."

It was with that last sentence foremost in his thoughts that Donald started early the next morning for Fort James. Yet with each of those three hundred and fifty miles over which he sped its potency diminished. Away from Janet, alone in the wilderness with his half-breed driver, fighting for each foot and each second, the fatigue of his body brought a weariness and a trembling of the spirit.

In those dreary miles he saw things as they were, as

he always had seen them, as they must irrevocably be unless— More and more he felt that the very strength and purity of Janet's love demanded a future untainted by the common tragedy of fur land; that somehow he must wring sanction from the man who had impressed all the north country with his hardness.

Yet when he reached Fort James another factor intruded itself. For the first time he saw clearly what he was about to do, understood that the man to whom he was going was his father and that he must tell him a story that could be only stunning and excruciating in its effect.

Corrigal himself came to the door when Donald drove up at the Hudson's Bay.

"Did you get him?" he demanded eagerly.

"Yes, the other side of Fort Bruce. I turned him over to the Mounted."

Corrigal led the way into the living room, asking questions rapidly as he did so.

"Wait," Donald protested. "I'll tell all that later. There's something else, something more important."

For five minutes Corrigal listened without interruption. Donald sought desperately not to color the story. He tried to repeat it exactly as Millington had told it to him, while he cringed there beside the campfire and the two half-breeds grumbled in the cold a hundred yards down the trail. He did not tell all the circumstantial facts in his own history and as he neared the end he eagerly searched the face of the man who sat opposite him.

But after the first startling statements Corrigal's expression had hardened and told nothing. When Donald reached the point where Nee-tah-wee-gan had described the murder of the helpless woman the district manager leaped to his feet with a sharp cry.

Donald was silent as he paced the floor.

"Go on," Corrigal said at last.

He continued his pacing when Donald had finished and for a full minute the younger man sat there with hope dwindling and heart sinking.

Back and forth Corrigal strode. His features were twisted by rage and pain and then he stopped directly before Donald and looked down at him.

"Lad," he said huskily, "that was a terrible thing to bring to me. For a moment I couldn't think of anything except the horror of it—of how she must have died there alone.

"But that is something we'll have to make each other forget. Some day I'll tell you about her. You'll want to hear—and I have never told anyone. But I know you can help me. You have already. There are thirty years we will have to wipe clean and —"

"You mean," Donald cried when he paused, "you mean that you believe it—that you believe I am—"

He had risen to his feet and Corrigal threw both arms around him.

"Great God!" he cried in a voice that touched Donald as nothing else ever had.

His head was down on Donald's shoulder and his body shook as the room echoed with his sobs.

But in a moment he got hold of himself. He leaned back, grasping the younger man by the arms and holding him away. The tears were running down his cheeks but through them there shone a smile that was like a child's, for it had broken through the repression of thirty years.

"Son!" he whispered. "My son! Mine!"

Everett McNeil

✬

READERS of juvenile fiction have long been acquainted with the stories of Everett McNeil. He is a native of Wisconsin, born at Stoughton, September 28, 1862. Mr. McNeil was educated at Milton College where he received his B.S. degree in 1887. He served in the Spanish-American War as a private in Company I, 9th New York Regiment. His books are largely of uniform type; an adventure series for boy readers. The stories are daring, imaginative, and full of action. All have an historical background and thus stimulate the youthful reader to learn more of the heroes and their contemporaries. Mr. McNeil died December 14, 1929 at the home of his sister in Tacoma, Washington.

His published works include: *Dickon Bend-The-Bow*, 1903; *The Hermit of the Culebra Mountains*, 1904; *The Lost Treasure Cave*, 1905; *The Boy Forty-Niners*, 1908; *In Texas with Davy Crockett*, 1908; *With Kit Carson in the Rockies*, 1909; *Fighting with Fremont*, 1910; *The Cave of Gold*, 1911; *The Totem of Black Hawk*, 1914; *The Lost Nation*, 1918; *Buried Treasure*, 1919; and *Tonty of the Iron Hand*, 1925. More recent works of this industrious writer are: *Daniel Duluth or Adventuring on the Great Lakes*, *For the Glory of France*, and *The Shadow of the Iroquois*. His last work, *The Shores of Adventure*, was written a short time before his death.

From DANIEL DU LUTH OR ADVENTURING ON THE GREAT LAKES, *by Everett McNeil. New York, E. P. Dutton & Company, Publishers. Reprinted by special permission of the publishers.*

CHAPTER II

"I HAVE made inquiries," Father answered, "of all the *coureurs de bois* who came out of the woods and of all the Fathers who came from their missions among the Indians and only this have I learned.

"Thirteen years ago that old bush-ranger, Pierre Ribault, came out of the wilderness to the northwest, with a wild tale of the Indians he had visited in the region of Lake Superior. He told of a girl he had seen in the camp of a band of Issati-Sioux on the south shore of Lake Superior, who, he was sure, was a white girl. He had only a glimpse of her; for, before he could come near, she had been suddenly whisked out of sight by an ugly old squaw, who appeared to have her in charge. He said this girl looked to be about seven years old, the age Carmela would then have been, had black hair and brown eyes, even as Carmela had, and was dressed in the whitest of tanned deerskin, adorned with differently colored porcupine quills and treated by the old squaw as if she were a little Indian princess.

"But, when he had made inquiries about her, a hideously ugly chief, with half of his nose sliced off and a great scar on one side of his face, had scowled so ferociously and had laid his hand so threateningly on his knife that Pierre declared he had felt the hair on top of his head prickling and had not dared to open his mouth again about the girl, nor had he ever caught a second glimpse of her. Evidently the Indians guarded her closely, as something most precious in their eyes; but Pierre did not understand why and dared not ask.

"Then, in 1667, two years later, the Jesuit missionary, Father Allouez, passed through Montreal on his way to Quebec. He was returning from two years of missionary work among the Indians at the western end of Lake Superior, where he had founded the mission of Saint Esprit.

I at once sought him out, as I did all who came out of the great wilderness to the northwest. He had a most marvelous tale to tell of his travels among the Indians and I listened to him spellbound for half the night; but, when I spoke of Carmela and told him my reasons for believing that she was still alive and held captive by the Indians, he started and his eyes turned quickly to my face.

"'Would to God I had known of this before!' he exclaimed, his face showing surprise and horror. 'Then I would have searched more deeply into the mystery of the girl queen I found ruling over a small band of Issati-Sioux encamped on Chagouamigong Bay, at the western end of Lake Superior, near my mission of Saint Esprit. I saw her but once and then but a short time; for she was most jealously guarded by an ugly old chief, called by a name that signifies Cutnose in their language, doubtless because the lower half of his nose had been cut off in some fight, leaving a great scar on his left cheek that gave to his twisted countenance a most hideous and ferocious expression. She did not appear to be over nine or ten years old and, at the first sight, I felt sure she was pure white; but, when I spoke to Cutnose about her, he scowled and declared that her mother, now dead, was his daughter and her father one of those roving French *coureurs de bois*, who had disappeared shortly after the girl's birth. I was still doubtful; but when I questioned him further, he became angry and told me, in the Indian way, which is not a pleasant way, to mind my own business. I never saw the girl again. Afterwards I learned that, young as she was, she was held in the greatest reverence by all the Indians of that region and was treated more like a princess than the granddaughter of a petty chief. This mystified me greatly; but I got only guttural grunts and ugly scowls when I sought to learn the reason why. Now I think of a surety, taking into consideration the things you have told me, that she must have been your lost daughter. If I ever go back to that mission, which I hope God will permit me to do, I will make certain whether or not she is your Carmela. If she is, I will take her under my care and restore her to you at the first opportunity.'" Father paused.

"But," I began at once, for I was greatly excited, "the girl must have been Carmela. She was the same age, had the same colored hair and eyes and the chief who held her captive had lost half of his nose and had a great scar on his left cheek, the same as the savage had who ran off with her. That is why the Indians were so afraid of letting a white man see her or talk to her. But, did not Father Allouez go back to the mission? Have you had no other word of this mysterious girl?"

"No," and Father's face clouded. "So far as I know Father Allouez never went back to the mission of Saint Esprit and not a word further of this mysterious girl has come to me from out the great wilderness to the northwest, although I have questioned all who came to Montreal from wandering among the Indians of that region. This happened eleven or more years ago; and even if the girl were Carmela, God alone knows whether or not she is still alive. That is what I want you to find out. I want you to learn what has become of the girl that Pierre and Father Allouez saw; and, if she is Carmela, I want you to bring her home to me. But think not I am asking you, who are but little more than a boy in years, to go on this dangerous mission without having taken thought of your safety. I have made arrangements with—"

"But, Father," I interrupted indignantly, "give not a thought to its dangers. I would go willingly, gladly, were they ten times as great. Now, when do I start?"

"My son, you are young; I am old. A youth goes forth into dangers rashly. It is the province of age to safeguard him from these dangers as much as possible. Accordingly I have planned your going carefully. All that I could do to prepare you for the perils to come, I have done. The rest lies in the hands of God."

"But when do I start?" I reiterated, with all of a boy's impatience of delay.

Father sat silent for a moment, his eyes going to the glowing fireplace, which drove some of the chill of that gloomy day out of the little office, while I waited impatiently for his answer.

"Last night," he at length began, turning his eyes to my face, "I had a long talk with my brave and good friend, Sieur Du Luth, who told me that he is about to start on a mission to the Indians of the far Northwest, going even beyond the shores of that great inland sea called Lake Superior. This I considered most providential and told him our story and how I wished you to go among these same Indians in search of your sister. He was deeply moved by my woful tale and most willingly promised to take you with him and to give every possible aid to your search."

"What?" I cried incredulously and vastly excited; for Daniel Du Luth was the hero of all the youths of Montreal. We looked upon him much, I fancy, as did the boys of Merrie Old England look upon that great *coureur de bois*, Robin Hood of Sherwood Forest; and the thought that I was to go with him on this great adventuring of his into the far wilds of this New World's wildernesses was like an elixir to my soul. "What!" I again cried, "am I really to go with Sieur Du Luth?"

"Yes," Father answered, smiling a little at my excitement. "It is all arranged. You are to start at sunrise on the third morning after this. Now as to your equipment" —Father arose slowly and went to a small closet back of his desk, the door of which was closed—"come here, son," and he opened the door.

I, now greatly excited, hurried to his side. In a corner of the closet, which was small, stood the finest gun I had ever seen. Not that its stock and barrel and lock were over-decorated with gold and silver and inlaid with pearl, as many guns are nowadays; but one look at its sturdy stock, made from the strongest and best wood, its heavy barrel of wrought steel and its stout lock told me that it was the product of the highest gunmaking skill.

"O Father!" and both my hands went out and caught hold of the gun and drew it to me, "is this beautiful gun for me?"

"Yes, son, I had it made to order especially for you by one of the most skilful gunmakers of Paris—that is to say, of the world," and a touch of pride came into his voice. "There are many handsomer guns; but not even the King himself has a better. I had it made unusually strong so that it would endure safely the rough usage you will be obliged to give it."

In the closet also hung a powder-horn and bullet-pouch, a double-barreled pistol, a strong-bladed hunting knife, a small hand-ax, to be carried in the belt, and a complete suit of deerskin clothes, with moccasin and coonskin cap —in short, all the personal equipment I would need for such a journey.

"Now, son," Father said, when all the marvels of the closet had been disclosed, "take all of these things to your room. Get inside the clothes, if you want to. Admire your looks as much as you please; but do not go out of your room without my permission. And remember not a word to anyone of this journey Du Luth is planning or of your going with him. He has enemies, who might conspire to do him harm, were his plans known. Tomorrow he is to call and then I will introduce you to him."

I gathered the things up in my arms and hurried to my room; for I was most eager to give them all a most thorough examination, more particularly the gun and pistol, and to try on the clothes. Never had I dreamed that such exciting things would happen to me, as had occurred since I opened the door of Father's little office and entered.

Charles D. Stewart

☼

CHARLES D. STEWART, who has lived at Pike Lake near Hartford, Wisconsin for nearly a quarter of a century, has had a cosmopolitan experience that is reflected in his many books and magazine articles. He was born in Zanesville, Ohio, March 18, 1868, but came with his parents to Milwaukee when a small boy, and grew up in the family home which was located where the Miller Hotel now stands. In a letter to the writer of this sketch, Mr. Stewart says: "The old Third Street home was in what was then a nice, quiet, elm-shaded neighborhood, and I used to play ball evenings on Third Street near Wisconsin Avenue after the teams had gone home and the street was deserted. Wisconsin Avenue was then called Spring Street."

His own account indicates that he was not enthusiastic about his school work, though his parents urged him to go away to school. He did attend Wayland Academy for a short time, but the desire to get out in the world was too great, and he left school rather unceremoniously. When he was sixteen, Mr. Stewart left home and got a job on a Missouri River steamboat,—*The General Meade*. In 1886-87 he was a ranch hand on a cattle range in central Texas. In 1887 he returned to Milwaukee where he resided until he went to Pike Lake in 1907.

While on the Texas cattle ranch Mr. Stewart did his first writing for publication,—some humorous articles for *Peck's Sun*. In March and July, 1890, his first magazine articles appeared in *The Century Magazine* under the title of *Reflections*. Since that time writing has been his profession except for a brief interruption when he served under Governor Emanuel L. Philipp as executive secretary.

His books include: *The Fugitive Blacksmith*, 1905; *Partners of Providence*, 1907; *Essays on the Spot*, 1910; *The Wrong Woman*, 1912; *Finerty of the Sand House*, 1913; *Buck*, 1919; and *Valley Waters*, 1922.

In addition to the books above mentioned, Mr. Stewart published in 1914 *Some Textual Difficulties in Shakespeare* (Yale University Press) which attracted wide attention. He has written also many short stories and magazine articles, a number of which have Wisconsin backgrounds. Of the stories and essays with scenes laid in Wisconsin may be mentioned: *On a Moraine*, 1909; *The Swimming Delegates*, 1909; *The Joke that was Practical*, 1909; *The Trouble at Schoenecker's*, 1909; *Since Shakespeare's Time*, 1909; *By Power of the President*, 1910; *The Dagger*, 1914; *Prussianizing Wisconsin*, 1919; *Belling a Fox*, 1921; *Those Wasps of Ours*, 1922; *The Arrow Maker*, 1923; *Reptiles and Angels*, 1924; and *Feathers to Burn*, 1929. These were first published either in the Atlantic Monthly or in The Century Magazine.

Mr. Stewart's books and short stories have more than ordinary merit. *The Fugitive Blacksmith* and *Valley Waters* will well repay a careful reading and rereading. The following selection from *The Fugitive Blacksmith* indicates his understanding of the psychology of endeavor and ultimate success.

From THE FUGITIVE BLACKSMITH, *by Charles D. Stewart, Published by The Century Co., New York, 1905. By permission of the publishers.*

CHAPTER XV

" 'But I ought to get along faster than most of them, because you are willing to show me all the tricks,' I said to Bill.

" 'Bein' a mechanic,' says he, 'ain't knowin' a certain number of tricks; it's bein' a certain kind of a man. After you've learned to be a mechanic you'll soon be a blacksmith.'

" 'I don't exactly understand what you mean,' I said.

" 'Well,' said Bill, 'when I'm setting an iron axle so the wheels will track, I tap it with the hammer and say, "Hit her there," don't I?'

" 'Yes.'

" 'Well, that's bein' a mechanic; it's thinkin'.'

"Bill sat quiet for a while. I guess he was thinking. Then he said: 'The best thing that ever happened to me was being put at the trade in a shop where they didn't want me to learn anything—although I didn't look at it that way at the time. And when I found that out I watched them like a hawk, and I kept thinking about everything they did. I had the satisfaction, as you might say, of stealing it. And the result was that when I had learned what the common every-day ones called the trade, I kept going ahead and thinking and trying to get the best of things, because I had had so much practice. I had so much practice getting the best of men that, when I came to dealing with things themselves, and on my own hook, I had the habit of watching them sharp and prying secrets out of them. Things don't tell you anything. You'll find that all you learn from them you've got to steal. What was your father?'

" 'He was a cooper,' said I.

" 'Maybe that will help some; but it's for you to do the thinkin' and the askin'. You've got the anvil to practice on now; and I'm there all the time to steal the trade from.'

"The next day Bill went away to Wilton to look over a printing-press and fix it. Before he left he gave me a tire to cut down and try to fit on the old wheel that was leaning against the front of the shop; and he said, 'Whenever I am gone be sure and keep busy. When you see a farmer coming along get a piece of red iron on the anvil, and, whatever you do, make a noise. And don't tell anybody you're just learning. When anybody brings a job in tell them you're so busy that they can't get it till tomorrow. Then when I come back I'll do it all. But, whatever you do, make a noise once in a while. The way to be a blacksmith is to start being one.'

"After Bill fixed the printing-press and they found he understood machinery, he got a call to go to another part of the county and tamp the flues in a leaky boiler. While he was there he took a look at the engine. He reset the eccentric and fixed the valve so that she would work with less steam. He was particular to explain the reason for it, so that the boss would see that he knew what he was doing. That way he got a reputation, and before long he was gone a day or two out of every week; and whenever he was going he would set me at a job. 'Whatever you do,' he would say, 'keep the place busy. If you run out of work, unmake a hook and make it over; you can always do it better.'

"Being left alone that way and having farmers call me 'blacksmith' was what put me to learning for myself. The jobs I took in seemed to be my own—although I couldn't do them. And the next day, instead of expecting to be shown, I would find myself stealing the trade from Bill. And the moment I would pick up an idea of my own he would notice it; and I would see him smiling to himself."

Charles Tenney Jackson

✧

ALTHOUGH born in St. Louis, Missouri, October 15, 1874, Charles Tenney Jackson came to Wisconsin when a boy and was educated in the Madison High School and in the University of Wisconsin. He left the university to enlist as a private in the 1st Wisconsin Volunteers for service in the Spanish-American War. While in the military service, he also acted as newspaper correspondent. In 1900 he became connected with the Milwaukee Sentinel, and in 1907-1908 was on the staff of the San Francisco Chronicle. Mr. Jackson has written a number of books, best known of which are: *Loser's Luck*, 1905; *Day of Souls*, 1910; *My Brother's Keeper*, 1911; *The Midlanders*, 1912; *The Fountain of Youth*, 1914; *Jimmy May in the Fighting Line*, 1919; and *Captain Sazarac*, 1922. He has also written many short stories and articles for magazines.

From THE DAY OF SOULS, *by Charles Tenney Jackson. The Bobbs-Merrill Company, Indianapolis, Publishers. 1910. Used by special permission of the publishers.*

ARNOLD crossed to the vestibule of the Security Building, where Police Commissioner Stillman awaited him. He was a brisk, alert-eyed man who had been of the "Handsome Harry" type in his university days, ten years ago, before he acquired his flesh; a joker, a raconteur, of flattering address, never at a loss for a quip, an indefatigable worker, a lieutenant of the boss, a shrewd attorney of the firm of Chatom, Bence and Company. But for politic reasons the police commissioner's name was not on the gilt legend across the windows of the great law offices, to a secluded room of which he now, in great joviality, conducted Arnold. He had sent messengers for the young man that morning and had scoured the city for him the previous night, unavailing, he said—and it was a matter of great importance. Stillman closed the opaque glass window to an outer room, where two clerks pored over papers and reports; the other window looked down on the spacious court of the building.

The politician offered a cigar and sat back easily in his desk chair, smiling over one of his witticisms. His manner was ingratiating, a patronizing more flattering than unpleasant; his study of the younger man was unobtrusive, but incessant.

Stillman was the right-hand man of the boss, as cool, wily, astute as the boss himself; he was known in the street as the "rent collector." Through his connections with the boss and his position on the police board, where his associates were merely puppets, he was the autocrat of the five thousand saloons and resorts in the city, and of their forty thousand denizens and habitués. From the millionaire liquor dealers—shining lights of San Francisco society—down the descending scale to the Barbary Coast, he, the overlord, drew power through his hidden and intricate associations. With the boss he assisted at extorting money from every evil traffic; their business genius founded and directed a score of enterprises that flourished through their connection with the mayor. With one man they were secretly associated in fire insurance, and it was seen that every saloon and dive-keeper took out policies with this concern; with another they established a great crockery and glass store, and every café and "French Restaurant" needing police acquiescence in its methods saw the logic of purchasing exclusively through this house; they founded a wholesale liquor store, and from it wise dealers purchased their goods;

they had relations with three different law firms, and soon every seeker of justice, from the public service corporations, the Six Companies of Chinatown down to the street drabs and *Pie gow* gamblers, saw the utility of retaining firms that could have it known, though with subtle circumspection, that they had peculiar resources in getting their clients' affairs favorably before the departments of government, the police courts and the superior bench. Under Stillman, the satrap, the tenderloin vote was a political power, astutely commercialized, organized for tribute; and from every source, none too small to be neglected, flowed an incalculable revenue to those Higher Up; and down again, rotting through the social fabric, flowed a portion of the mighty spoils. Stillman, the specialist in elaborating the night life of the town, was answerable to none save the boss and Barron Chatom, the attorney for the railroad, who represented in the secret government of the city the big money, the bribe-giving boards of directors, managers, takers of profit, as Stillman did the liquor men and the gamblers of the track and the "fight combine;" and against this power nothing in the city could stand. Behind Stillman's smiling camaraderie, his blithe democracy and power with men, stood the vague figures of the secret rulers of the town, as of America, the money-getters. Stillman looked at the young man in the chair across from him, talking on the San Franciscan's ever-present topic of the prize-ring and the races, before he disclosed deeper affairs.

"Haven't been to Sacramento of late?" he queried, at length, more leisurely.

"Not since the session began," answered Arnold.

Stillman laughed placidly. John Arnold was on the pay-rolls of the state of California at six dollars a day as a clerk in the senate—but he had not been near the capitol except to be sworn in. The people paid for his efficient services of last November to the "push," in rather good measure.

"You're worth something better, boy," resumed the commissioner, patting his paunch with breakfast content. "You haven't been around the city hall much since the campaign—I've been in shape to find things for you several times. We've been pretty good friends, Ham."

"Yes?" said Arnold leisurely.

"What I'm getting at is this," continued the commissioner: "there's a trick to be turned that's needed badly. Of course you know the grand jury's beginning to push into a lot of things—McMahon would like to land Weldy on this registration business—and one way and another we can't control 'em."

"They can't get Fred." Arnold's voice was indifferent.

"They can," retorted the commissioner emphatically. "They'll indict him to-morrow for fraudulent registration."

The younger man stared incredulously. Weldy, assemblyman from the Fifty-Second, was his friend. In the old days, when his father was going down in the battle of millions over the San Joaquin water rights, Ham used to go every night from the court room to the Star printing office, where Fred Weldy kicked a job press. After Selden Arnold was convicted, and his friends and acquaintances fell away from the felon's son, it was Fred's mother who offered him lodgings in an obscure street; and when he returned from the wars, nursing the bullet he got through a leg in Samar, it was the simple old woman and her apprentice son who took him in when he was again friendless and alone. Two years later Arnold got the union printer into politics, brought him to Stillman's notice, and he was sent to the legislature, wholly untried and inexperienced except for the two months in the registrar's office before the primaries.

Fred was somewhat sheep-headed, and Arnold had been his sponsor in his brief, uneventful political essay in the tenderloin district. But Mother Weldy was proud of the statesman; Arnold had met her only the other day and she showed him her new hat with the shiny black cherries, and told him when Fred was governor she should go back to Bavaria to visit the *Grossmutter*.

"That's the rub," Stillman was resuming. "I can't shut McMahon off and he's put the grand jury on Fred—he was so sore over the beating he got in the district. And it happens that five or six of the jurymen are from the Fifty-Second and are standing with Mac." The commissioner reached to a memorandum pad: "Selig, O'Grady, Brown—that's the coal dealer Brown, isn't it?—Mayo and Landry." He rubbed his nose. "It's a tough nut to crack. You know the registration was a little raw in spots, and it's certain to furnish an indictment."

"Can't you hold the jury?"

"Not in the Weldy matter. It's McMahon's personal spite to indict him. And we want him badly in the legislature—the anti-race-track bill, and then—Well, I don't mind telling you. We're behind Chatom for the United States senate next year, and it'll be a scratch fight. We can't afford to have Weldy indicted."

"No," said Arnold, "it would kill his mother."

The commissioner looked on his averted face with sudden cunning.

"It would," he answered solemnly, "and that would be a dirty deal. Weldy's got a future—and the old lady's proud of him." It was the first time Stillman had heard Fred Weldy had a mother.

The younger man sat in some perplexity, while the little square leather clock on Stillman's desk ticked with business haste.

"It's funny about those jurors," Arnold muttered. "Can't they be held in line? Of course I don't know, but I thought you had a drag."

"Son," Stillman leaned to him and tapped his knee, "they wouldn't touch you in a century—but I can't hold them on Weldy. That's why I'm talking to you. You're the straightest man we've got—everybody your friend about town. Now, Ham, you and Fred were the two clerks who passed all those registration applicants last summer about whom the big squeal is on, but you notice that your name is never brought into it, don't you? The mayor and I were talking about you last night. We decided that the thing to do is to have you summoned before the grand jury and swear that you handled all those registration lists—*all* on the day the specified instances of fraud are charged against Fred."

Arnold sat upright, staring at the other.

"Great and glorious!" he said at length, "you don't want much do you?"

"We want to keep Weldy in his seat—we're going to need him badly."

"And I'm to commit perjury?"

"Jack, we'll guarantee your immunity. We can swing the grand jury in your case. You can hold men that would eat Weldy. I'll deposit ten thousand dollars in any bank you name as a bond and a wager that they won't touch you. I know *my* men!"

"Harry, I'm out of politics. I've done a lot of dirty work for you, but I quit last night for good."

The commissioner smiled. Arnold's face was averted.

"Well, Fred goes over the road. He'll get five years on every count, if they get it before Judge Ransome or Dolan—and they will. If he's indicted, and it gets into court, I throw up my hands and leave him—I can't afford to stir the matter further."

Arnold laughed grimly. "Sometime the lid will rip up and we'll all be blown to hell!" said he. "I see it coming."

The commissioner sighed. "Well, here's a good man—your friend—going in stripes. Fred swears by you—he'll take your word now when I couldn't program him a minute."

The younger man rose and went to the window to stare down an air shaft. He was thinking of Mrs. Weldy and the way the shiny black cherries had nodded above her kindly face; and of Fred—he had intended to put Fred "right" in his budding career. After all Fred had done little of the registration; Ham, himself, a lieutenant of the tenderloin push, had sworn in the "floaters" last summer, brazenly, cynically—assured that he would be "protected"—that this, indeed, was what he was there for. Fred's wrong-doing in the matter had been a mere looking on and grinning at the audacity of it all—this revelation of practical politics at the city hall.

"Ham, it's safe as lying in bed," said Stillman steadily. "You know me—I couldn't operate long if my word wasn't good as a bond, could I? Well I say you'll be protected, if you exonerate Fred. I control enough of the jurors to stop the investigation right there. And you keep the best friend you ever had out of state prison."

The police commissioner's voice had the emphasis of truth. Arnold was scratching on the window glass. Then he turned: "Harry, if I do this thing, I'm done for."

"Ham, you're safe. I can put behind you bigger things than you ever dreamed of!"

"I wasn't thinking of my safety. I'm not afraid of any indictments by that grand jury push—but, well, I thought I was out of it all—I've gone pretty deep, but never to perjury."

"It's up to you whether or not Fred goes over the bay. I tell you, we daren't make any fight in court for him."

"I'm just thinking," mused the other, "what I ever got out of this game. Harry, you put me into politics. I was pretty clean until you got me to working in the district, and I only started it to help my old man—because you said you'd see that that pardon of his went through. That was three years ago."

"Arnold," retorted the commissioner, "turn this trick

for me and I'll have that matter before the governor in forty-eight hours."

"You will?"

"You know the man who can? That's Chatom."

"Chatom? He's cold as death!"

"Chatom wants Weldy left alone for that senatorship fight next session. Didn't I say that I could put bigger things behind you than you ever dreamed of? Why, boy, come out of your daze! Don't you see it—don't you *see*?"

Arnold stirred as Stillman's hand struck his shoulder. He wheeled in the revolving chair and stared at the white farther wall of the court. In the outer office he heard the clicking of the typewriter, somewhere else the muffled drone of a voice dictating to a stenographer.

William Henry Bishop

☼

FIFTY or sixty years ago William H. Bishop was one of the best known residents of Milwaukee. He was born in Hartford, Connecticut, January 7, 1847, and was graduated at Yale in 1867. Soon after completing his college work he came to Milwaukee and became one of the editors and proprietors of the *Daily Commercial-Times*, with which he was connected until 1877. From 1892 to 1902 Mr. Bishop was an instructor in Yale College. In 1903 he was appointed United States Consul to Genoa, Italy by President Roosevelt. He was transferred to Palermo, Italy in 1905, where he continued as consul until his resignation in 1910. Mr. Bishop rendered distinguished service during the disastrous Messina earthquake in 1908 and was decorated by the King of Italy. Since 1910 much of his time has been spent abroad. Milwaukee gave Mr. Bishop the inspiration for some of his stories. The scene of *The Golden Justice* is laid in the Wisconsin metropolis. In the extended list of his published works are found: *Detmold*, 1879; *The House of a Merchant Prince*, 1882; *Old Mexico and Her Lost Provinces*, 1884; *The Golden Justice*, 1887; *A House Hunter in Europe*, 1893; *Sergeant Von*, 1889; *A Pound of Cure*, 1894; *Writing to Rosina*, 1894; and *Queer People*, 1902.

From THE HOUSE OF A MERCHANT PRINCE, *by William Henry Bishop. Published by Houghton, Mifflin and Company, Boston, 1884.*

"TO MEET THE PRESIDENT OF THE UNITED STATES"

The list of invitations, "To meet the President of the United States," as the inscription on an impressive large square of pasteboard ran, was sufficiently large to include Russell Bainbridge. The young man considered it desirable to appear at the reception of a patron, who might be a more useful patron yet. He had a certain interest, besides, in the new chief magistrate of the country, then but lately installed into office.

He first paid a call or two, dropped in at a regular weekly reception of the same date, and arrived at Rodman Harvey's at about eleven o'clock. A fine, drizzling rain was falling. The glowing roof of the picture-gallery could be seen from a distance, lighting up the humid atmosphere above it. A striped canvas awning stretched down from the portal of the house and across the sidewalk. Similar awnings were out to-night at the fashionable restaurants and theatres.

By the awning's mouth lingered a few spectators, kept in check by a policeman, watching patiently under their umbrellas the arrival of the guests. The elegant men got down, with the collars of their great-coats turned up and silk mufflers about their throats. Wonderful creatures, in voluminous draperies of white, pale pink, blue, and saffron, followed. Their skirts were gathered close about them, and they alighted upon the carpeted stone with dainty rebounds. The carriages were ranged in an interminable file on either side of the street. Their wet varnish glistened in the gas-light. The gas-lights themselves were reflected mysteriously from the wet sidewalks, as if black streams of fathomless depth, somehow curiously solidified to bear the weight of the figures which trod them.

The gloom without gave but the more effect to the

brightness within. Two orchestras were playing: one in the music-gallery of the principal drawing-room; the other in a spacious temporary apartment formed, for the convenience of the dancers, by roofing over the yard at the rear of the mansion. The banisters of the grand staircase were adorned with a wreathing of smilax and roses. A deep cornice and wainscot belt of white flowers, starred with others in color, extended around the small drawing-room. Over the spot where the President stood, with the hostess and her daughter beside him, hung a mammoth ball of violets.

No expense had been spared, as the saying is. Some elderly guests, brushing up their mature whiskers at the mirror in the dressing-room, endeavored, in a practical way, to compute it. There were those who said,—"Harvey is not doing all this without an object, either. He has his designs upon the distinguished guest of the evening. He hopes to obtain from him the office of secretary of the treasury. He has long intrigued for it. This, chiefly, is what his late political activity means. He considers a seat in Congress from the foremost district of New York, as a stepping-stone. No doubt his not having taken part in national affairs before has been construed against him."

"The health of the present incumbent is not good," said one speaker. "In case of the appointment of a successor, it is eminently proper that a secretary should be chosen, for once, from the commercial metropolis of the country. Who more suitable, in that event,—so Harvey thinks,—than himself?"

"He knew the President of old, it seems," said another. "He employed him in some railroad case in the West. Well, I do not say that Harvey would be my choice, but stranger things have happened than that he should get it."

"I see that General Burlington is here," remarked another. "He and the President were in the war together.

I suppose he has laid aside his difference with Harvey for the time being, to come and pay his respects. He is quite right. He is a level-headed person, Burlington."

These elderly gossips were not above comments, also, on feminine points and on the current social scandals. They retailed two late Huyskamp escapades. A granddaughter had run away with an adventurer, whom she had been in the habit of meeting in Central Park, instead of going to Madame Bellefontaine's school, for which she started with her books regularly. The second Mrs. Huyskamp, Mrs. James, had also been seen coming out of a cemetery with her head on the shoulder of Northfleet, a man much younger than herself.

"That I deny *in toto*," said Watervliet, availing himself of an opportunity to repeat a witticism which had met with success at the club. "It stands to reason. You cannot have old heads on young shoulders."

The indifferent feeling with which Bainbridge had come to the party changed to something much more like pleasure when he unexpectedly found Ottilie there. That young woman colored a little on meeting him. She was reflecting as to what he would think of her vacillation of purpose.

She was with Mrs. Hastings, who had presented to her a number of young men. Among these was young Stillsby, whose repute for wisdom was not of the most profound. She had been impressed at first by this person's air of fashion, then wondered, and been amused, at the character of many of his sayings. The new acquaintances hovered about her, and Bainbridge at first could have her to himself but little.

"You did not write to me, as you promised," he said, seizing one of the opportunities. "I have lived for nothing else ever since."

"You have lived very well then, apparently. *Did* I promise to write? Well, I have been busy. It is but a short time now till our Commencement. And by the way, since you remind me of it, I have used your pamphlets in the preparation of my graduating essay. It is to be 'The Reformation of Criminals.'"

"Bravo! At last we have the matter settled. So you are to graduate. And then—?"

"I return to my home in the West. Glad enough I shall be to get back to dear old Lone Tree again."

"I am sorry for that.—I thought perhaps you might be intending to come here.—Your uncle would not leave you a great fortune, I dare say, but he would not be bad to live with. If you should get on as well with the rest as with him, I think you might count on a very tolerable existence. Why not return?"

"Nobody has axed me, sir," she said, misquoting the old ballad. Then, as if the subject were not a wholly comfortable one, she changed it, with "Well, you cannot deny that *this* is palatial."

"Oh yes, I can. Do not limit my capacity for denying too hastily. In the palace there should be a noble poverty of effect. They understand it in Italy. There should be a few handsome things along the walls, and the central spaces left free, for the noble occupants to walk up and down in, with their hands behind their backs, planning statecraft, wars, and matrimonial alliance, with the princes, their neighbors."

They were favorably posted for observing the guest of the evening.

"I think I should wish to be like that," said Ottilie, contemplating him. "If I were a man I should want to be very ambitious, and have as many bowing down before me as possible."

"Oh, the point is to *be* something; not to make a lot of people think you are," said Bainbridge.

It was a fine and somewhat startling sentiment, from him, but he delivered it with an air implying that the object was of course impossible, and nothing less was worth striving for.

The President was in some sense a type of his kind. He had risen honorably from humble beginnings. He had been farmer's lad, school-master, general in the civil wars, representative, governor of his state, and diplomat. He was a person of sterling worth; yet he was hardly of merit sufficient in itself to command the imposing recognition he had received. He had been chosen rather as a compromise candidate, in the discords of greater leaders, who often destroy one another, under our system, and rarely attain the coveted prize. His whole presence disclosed a calm, well-regulated life. He was of a good, robust figure, and neat and plain in attire. His dignity was of a genuine, simple sort, arising apparently from consciousness of his exalted success, but it had traces of angularity. He gave all who were presented to him a somewhat stiff shake of the hand. He had no great fund of ingenious or gallant discourse at command, but uttered now and then one of those mild pleasantries, which pass on such an occasion and from such a source as brilliant scintillations of wit.

As the pressure of new arrivals slackened, Rodman Harvey, the host, was to be seen conversing with him confidentially, and even giving slight taps on his sleeve, by way of emphasis.

"Ah, yes, indeed," said lookers on, "he will have his secretaryship, sure enough."

Angelica, slender, erect, with a long, simple "train" of rich material stretched out behind her, stood like some rare proud bird. Mrs. Harvey was in brocaded satin, its front embroidered with seed pearls, garnets, and other precious stones. From a collar of large diamonds of the purest water depended a splendid ornament of opal and diamonds. Her full bosom, heaved with the pride natural to such an occasion. She was all smiles and comely condescension. When the guests had finally been received, she took the arm of the President and walked through the rooms. Angelica, had withdrawn with Kingbolt of Kingboltville, to take a turn in the dancing-hall.

It was at such times that Rodman Harvey was especially content with his spouse. This was her element. It was what he had in mind when, at a certain stage of his increasing prosperity, caught by the subtle taste for fashion and display, he had married the widow of the elegant Charles Battledore. Perhaps, as he contemplated her, his thoughts may have gone back to an earlier helpmate in the day of small things,—to her with whom he had trodden ingrain carpets, and sat upon horse-hair furniture. Conference with that wife had always been a matter of the calmest reason. *She* had had no petulances of a spoiled child, no preposterous stormings-about, arising from slight cause and abating as easily. She had been inclined to look upon his growing wealth as a delusion and a snare, and had hardly increased her scale of personal expenses to the last.

The young children by that marriage were dead, with her. He thought of the group buried away together in the rural graveyard of his native place. He had been accustomed to alight from the train there, on summer days, at long intervals, to pass an hour beside their graves. There were wooden urns on the posts of the gate, through which you entered from the village green. The headstones were stained now and awry, the low mounds grown over with tall grass and wild flowers. How very far away that earlier life all seemed! Could it be that he had ever been bound in such intimate ties with so different a circle? Was it to be that in some vague future state the relation was again to be renewed?

Edna Ferber

☼

EDNA FERBER was born in Kalamazoo, Michigan, August 15, 1887, the daughter of Jewish parents. Her father was a Hungarian, her mother a native of Milwaukee. During her early childhood the family moved to Appleton, Wisconsin, where Miss Ferber received her education in the public schools and in the Ryan High School from which she was graduated. She began her literary career as reporter for the Appleton Crescent. Later she was employed successively by the Milwaukee Journal and by the Chicago Tribune. Some of her earlier books were the outgrowth of her newspaper experience. She now resides in New York City.

Best known of her writings are, *Dawn O'Hara*, 1911, *Buttered Side Down*, 1912, *Roast Beef Medium*, 1913, *Personality Plus*, 1914, *Emma McChesney & Co.*, 1915, *Fanny Herself*, 1917, *Cheerful by Request*, 1918, *Half Portions*, 1919, *The Girls*, 1921, *Gigola*, 1922, and *So Big*, 1924. It is probable that So Big is more widely read than any of her other books.

(The writer regrets his inability to obtain from either Miss Ferber or her publishers permission to reprint even a brief excerpt from her works.)

Elizabeth F. Corbett

※

UP TO date Elizabeth F. Corbett has spent most of her active life in Wisconsin although Illinois is her native state and she is now a resident of New York City. She was born at Aurora, Illinois, September 30, 1887, came to Wisconsin and received her A. B. degree from the University of Wisconsin in 1910. During her student years at Madison she was distinguished for scholarship and was elected to Phi Beta Kappa. For a number of years and until recently, Miss Corbett resided in Milwaukee. In a letter to the writer of these sketches, she says: "Although I've lived the greater part of my life in Wisconsin, I'm now technically a resident of New York. However, it always makes me proud to be alluded to as a Wisconsin author."

Miss Corbett has written many magazine articles and a number of books. Among the latter are: *Cecily and the Wide World*, 1916; *The Vanished Helga*, 1918; and *Puritan and Pagan*, 1920.

Dr. Victor Kutchin

☼

DR. VICTOR KUTCHIN of Green Lake, Wisconsin has written and published both prose and poetry. Although he has lived nearly four score years, his pen is still busy. Always a lover of birds and flowers and of the great out-doors, Dr. Kutchin is secretary-treasurer of the Wisconsin Audubon Society. In addition to this interest, he is an outstanding advocate of the conservation of Wisconsin's natural resources and of its beauty spots.

Among the books he has written are: *Leaves Caught in an Eddy*, (poems), *Love Among the Ruins*, *What Birds Have Done for Me*, and *The Strange Case of John R. Graham*.

Dr. Kutchin is a curator of the Wisconsin Historical Society.

Ira A. Kenyon

✥

IRA A. KENYON was born in Sanilac County, Michigan in 1884. When the boy was a year old, his father, a woodsman, moved to Phillips, Wisconsin. Ira Kenyon attended the public schools in Phillips, but when he reached high school age he found it necessary to work in the saw-mills, on drives and in the forests. This made his attendance at the high school irregular and it was not until 1907 that he was graduated from the Phillips High School.

Mr. Kenyon learned the printer's trade in the office of the Phillips Times, and worked as an itinerant printer to pay his expenses while making a tour of the western states. Upon his return he worked on the Phillips Bee and the Park Falls Independent, and was again with the Phillips Bee when America entered the World War.

Mr. Kenyon organized the Phillips and Park Falls company that became a part of the 32nd Division, and was commissioned first lieutenant. He went to France with the 119th machine gun battalion and was promoted to captain in 1918.

After the war he returned to the Phillips Times where he remained until January, 1924. He then went to Mellen as editor of the Mellen Weekly. In 1925 he started the Mellen Record of which he is editor and publisher.

Mr. Kenyon has written four novels, all dealing with northern Wisconsin: *The Lake of Pine*, *The Homestead on Popple Creek*, *Fangs of the Pack*, and *Isle of the Devil*.

Margery Bodine Latimer

☼

AMONG the younger writers of Wisconsin none gives greater promise of an eminent career in letters than Margery B. Latimer. And Miss Latimer's work is not wholly prospective. She has already secured a position among literary folk and recognition has come from far distant sections of the country.

Miss Latimer was born in Portage, Wisconsin, February 6, 1899. After receiving her elementary education in the public schools of her native city, she was successively a student at Wooster (Ohio) College, the University of Wisconsin and Columbia College.

It was only after a considerable period of preparation that Miss Latimer in 1928 gave her first work, *We Are Incredible*, to the public. This was followed by *Nellie Bloom and Other Stories*, 1929; and *This Is My Body*, 1930. She has also contributed largely to the leading magazines and newspapers. Of her story called *The Family*, included in her *Nellie Bloom and Other Stories*, the New York Times book review said: "It is one of the most important stories published in America in twenty-five years." Miss Latimer resides in Portage, Wisconsin.

Part II

WISCONSIN POETS AND SONG WRITERS

Ella Wheeler Wilcox

☼

WISCONSIN has produced no great poets although much creditable verse has been written by Wisconsin people. Among these Ella Wheeler Wilcox undoubtedly occupies first place in the public mind, though present day critics are less favorable in their estimate of her work than were those of two score years ago.

Ella Wheeler was born at Johnsburgh Center, Wisconsin, in 1855. When the future poet was a year old the family moved to the township of Westport on the north side of Lake Mendota. In this humble farm home she lived until her marriage to Robert M. Wilcox in 1884. In her autobiography, published under the title of *The World and I*, she tells of the long years spent in an unpleasant home environment, while she struggled for fame and a living. The prosaic countryside, with the nearest postoffice five miles away, was almost intolerable to the romantic and emotional girl who "saw visions and dreamed dreams." With unbounded faith and ambition she worked on and her poems gradually brought her a modest income. In 1883 she gave to the world *Solitude*, best known of her shorter poems. A volume of verse published in the early eighties under the title of *Poems of Passion* aroused a storm of protest. It was classed anywhere from daring to immoral. A perusal of the book does not indicate to the present day reader any basis for this denunciation. It may have been partly due to adverse criticism that within two years after the publication of *Poems of Passion*, over sixty thousand copies had been sold. If not distinctly religious, many of her short poems have a substratum of ethics and morality combined with a genuine sympathy for suffering and sorrowing humanity. The Wheeler household were uncompromising opponents of the liquor traffic; some of Ella Wheeler's early poems indicate that on this question, at least, she was in harmony with her family. Her *Two Glasses* was at one time a favorite recitation in schools and temperance gatherings.

Ella Wheeler's marriage to Robert Wilcox in 1884 marked the end of her residence in Wisconsin. After the death of Mr. Wilcox in 1916, Mrs. Wilcox spent some time in France where she was engaged in war-time service. She died at South Beach, Connecticut, October 30, 1919.

From SHELLS, *by Ella Wheeler, Published by Hauser & Storey, Milwaukee, Wisconsin, 1873.*

THE TWO GLASSES

There sat two glasses, filled to the brim,
On a rich man's table, rim to rim.
One was ruddy, and red as blood,
And one was as clear as the crystal flood.

Said the glass of wine to his paler brother,
"Let us tell tales of the past to each other;
I can tell of banquet, and revel, and mirth,
Where I was king, for I ruled in might.
And the proudest and grandest souls on earth
Fell under my touch, as though struck with blight.
From the heads of kings I have torn the crown,
From the heights of fame I have hurled men down;
I have blasted many an honored name,
I have taken virtue, and given shame;

I have tempted the youth, with a sip, a taste,
That has made his future a barren waste.
Far greater than any king am I,
Or than any army beneath the sky.
I have made the arm of the driver fail,
And sent the train from its iron rail.
I have made good ships go down at sea,
And the shrieks of the lost were sweet to me;
For they said, 'Behold, how great you be!
Fame, strength, wealth, genius, before you fall,
And your might and power are over all.'"
"Ho! Ho! pale brother," laughed the wine,
"Can you boast of deeds as great as mine?"

Said the water glass, "I cannot boast
Of a king dethroned or a murdered host;
But I can tell of hearts that were sad,
By my crystal drops made light and glad.
Of thirsts I have quenched, and brows I've laved;
Of hands I have cooled, and souls I've saved.
I have leaped through the valley, dashed down the mountain;
Slept in the sunshine, and dripped from the fountain.
I have burst my cloud fetters, and dropped from the sky,
And everywhere gladdened the landscape and eye.
I have eased the hot forehead of fever and pain,
I have made the parched meadows grow fertile with grain;
I can tell of the powerful wheel of the mill,
That ground out the flour, and turned at my will;
I can tell of manhood, debased by you,
That I have uplifted, and crowned anew.
I cheer, I help, I strengthen and aid;
I gladden the heart of man and maid;
I set the chained wine-captive free,
And all are the better for knowing me."

These are the tales they told each other,
The glass of wine, and his paler brother,
As they sat together, filled to the brim,
On the rich man's table, rim to rim.

* * * * *

From POEMS OF PASSION, *by Ella Wheeler. Published by W. B. Conkey Company, Chicago.*

SOLITUDE

Laugh, and the world laughs with you;
    Weep, and you weep alone,
For the sad old earth must borrow its mirth,
    But has trouble enough of its own.
Sing, and the hills will answer;
    Sigh, it is lost on the air,
The echoes bound to a joyful sound,
    But shrink from voicing care.

Rejoice, and men will seek you;
    Grieve, and they turn and go.
They want full measure of all your pleasure,
    But they do not need your woe.
Be glad, and your friends are many;
    Be sad, and you lose them all,—
There are none to decline your nectar'd wine,
    But alone you must drink life's gall.

Feast, and your halls are crowded;
    Fast, and the world goes by.
Succeed and give, and it helps you live,
    But no man can help you die.
There is room in the halls of pleasure
    For a large and lordly train,
But one by one we must all file on
    Through the narrow aisles of pain.

The following one stanza poem, from POEMS OF POWER, *indicates the sympathetic attitude of the poet:*

THE WORLD'S NEED

So many gods, so many creeds;
So many ways that wind and wind;
While just the art of being kind,
Is all this sad world needs.

* * * * *

From POEMS OF POWER *by Ella Wheeler Wilcox. Published by W. B. Conkey Company, Chicago.*

I AM

I know not whence I came,
　I know not whither I go;
But the fact stands clear that I am here
　In this world of pleasure and woe.
And out of the mist and murk
　Another truth shines plain—
It is my power each day and hour
　To add to its joy or its pain.

I know that the earth exists,
　It is none of my business why;
I cannot find out what it's all about,
　I would but waste time to try.
My life is a brief, brief thing,
　I am here for a little space,
And while I stay I would like, if I may,
　To brighten and better the place.

The trouble, I think, with us all
　Is the lack of a high conceit.
If each man thought he was sent to this spot
　To make it a bit more sweet,

How soon we could gladden the world,
　　How easily right all wrong,
If nobody shirked, and each one worked
　　To help his fellows along.

Cease wondering why you came—
　　Stop looking for faults and flaws.
Rise up to-day in your pride and say,
　　"I am a part of the First Great Cause!
However full the world,
　　There is room for an earnest man.
It had need of me or I would not be—
　　I am here to strengthen the plan."

TWILIGHT

The God of the day has vanished,
　　The light from the hills has fled,
And the hand of an unseen artist,
　　Is painting the West all red.
All threaded with gold and crimson,
　　And burnished with amber dye,
And tipped with purple shadows,
　　The glory flameth high.

Fair, beautiful world of ours!
　　Fair, beautiful world, but oh,
How darkened by pain and sorrow,
　　How blackened by sin and woe.
The splendor pales in the heavens
　　And dies in a golden gleam,
And alone in the hush of twilight,
　　I sit, in a checkered dream.

I think of the souls that are straying,
　　In shadows as black as night,

Of hands that are groping blindly
  In search of the shining light;
Of hearts that are mutely crying,
  And praying for just one ray,
To lead them out of the shadows,
  Into the better way.

I think of the Father's children
  Who are trying to walk alone,
Who have dropped the hand of the Parent,
  And wander in ways unknown.
Oh, the paths are rough and thorny,
  And I know they cannot stand:
They will faint and fall by the wayside,
  Unguided by God's right hand.

And I think of the souls that are yearning
  To follow the good and true;
That are striving to live unsullied,
  Yet know not what to do.
And I wonder when God, the Master,
  Shall end this weary strife,
And lead us out of the shadows
  Into the deathless life.

ANSWERED PRAYERS

I prayed for riches, and achieved success—
  All that I touched turned into gold. Alas!
My cares were greater, and my peace was less
  When that wish came to pass.

I prayed for glory; and I heard my name
  Sung by sweet children and by hoary men.
But ah! the hurts, the hurts that come with fame!
  I was not happy then.

I prayed for love, and had my soul's desire;
   Through quivering heart and body and through brain
There swept the flame of its devouring fire;
   And there the scars remain.

I prayed for a contented mind. At length
   Great light upon my darkened spirit burst;
Great peace fell on me, also, and great strength.
   Oh! had that prayer been first!

James Gates Percival

※

THE wayfaring stranger who finds himself in Hazel Green, Grant County, Wisconsin, should not leave that charming village until he has strolled through the old cemetery, only a few rods from the business center of the hamlet. There in the "silent city" he will see a monument the inscription on which tells briefly the life story of a man who, a century ago, attracted the attention of the best literary critics in America.

The record, graven in stone, reads as follows:

JAMES GATES PERCIVAL
LEARNED AND ACUTE IN SCIENCE
BORN IN
BERLIN, CONNECTICUT
SEPTEMBER 15, 1795
GRADUATED AT YALE COLLEGE
B.A. 1815 M.D. 1820
STATE GEOLOGIST
OF
CONNECTICUT, 1833-1842
STATE GEOLOGIST
OF
WISCONSIN, 1854-1856
DIED IN HAZEL GREEN
MAY 2, 1856
EMINENT AS A POET
RARELY ACCOMPLISHED AS A
LINGUIST
LEARNED AND ACUTE IN SCIENCE
A MAN WITHOUT GUILE

The literary career of J. G. Percival does not belong to Wisconsin; his poems were all written in early life while he was yet a resident of his native state. His last years only were spent in Wisconsin; here he died, and here his mortal remains were interred in the soil of his adopted state.

His life may be divided roughly into two periods, the earlier or literary period ending about 1831, and the later period, continuing to the time of his death, during which he devoted himself to science and the languages. It is worthy of note that Percival collaborated with Noah Webster in the great task of compiling the early edition of Webster's dictionary.

Sixty or seventy-five years ago every well stocked book store had on its shelves copies of Percival's Poems; to-day they are no longer read, although a few of his shorter poems are found in almost every American anthology. During Percival's lifetime literary critics were divided in regard to his rank as a poet. William Cullen Bryant compared Percival with Moore for "brilliancy of imagery and sweetness of versification," and cited the "Coral Grove" in support of his statement. On the other hand, James Russell Lowell was unsparing in his condemnation of Percival's style. Perhaps both these eminent writers were in part correct in their estimate. Bryant was referring to the shorter poems, many of which are gems. Lowell analyzed the longer efforts of Percival, which in some cases are a hopeless jumble of beautiful language.

A few of the beter known short poems of Percival are reprinted with this sketch.

THE CORAL GROVE

Deep in the wave is a coral grove,
Where the purple mullet and gold-fish rove,
Where the sea-flower spreads its leaves of blue,

That never are wet with falling dew,
But in bright and changeful beauty shine,
Far down in the green and glassy brine.
The floor is of sand like the mountain drift,
And the pearl-shells spangle the flinty snow;
From coral rocks the sea plants lift
Their boughs, where the tides and billows flow;
The water is calm and still below,
For the winds and waves are absent there,
And the sands are bright as the stars that glow
In the motionless fields of upper air:
There, with its waving blade of green,
The sea-flag streams through the silent water,
And the crimson leaf of the dulse is seen
To blush, like a banner bathed in slaughter:
There, with a light and easy motion,
The fan-coral sweeps through the clear, deep sea;
And the yellow and scarlet tufts of ocean
Are bending like corn on the upland lea:
And life, in rare and beautiful forms,
Is sporting amid those bowers of stone,
And is safe, when the wrathful spirit of storms
Has made the top of the wave his own:
And when the ship from his fury flies,
Where the myriad voices of ocean roar,
When the wind-god frowns in the murky skies
And demons are waiting the wreck on shore;
Then far below, in the peaceful sea,
The purple mullet and gold-fish rove,
Where the waters murmur tranquilly,
Through the bending twigs of the coral grove.

EVENING

O Evening! I have loved thee with a joy
 Tender and pure, and thou hast ever been
A soother of my sorrows. When a boy,

I wandered often to a lonely glen,
  And, far from all the stir and noise of men,
Held fond communion with unearthly things,
  Such as come gathering brightly round us, when
Imagination soars and shakes her wings.

Yes, in that secret valley, doubly dear
  For all its natural beauty, and the hush
That ever brooded o'er it, I would lay
  My thoughts in deepest calm, and if a bush
  Rustled, or small bird shook the beechen spray,
There seemed a ministering angel whispering near.

LOVE

If on the clustering curls of thy dark hair,
And the pure arching of thy polished brow,
We only gaze, we fondly dream that thou
Art one of those bright ministers who bear,
Along the cloudless bosom of the air,
Sweet, solemn words, to which our spirits bow,
With such a holy smile thou lookest now,
And art so soft and delicately fair.
  A veil of tender light is mantling o'er thee;
Around thy opening lips young loves are playing;
And crowds of youths, in passionate thoughts delaying,
Pause as thou movest by them, to adore thee;
By many a sudden blush and tear betraying
How the heart trembles, when it bends before thee.

NIGHT

Am I not all alone? The world is still
  In passionless slumber; not a tree but feels
  The far-pervading hush, and softer steals
The misty river by. Yon broad, bare hill
  Looks coldly up to heaven, and all the stars
    Seem eyes deep fixed in silence, as if bound

By some unearthly spell; no other sound
 But the owl's unfrequent moan. Their airy cars
The winds have stationed on the mountain peaks.
Am I not all alone?—A spirit speaks
 From the abyss of night, "Not all alone—
Nature is round thee with her banded powers,
And ancient genius haunts thee in these hours;
 Mind and its kingdom now are all thine own."

TO SENECA LAKE

On thy fair bosom, silver lake,
 The wild swan spreads his snowy sail,
And round his breast the ripples break,
 As down he bears before the gale.

On thy fair bosom, waveless stream,
 The dipping paddle echoes far,
And flashes in the moonlight gleam,
 And bright reflects the polar star.

The waves along thy pebby shore,
 As blow the north-wind, heave their foam,
And curl around the dashing oar,
 As late the boatman hies him home.

How sweet, at set of sun, to view
 Thy golden mirror spreading wide,
And see the mist of mantling blue
 Float round the distant mountain's side!

At midnight hour, as shines the moon,
 A sheet of silver spreads below,
And swift she cuts, at highest noon,
 Light clouds, like wreaths of purest snow.

On thy fair bosom, silver lake,
 O, I could ever sweep the oar,

When early birds at morning wake,
  And evening tells us toil is o'er!

THE EAGLE

Bird of the broad and sweeping wing,
  Thy home is high in heaven,
Where wide the storms their banners fling,
  And the tempest clouds are driven.
Thy throne is on the mountain top;
  Thy fields, the boundless air;
And hoary peaks, that proudly prop
  The skies, thy dwellings are.

Thou sittest like a thing of light,
  Amid the noontide blaze:
The midway sun is clear and bright;
  It cannot dim thy gaze.
Thy pinions, to the rushing blast,
  O'er the bursting billow, spread,
Where the vessel plunges, hurry past,
  Like an angel of the dead.

Thou art perched aloft on the beetling crag,
  And the waves are white below,
And on, with a haste that cannot lag,
  They rush in an endless flow.
Again thou hast plumed thy wing for flight
  To lands beyond the sea,
And away, like a spirit wreathed in light,
  Thou hurriest, wild and free.

Lord of the boundless realm of air,
  In thy imperial name,
The heart of the bold and ardent dare
  The dangerous path of fame.
Beneath the shade of thy golden wings,
  The Roman legions bore,

From the river of Egypt's cloudy springs,
    Their pride, to the polar shore.

And where was then thy fearless flight?
    O'er the dark, mysterious sea,
To the lands that caught the setting light,
    The cradle of liberty.

MAY

I feel a newer life in every gale,
    The winds that fan the flowers,
And with their welcome breathings fill the sail,
    Tell of serener hours—
Of hours that glide unfelt away
Beneath the sky of May.

The spirit of the gentle south-wind calls
    From his blue throne of air,
And where his whispering voice in music falls,
    Beauty is budding there;
The bright ones of the valley break
Their slumbers, and awake.

The waving verdure rolls along the plain,
    And the wide forest weaves,
To welcome back its playful mates again,
    A canopy of leaves,
And from its darkening shadows floats
    A gush of trembling notes.

Fairer and brighter spreads the reign of May;
    The tresses of the woods,
With the light dallying of the west-wind play;
    And the full-brimming floods,
As gladly to their goal they run,
Hail the returning sun.

William Ellery Leonard

☆

WILLIAM ELLERY LEONARD, poet and educator, was born in Plainfield, New Jersey, January 25, 1876. He was graduated from Boston University in 1898, received his A.M. degree from Harvard, 1899, and his Ph.D. degree from Columbia in 1904. Dr. Leonard came to the University of Wisconsin in 1906 as instructor in English and has since been a member of the faculty, being associate professor of English at the present time. He has written much, both verse and prose. It has been said that his poetical works are too scholarly to be popular with the ordinary reader. Whether this be true or not, Dr. Leonard is undoubtedly the foremost Wisconsin poet of his time. His published works include: *Sonnets and Poems*, 1906; *The Poet of Galilee*, 1909; *The Vaunt of Man and Other Poems*, 1912; *Glory of the Morning* (an Indian play), 1912; *The Red Bird* (an Indian play), 1923; and *Two Lives*, 1915. This last is read more widely perhaps than any of his other publications. Recent productions from the pen of this gifted writer are *The Locomotive God*, and *A Son of Earth*, the latter just off the press. This latest work is a collection of his poems, both early and late in point of time, which gives the reader an opportunity to judge of the development of his genius. Dr. Leonard leads a secluded life, and, except for his class-room and student contacts, is not known personally to a large number of people, even in Madison where he has so long resided.

WILLIAM ELLERY LEONARD

From TWO LIVES, *A Poem. By William Ellery Leonard.*
B. W. Huebsch, Inc. New York, Publishers.

Illustrative of the poet's style we have selected for this work the first two stanzas from his *Two Lives*.*

The shining City of my manhood's grief
Is girt by hills and lakes (the lakes are four),
Left by the ice-sheet which from Labrador
Under old suns once carved this land's relief,
Ere wild men came with building and belief
Across the midland swale. And slope and shore
Still guard the forest pathos of dead lore
With burial mound of many an Indian chief,
And sacred spring. Around me, Things-to-come
Are rising (by the plans of my compeers)
For art and science, like a wiser Rome
Upon a wiser earth for wiser years.—
Large thoughts, before and after; yet they be
Time's pallid backgrounds to my soul and me.

'Tis no mean city: when I shut my eyes,
To thought she seems memorial as they,
The world's white cities famous far away,
With her own beauty, her own sunset skies
Across her waters, her own enterprise
Beside her woodlands, with her thousand homes,
Her squares and flowering parks, and those two domes
Of Law and Learning, and her bold and wise.
She too shall have, and has even now, her fame
(Like Florence or Geneva, once the fair
Sojourn of worthy men), and of the same
A solemn part, perhaps, shall be that there,
By house and tree, to flesh and blood befell
The things whereof this story is to tell.

**By permission of the author.*

From A SON OF EARTH, *Collected Poems, by William Ellery Leonard. Published by The Viking Press, New York, 1928. Reprinted by permission of the author.*

NATURA MAGNA

Gaze not at hearth-flame nor at funeral pyre
Too long in dreams or tears; but rise and bare
Your souls to lightning; see the mountain flare
Forth its wild torrents of essential fire!
Sit not too long by well-springs of desire
In shadowy woodlands with the white nymphs; fare
Out to blue ocean and the sun-bright air!—
Hark! the deep voice: "Exult ye, and aspire!

"As some god's festival on holy ground
Ye shall approach my universe afar,
Naked and swift as heroes, from all climes;
Thus ye shall fill an epos with new sound,
Thus ye shall yield new names for many a star,
And thus from ye shall date the aftertimes."

WANDERERS

What makes us wander? The west wind's call and cry
When frost is on the stubble? The harvest moon
Crowning the hill-road? The diffused moon
Of summer and reaches of unruffled sky?
Sunset? Or sea? Or rivers gliding by
Around the bluffs? Or snow against the face?
Or some dim sense of earth itself in space,
When at the spring the wild geese northward fly?

Is it in the blood?- impulse of veined feet
And sinewy thighs that wither if they rest?
Is it in the soul?- to whom the Incomplete
Is challenge to the immemorial quest,
The soul that leaves To-day in winding sheet
For some To-morrow with stars upon its breast.

MIGNON (For Helen)

Know'st thou the land where bloom the citron rows,
In dusky leaves the golden orange glows,
And soft a wind is borne from bluest sky,
And stands the myrtle still, the laurel high?
Know'st thou the land?
                    Oh there, O there
Would I with thee, O my beloved fare!

Know'st thou the house? On pillars rest the beams.
The hall it shines; the shimmering room it gleams;
And marble statues stand and look at me:
"What have men done, O my poor child, to thee!"
Know'st thou the house?
                    O there, O there
Would I with thee, O my protector, fare!

Know'st thou the hill, its path in clouds and gray?
The mule he seeks through mountain mist his way;
In caverns dwell the dragons' ancient broods;
Down plunge the cliffs, and over them the floods.
Know'st thou the hill?
                    O there, O there
Lies our own way. O father, let us fare!

WALT WHITMAN

In Washington in war-times, once I read,
When down the street the good gray poet came—
A roving vagabond unknown to fame—
From watches by the dying and the dead,
The old slouch hat upon his shaggy head,
His eyes aglow with earth's immortal flame,
Lincoln, who marked him from the window frame,
The judge of men, the deep-eyed Lincoln, said:
"That is a man."—

What poet has juster meed
Whose brazen statue in the morning stands
On marble avenues of elder lands?—
In life, in death, that was a man indeed.—
O you who 'gainst him lift your righteous hands,
And you, the fops that ape his manhood, heed!

WITH MOTHER EARTH

'Tis well to spend a lucid afternoon
In the long silvery grass, with upturned eye
Noting the leaves that fret the azure sky;

'Tis well to wait the coming of the moon,
Out on the hillside, over fields of June.

'Tis well to listen, when abed we lie,
To midnight murmurs of the rain and try
To mark therein the world's primeval tune.

'Tis well to know that (spite of death and dearth
And evil men in cities plotting ill
And friends that leave us when our thoughts are new.)

The good man may abide with Mother Earth
And dream his dreams and have his visions still
And trust the Infinite to see him through.

Hattie Tyng Griswold

☼

(This sketch of the life of Hattie Tyng Griswold was contributed by her daughter, Mrs. Florence Griswold Buckstaff of Oshkosh, Wisconsin, who also selected the following poems as illustrative of her mother's literary work.)

MRS. HATTIE TYNG GRISWOLD, poet, newspaper writer and novelist of Wisconsin's early days, was a typical New Englander, transplanted to the West. She knew the hunger of the early settlers for books and beauty. She anticipated present-day writers in her descriptions of pioneer days in Wisconsin, and she was both ardent and persuasive in newspaper articles advocating various reforms and improvements in ways of living. She wrote continuously for many years to the newspapers, letters on temperance, health, law enforcement, charity, religion and literature.

A series of letters to the *Chicago Tribune* on *The Home Life of Great Authors* was published later (1886) in two volumes by McClurg and remained a standard book of reference for many years.

Mrs. Griswold's books of poems, *Apple Blossoms*, (1874) (1878) went through two editions. Several stories for girls, *Waiting on Destiny*, (1889), *Fencing with Shadows*, (1892), *and Lucille and her Friends*, (1892), were well received.

Hattie Tyng was born in Boston in 1840, and came to Wisconsin about 1850 with her father, Dudley Tyng, who was a Universalist missionary. She was married in 1863 in Columbus, Wisconsin, to Eugene Sherwood Griswold, and lived in Columbus until her death in 1909.

They had three daughters, Mrs. Florence Griswold Buckstaff, Miss Ada Tyng Griswold and Mrs. Edith Griswold Williams, all of whom reside in Oshkosh.

DEAD!

Dead! dead on the field of battle,
   'Mid its awful crash and roar;
Dead! gone on the last long marching,
   To the land where nevermore
Shall the bugle sound reveille,
   Or the dreadful cannon roar.

Dead! dead on the field of battle,
   A gallant heart, and tried;
Close, close to the foremost standard,
   Where the fiercest warriors ride,
Where men fell like leaves in autumn,
   And where he fell, and died.

Dead! dead on the field of battle,
   With his name and his honor white—
There's nothing on earth so glorious
   As dying for the Right,
Thank God he died 'mid the foremost,
   In the fiercest of the fight.

Dead! dead on the field of battle;
   Could he be alive once more,
We would bid him go, and do, and die,
   'Mid the battle's rush and roar.
He who for country dies, dies not,
   But lives forevermore.

The foregoing was written by Mrs. Griswold during the Civil War and was widely read in camps and hospitals at the time.

HATTIE TYNG GRISWOLD

UNDER THE DAISIES

I have just been learning the lesson of life—
    The sad, sad lesson of loving,
And all of its power for pleasure or pain
    Been slowly, sadly proving;
And all that is left of the bright, bright dream
    With its thousand brilliant phases,
Is a handful of dust in a coffin hid—
    A coffin under the daisies.
    The beautiful, beautiful daisies,
    The snowy, snowy daisies.

And thus forever throughout the world,
    Is love a sorrow proving;
There's many a sad, sad thing in life,
    But the saddest of all is loving.
Life often divides far wider than death,
    Stern fortune the high wall raises;
But better far than two hearts estranged,
    Is a low grave starred with daisies.

And so I am glad that we lived as we did,
    Through the summer of love together,
And that one of us, wearied, lay down to rest,
    Ere the coming of winter weather;
For the sadness of love is love grown cold,
    And 'tis one of its surest phases;
So I bless my God, with a breaking heart,
    For that grave enstarred with daisies:
    The beautiful, beautiful daisies,
    The snowy, snowy daisies.

THE SUNDERING FLOOD

How shall I bear me in the hour to be,
    When the great Sundering Flood comes rushing down,
And I shall feel the coldness of that sea
    In which all mortal men shall one day drown?

Shall I be glad who have been sad so long,
　So weary of life's ceaseless care and fret,
Shall I be blithe and sing a careless song
　When with that icy foam my feet are wet?

Or will the sweetness of the happy earth
　Sweep over me, and friends hold me in chain,
And shall I feel that love has had new birth,
　And every rose of life will bloom again?

God knows I have been brave up to this hour,
　No coward drop in all my valiant blood,
Bid me not part from courage, O thou Power
　That hold'st in leash e'en thy great Sundering Flood.

MOUNTAIN MIST

Upon the distant mountain's crest,
　Day after day I saw the blue;
About me all was cloudy, gray—
　I longed so for the mountain hue.

I climbed to reach it glad of heart,
　Though weary, slow my footsteps grew;
The rocky heights were grim and bare,
　The bluebells held the only blue.

The top I reached, nor saw it there,
　The sweet mirage fled on before;
Yet at the foot I found it still
　Hanging the silent summit o'er.

I seek and seek, but shall not reach
　That hue alluring as the sea—
The blueness which was never there,
　But which forever there will be.

From HOME LIFE OF GREAT AUTHORS, *by Hattie Tyng Griswold. Published by A. C. McClurg and Company, Chicago*, 1887.

WASHINGTON IRVING

IT is a little over one hundred years since Washington Irving was born; and it is nearly thirty years since he ceased to charm the reading world by the work of his genial and graceful pen. For fifty long and fruitful years he was our pride and boast, and his memory will for many a long year yet be green in the hearts of his countrymen. He was our first and best humorist. Before his advent, what little writing had been done in this country was mostly of the sentimental and tearful sort. And for many years after he began to write, it was much the same. Weeping poetesses filled whole columns with their tears, and in every local sheet new Werthers were trying to tell of the worthlessness of life and the beauties of dying. Young bards were inditing odes to melancholy, and everybody was chanting in chorus, if not the words, at least the sentiment of, "how sublime a thing it is to suffer and be strong." There was no laughter in the land.

* * * * *

Washington Irving was born in the city of New York in 1783, the youngest of eleven children born to his parents. At that time New York was a rural city of twenty-three thousand inhabitants clustered about the Battery. The Irvings were descendants of the old Scotch Covenanters, and were strict Presbyterians. The home rule was one of austerity and repression. The children were brought up on the catechism and the Thirty-Nine Articles. As they grew older all were repelled from the church of the father by the severity of its dogmas, and all except one attached themselves to the Episcopal Church. Washington, we are told by Mr. Warner, "in order to make sure of his escape and feel safe, while he was still constrained to attend his father's church, went stealthily to Trinity Church at an early age and received the rite of confirmation." He was of a joyous and genial temperament, full of life and vivacity, and not at all inclined to religious seriousness. He was born with a passion for music, and was also a great lover of the theatre. These things, in the eyes of his father, were serious evils, and he felt great anxiety for the son's spiritual welfare. The gladsomeness and sportiveness of the boy's nature were things which he could not understand, and he feared that they were of the Evil One. There was no room in the darkness of his religious creed for anything that was simply bright and joyous. To save one's soul was the business of life; all things else were secondary and of small importance. Of course, he worried much over this handsome, dashing, susceptible, music-loving, laughter-loving son, and doubtless shed many tears over his waywardness. Yet there was nothing wild about the boy. The writing of plays seems to have been his worst boyish offense. His first published writings were audacious satires upon the theatre, the actors, and the local audiences. They had some promise, and attracted some attention in the poverty of those times.

At the age of twenty-one he was in such delicate health that a voyage to Europe was looked upon as the only means of saving his life. He accordingly embarked for Bordeaux and made an extended tour of Europe, loitering in many places for weeks at a time, and laying up a store of memories which gave him pleasure throughout life. In Rome he came across Washington Allston, then unknown to fame. He was about three years older than Irving, and just establishing himself as a painter. Irving was completely captivated with the young Southerner, and they formed a very romantic friendship for each other.

Irving even dreamed of remaining in Rome and turning artist himself, that he might always be near his friend. He had a great dread of returning to the New World and settling down to the uncongenial work of the law, and he fancied he had some talent for art.

* * * * *

But the art scheme was soon abandoned, and he went on to London, where he began his literary work. His name of Washington attracted considerable attention there, and he was frequently asked if he were a relative of General Washington. A few years later, after he had written the "Sketch Book," two women were overheard in conversation near the bust of Washington in a large gallery. "Mother, who was Washington?" "Why, my dear, don't you know?" was the reply, "he wrote the 'Sketch Book'."

* * * * *

He returned to New York in 1806, and was much sought after in society from that time on. It was a very convivial company, that of old New York in the early part of the century, and Irving entered into its pleasures with the rest of his friends. * * * "Who would have thought," said Irving to Governor Kemble, in alluding, at the age of sixty-six, to these scenes of high jollity, "that we should ever have lived to be two such respectable old gentlemen!"

It was during these years that he made the acquaintance and learned to love so deeply Matilda Hoffman, a beautiful young girl, daughter of one of his older friends. She was a most lovely person, in body and mind, and in his eyes the paragon of womanhood. He was young, romantic, full of sensibility, and his love for this beautiful girl filled his whole life. He was poor and could not marry, but he had many arguments with himself about the propriety of doing so even without an income. "I think," he finally writes, "that these early and improvident marriages are too apt to break down the spirit and energy of a young man, and make him a hard-working, half-starving, repining animal all his days." And again: "Young men in our country think it a great extravagance to set up a horse and carriage without adequate means, but they make no account of setting up a wife and family, which is far more expensive." But while he was looking about on every side for some way to better his fortunes, that he might take to his home this woman he loved so tenderly, her health began to fail, and in a short time he was deprived by death of her companionship. His sorrow was life-long, and it was a sorrow which he held sacredly in his own heart. He never mentioned her name, even to family friends, and they learned to avoid any allusion to her, he was so overcome with emotion when merely hearing her name spoken. This was in his early youth, and throughout a long life he held himself faithful to her memory,—never, it is believed, wavering once in his allegiance. Thackeray refers to this as one of the most pleasing things he knew of Irving.

His countenance long retained the trace of his melancholy, and he was ever after a more subdued and quiet man. After his death a beautiful picture and lock of hair were found among his private papers marked in his handwriting, "Matilda Hoffman." He also kept by him throughout life her Bible and Prayer-Book. He lay with them under his pillow in the first days of his anguish, and carried them with him always in all lands to the end of his life. In a little private notebook intended only for his own eye were found these words after his death: "She died in the beauty of her youth, and in my memory she will ever be young and beautiful." Truly, not an unhappy fate as the world goes,—to live thus in the memory of such a man. What would years and cares and the commonplace of existence have done for such a love as this, we wonder? We shall never know. But we have all seen loves apparently as pure and as strong, worn away by the attritions of life,—by the daily labor for daily bread, by little incessant worries and faults and foibles upon the part of one or both,—until there was nothing left of the early color of romance; only a faded web of life where once was cloth of gold. How sweet to many a faded and careworn woman would be the thought of being always young and beautiful to the man she loved. Fortunate Matilda Hoffman of the olden time!

In 1817 he went again to Europe, and while there definitely made up his mind to look upon literature as his profession,—an almost unheard of thing in America at that time.

In his fiftieth year he returned to America, far from rich, though he had made money from his books. Although he had thought he could not support a family of his own, he found himself with two brothers and several nieces upon his hands for whom he must provide. He was very fond of them all; and, being the least selfish of men, enjoyed making them all comfortable. But to do so, he had to be industrious with his pen, and he never gave himself much rest. He bought a home at Tarrytown, upon the Hudson, which he called Sunnyside, and where he resided till his death. The farm had on it a small Dutch cottage, built about a century before, and inhabited by the Van Tassels. This was enlarged, still preserving the quaint Dutch characteristics; it acquired a tower and a whimsical weathercock, the delight of the owner, and became one of the most snug and picturesque residences on the river. A slip of Melrose ivy was planted, and soon overrun the house; and there were shaded nooks and wooded retreats, and a pretty garden.

It soon became the dearest spot on earth for him; and although it ate up his money almost as fast as he could earn it, he never thought of parting with it. The little cottage soon became well stocked. He writes:—

"I have Ebenezer's five girls, and himself also whenever he can be spared from town, sister Catherine and her daughter, and occasional visits from all the family connection."

Thackeray describes him as having nine nieces on his hands, and makes a woeful face over the fact. He dispensed a charming hospitality here, and no friend who ever visited him forgot the pleasure. He was a most genial and cordial host, and loved much to have his friends bring the children, of whom he was passionately fond. His nieces watched over his welfare with most tender solicitude; and the cottage at Sunnyside, although without a mistress, was truly a home.

It was with great reluctance that he left it after his appointment as minister to Spain, and all the pleasure he received from that high mark of the appreciation of his country did not compensate him for the hardship of leaving home. During this third visit to Europe "it is easy to see that life has grown rather sombre to Irving,— the glamour is gone, he is subject to few illusions. The show and pageantry no longer enchant; they only weary." He writes home: "Amidst all the splendors of London and Paris I find my imagination refuses to take fire, and my heart still yearns after dear little Sunnyside." Those were exciting times in Spain, and Irving entered into all the dramatic interest of the situation with a real enthusiasm, and wrote most interesting letters to friends at home, describing the melodrama in which he had sometimes an even perilous interest. Throughout his four years' stay the excitement continued, and the duties of minister were sometimes perplexing enough.

Through all the honors which he received—and he was one of the most honored men of his day—he was always modest, unassuming, and even diffident. He was the most cheerful of men, and seemed to diffuse sunshine wherever he went. He was essentially lovable, and could hardly be said to have made an enemy during his life. Indeed, one of his lacks was that of aggressiveness; it would have given a deeper force to his character and brought out some qualities that were latent in him.

He died on the 28th of November, 1859, at the close of a lovely Indian-summer day, and was buried on a little elevation overlooking Sleepy Hollow. Near by winds the lovely Hudson, up and down which go the white-winged boats bearing tourists to view the river he so loved, and over which hangs the blue haze he has so often described, softening everything in its gauzy folds. The feet of those he loved go in and out at Sunnyside, and his memory is a benediction.

Elizabeth Farnsworth Mears

☼

ELIZABETH FARNSWORTH spent her early years in Fond du Lac, but moved to Oshkosh after her marriage to John Mears. She wrote under the pen-name of Nellie Wildwood. It is generally stated that she was the first Wisconsin writer to publish a volume of verse. She wrote a play, *Black Hawk*, that drew full houses in some of the larger cities of the state. Her most pretentious work was a poem entitled, *Voyage of Pere Marquette, and Romance of Charles de Langlade, or The Indian Queen. An Historical Poem of the Seventeenth and Eighteenth Centuries*. Descriptive of the unbroken wilderness of the shores of Lake Winnebago in the period of this poem, the following selection is given;

"Tis early morn—the heavens are softest blue,
And the broad lake has caught the same fair hue;
While from the dreamy West the cooling breeze
Waves the green drapery of the lofty trees,
Amid whose cool and leafy shade is heard
The matin-song of many a bright-winged bird.
The robin's note from hedge of wilding rose—
The mourning dove pours forth her loving woes—
The thrush, with joyous gratitude elate—
The speckled partridge, whistling to its mate—
And all the feathered choristers of song,
Rouse the clear echoes, vales and groves among.
The fragrant zephyrs, 'mid the flowers that sleep
With morning freshness on the senses sweep.
The rising sun gilds tree and headland tall—

The crimson beams soft ling'ring where they fall,
Till earth and arching skies in splendor bright
Mingle in one, thus bathed in golden light."

Mrs. Mears had two daughters who became known far beyond the borders of their native Wisconsin; Helen Farnsworth Mears, famed artist and sculptor and Mary Mears, who excelled her mother in the field of literature.

Eben E. Rexford

※

EBEN E. REXFORD, poet, song writer and authority on floriculture, was born at Johnsburgh, New York in 1848. Like many of the Wisconsin writers he came to this state in early childhood, his parents having emigrated from their New York home to the Wisconsin wilderness in 1855. After the rural school training common to farm boys, he received his higher education at Lawrence College, Appleton. In 1908 the Appleton institution conferred upon him the degree of Doctor of Literature. For many years Mr. Rexford resided in the village of Shiocton, beloved by all who knew him. He died in Shiocton, October 16, 1916.

With his growing recognition as a literary man, Mr. Rexford clung to his habits of retirement. He traveled little and during the last forty years of his life never wandered far from his village home. He preferred to spend his time among the flowers and trees in his garden. It is said that he once rejected the offer of an honorary degree from the University of Wisconsin because it would necessitate a trip to Madison.

Aside from his articles on flower culture, Mr. Rexford wrote a number of poems that found favor with his readers. Some of his verses undoubtedly have merit, but it is hardly possible that Rexford's poetical work would be long remembered but for his remarkably popular song, "Silver Threads Among the Gold." It is sung and played everywhere, yet so little were its possibilities recognized by the author that he sold the poem to a Frank Leslie publication for three dollars. Two years later it was set to music. At the time Mr. Rexford wrote this, his best known poem, he was a student at Lawrence College and only 18 years of age. Another popular song of a generation ago, "Only a Pansy Blossom" was written by Mr. Rexford.

On July 16, 1930 a granite memorial was dedicated to the memory of the best known citizen that Shiocton has ever had. The memorial is set in the yard of the Congregational Church with which Mr. Rexford was connected.

SILVER THREADS AMONG THE GOLD

Darling, I am growing old,—
Silver threads among the gold,
Shine upon my brow today;—
Life is fading fast away;
But, my darling, you will be
Always young and fair to me,
Yes! my darling you will be—
Always young and fair to me.

When your hair is silver white,—
And your cheeks no longer bright
With the roses of the May,—
I will kiss your lips, and say;
Oh! my darling, mine alone,—
You have never older grown,
Yes, my darling, mine alone,—
You have never older grown.

Love can nevermore grow old,
Locks may lose their brown and gold;
Cheeks may fade and hollow grow;
But the hearts that love, will know
Never, winter's frost and chill;
Summer warmth is in them still,

Never winter's frost and chill,
Summer warmth is in them still.

Love is always young and fair,—
What to us is silver hair,
Faded cheeks or steps grown slow,
To the hearts that beat below?
Since I kissed you, mine alone,
You have never older grown,
Since I kissed you, mine alone,
You have never older grown.

  Chorus to last verse,
Darling, we are growing old,
Silver threads among the gold,
Shine upon my brow today;—
Life is fading fast away.

THE UNFRUITFUL TREE

There stood in a beautiful garden
A tall and stately tree.
Crowned with its shining leafage
It was wondrous fair to see.
But alas! it was always fruitless;
Never a blossom grew
To brighten its spreading branches
The whole long season through.

The lord of the garden saw it,
And he said, when the leaves were sere,
"Cut down this tree so worthless,
And plant another here.
My garden is not for beauty
Alone, but for fruit, as well,
 And no barren tree must cumber
The place in which I dwell."

The gardener heard in sorrow,
For he loved the barren tree
As we love some things about us
That are only fair to see.
"Leave it one season longer,
Only one more, I pray,"
He plead, but the lord of the garden
Was firm, and answered, "Nay."

Then the gardener dug about it,
And cut its roots apart,
And the fear of the fate before it
Struck home to the poor tree's heart.
Faithful and true to his master,
Yet loving the tree as well,
The gardener toiled in sorrow
Till the stormy evening fell.

"Tomorrow," he said, "I will finish
The task that I have begun."
But the morrow was wild with tempest,
And the work remained undone.
And through all the long, bleak winter
There stood the desolate tree,
With the cold white snow about it,—
A sorrowful thing to see.

At last, the sweet spring weather
Made glad the hearts of men,
And the trees in the lord's fair garden
Put forth their leaves again.
"I will finish my task tomorrow,"
The busy gardener said,
And thought, with a thrill of sorrow,
That the beautiful tree was dead.

The lord came into his garden
At an early hour next day,
And to the task unfinished
The gardener led the way.
And lo! all white with blossoms,
Fairer than ever to see,
In the promise of coming fruitage
Stood the sorely-chastened tree.

"It is well," said the lord of the garden.
And he and the gardener knew
That out of its loss and trial
Its promise of fruitfulness grew.
It is so with some lives that cumber
For a time the Lord's domain.
Out of trial and bitter sorrow
There cometh countless gain,
And fruit for the Master's harvest
Is borne of loss and pain.

S. F. Bennett and Joseph P. Webster

☼

S. F. BENNETT who wrote the words, and Joseph P. Webster who composed the music of "In The Sweet Bye and Bye" were both residents of Elkhorn, Wisconsin, when the hymn was written. No sacred song is better known than this production of sixty years ago.

IN THE SWEET BYE AND BYE
There's a land that is fairer than day,
And by faith we can see it afar,
For the Father waits over the way,
To prepare us a dwelling place there.

We shall sing on that beautiful shore
The melodious songs of the blest;
And our spirits shall sorrow no more—
Not a sigh for the blessings of rest.

To our bountiful Father above,
We will offer the tribute of praise,
For the glorious gifts of his love,
And the blessings that hallow our days.

Chorus,
In the sweet bye and bye,
We shall meet on that beautiful shore;
In the sweet bye and bye,
We shall meet on that beautiful shore.

William S. Pitts

✧

FEW songs are better known than "The Little Brown Church in the Vale." For more than sixty years it has been sung all over the English speaking world; yet there is no indication that it is growing less popular with the lapse of time. It was written in Rock County, Wisconsin by Dr. William S. Pitts who so little realized its possibilities that for several years thereafter the manuscript lay buried in his desk, unknown to all save the author.

Dr. Pitts was born in Orleans County, N. Y. in 1830. He came to Rock County, Wisconsin, with his parents in 1847. There he married in 1857 and there he resided until 1862 when he removed to Fredericksburg, Chickasaw County, Iowa.

The church which he immortalized is located in the one-time village of Bradford, not far from Fredericksburg. A visit to Bradford reveals a long deserted village wherein nothing remains except the well-kept church. Crumbling basement walls, from which the superstructures have long since disappeared, meet the eye in every direction.

Dr. Pitts made his first visit to Bradford in June, 1857. The beauty of this spot in the Little Cedar Valley made a deep impression on the visitor from Wisconsin. He returned to his Rock County home where he wrote the song, although at the time it was written, there was no "church in the vale." Not until December, 1864, when the present church was dedicated, did Dr. Pitts see his song vision realized. While the church was still unfinished, the song which had been written years before was first sung within its walls.

Regular services are no longer held in the sacred edifice, but sentiment has made it a shrine for visitors from distant places. Within the past year more than 16,000 people visited the church. The building is carefully preserved by a society organized for that purpose. Each year an increasing number of couples journey to the old church to take their nuptial vows. In the month of June, 1927, eighty five marriages were solemnized in the Little Brown Church. A fee of five dollars is charged for the use of the church for each wedding. This enables the society to keep the building and grounds in excellent condition and to maintain a resident pastor who has no congregation other than transients. There is a charm about the place that every visitor, who knows its history, must remember after he takes his departure.

Dr. Pitts lived to the age of eighty-nine years, beloved by all who knew him. In 1916 he attended a reunion of the former members of the congregation. Not one of these former communicants now lives in the neighborhood.

THE LITTLE BROWN CHURCH IN THE VALE

There's a church in the valley by the wildwood,
    No lov'lier place in the dale:
No spot is so dear to my childhood
    As the little brown church in the vale.

How sweet on a bright Sabbath morning
    To list to the clear ringing bell;
Its tones so sweetly are calling,
    O come to the church in the vale.

Chorus

Come, come to the church in the wildwood,
O come to the church in the dale;
No spot is so dear to my childhood
As the little brown church in the vale.

Carrie Jacobs Bond

☼

ANOTHER native of Wisconsin who has become widely known as a song writer is Mrs. Carrie Jacobs Bond who was born in Janesville, Wisconsin, August 11, 1862. Her father was Dr. Hannibal Jacobs, a well-known and highly respected resident of the southern Wisconsin city. Carrie Jacobs early showed a talent for music; when a mere child it is said that she could play by ear any piece of music she had once heard.

After her marriage to Dr. Bond they lived seven years at Iron Mountain, Michigan where the husband practiced medicine. Then Dr. Bond was killed in an accident, and the young wife was thrown on her own resources with an infant son to care for. In the years preceding, she had written a number of simple songs, and a few of them had sold at insignificant prices. However, they pointed the way, and the young mother turned seriously to song-writing as a means of livelihood. Her struggles and final success are too well known to need comment.

Of her many songs the best known are: *A Perfect Day*, *Just A Wearying for You*, *I Love You Truly*, *Do You Remember*, and *God Remembers When The World Forgets*. It has been said that *A Perfect Day* is sung around the world. Between five and six million copies have been sold. An inscribed boulder marks the birthplace of Mrs. Bond in Janesville.

A PERFECT DAY

When you come to the end of a perfect day
And you sit alone with your thought,

While the chimes ring out with a carol gay,
For the joy that the day has brought!
Do you think what the end of a perfect day
Can mean to a tired heart,
When the sun goes down with a flaming ray,
And the dear friends have to part?

Well, this is the end of a perfect day,
Near the end of a journey too;
But it leaves a thought that is big and strong,
With a wish that is kind and true.
For mem'ry has painted this perfect day
With colors that never fade,
And we find, at the end of a perfect day,
The soul of a friend we've made.

DO YOU REMEMBER?

Do you remember the days in the mountains?
  Do you remember the mist on the lea?
Do you remember the scent of the wild flow'rs?
  And are these memories still memories of me?

Do you remember the dew on the fern leaves
  Down by the brook that flows on to the sea?
Do you remember the songs sung together,
  And, thus remembering, think sometimes of me?

Do you remember the days in the mountains?
  Do you remember the sky's wondrous blue?
Do you remember the meadow-lark singing?
  To me these memories are memories of you.

Do you remember the song of the cricket,
  And the soft moonbeams aslant on the hill?
Do you remember the soft winds a-sighing
  Down thro' the cañons so peaceful and still?

Remember, remember,
Altho' we're apart,
Thro' silence and distance
You still hold my heart.

GOD REMEMBERS WHEN THE WORLD FORGETS*

How many gardens in this world of ours
   Hold blossoms that have never come to flowers?
A sudden wind comes coldly by—
   The rose tree bids its fairest bud good-bye.

How many ships of ours go out to sea
   In search of havens that shall tranquil be?
The storms of fate their fairest hopes o'er set,
   And there is naught to do except forget.

How many wear a smile upon their face
   Although their hearts may hold an empty place?
None knows the heights nor depths of their regrets,
   But God remembers when the world forgets.

JUST A-WEARYIN' FOR YOU†

Just a-wearyin' for you,
All the time a-feelin' blue,
Wishin' for you, wond'rin' when
You'll be comin' home again.
Restless, don't know what to do,
Just a-wearyin' for you.

*Music by Carrie Jacobs Bond
Poem by Clifton Bingham.

†Music by Carrie Jacobs Bond.
Verses by Frank Stanton.

Mornin' comes, the birds awake,
Used to sing so for your sake—
But there's sadness in the notes
That come trillin' from their throats.
Seem to feel your absence, too,
Just a-wearyin' for you.

Evenin' comes, I miss you more
When the dark gloom's round the door,
Seems just like you orter be
There to open it for me.
Latch goes tinklin', thrills me through,
Sets me wearyin' for you.

William T. Purdy and Carl Beck

☼

"ON, WISCONSIN" is the most stirring piece of music ever written by a Wisconsin composer. It has been said that its martial strains can win a foot-ball game or send a company of soldiers up to the cannon's mouth. And mostly the inspiration is in the music. The words, as in many popular songs, are not important,—as a matter of fact they have been changed a number of times and adapted to many different occasions.

Since 1909 when the words were written by Carl Beck and the music composed by William T. Purdy, "On Wisconsin" has been a part of every foot-ball game played by the University of Wisconsin teams. During the World War it was the battle song of the Fighting Thirty-second.

William Purdy died at Auburn, N. Y. in 1919 after a losing fight against tuberculosis. Carl Beck lives in the East, but the dead and the living are gratefully remembered in the state to which they gave its battle song.

The words of the original "On Wisconsin" follow:

ON, WISCONSIN

On, Wisconsin, On, Wisconsin;
Plunge right thru' that line,—
Run the ball clear 'round Chicago—
A touchdown sure this time;

On, Wisconsin, On, Wisconsin;
Fight on for her fame;

Fight, fellows, fight and
We will win this game.

On, Wisconsin, On, Wisconsin;
Grand old Badger State,—
We, thy loyal sons and daughters
Hail thee, good and great;
On, Wisconsin, On, Wisconsin;
Champion of the right;
Forward our motto,
We will win the fight.

W. D. Cornell

☼

REV. W. D. CORNELL, who for a number of years ministered to a congregation in Fond du Lac, is the author of the well-known hymn, "Wonderful Peace." The hymn was written in July, 1892 at the close of a camp meeting at West Bend, Wisconsin, of which Rev. Cornell had been in charge. The fourth stanza was contributed by a co-worker, Rev. Cooper of the West Bend Methodist Church. Rev. Cornell sold the hymn for five dollars before he realized that it was destined to become popular. The author of "Wonderful Peace," now resides in New York, but the active years of his life were spent in the ministry in Wisconsin.

WONDERFUL PEACE

Far away in the depths of my spirit to-night,
Rolls a melody sweeter than psalm;
In celestial-like strains it unceasingly falls
O'er my soul like an infinite calm.

What a treasure I have in this wonderful peace,
Buried deep in the heart of my soul;
So secure that no power can mine it away,
While the years of eternity roll.

I am resting to-night in this wonderful peace,
Resting sweetly in Jesus' control;
For I'm kept from all danger by night and by day,
And His glory is flooding my soul.

And me-thinks when I rise to that City of peace,
Where the Author of peace I shall see,
That one strain of the song which the ransomed will sing,
In that heavenly kingdom shall be:—

Ah! soul, are you here without comfort or rest,
Marching down the rough pathway of time?
Make Jesus your friend ere the shadows grow dark;
Oh, accept this sweet peace so sublime.

Chorus

Peace! peace! Wonderful peace,
Coming down from the Father above;
Sweep over my spirit forever, I pray,
In fathomless billows of love.

Carl Sandburg

☼

CARL SANDBURG, poet, essayist and biographer, was born at Galesburg, Illinois, January 6, 1878. His higher education was received at Lombard College in his native city. His ancestors were working people of the solid reliable Swedish type; the father was a railway shop blacksmith, and prosperity and plenty were only relative terms in the humble home. It is said that the boy's first interest in Lincoln was aroused by a tablet on the campus of Lombard College which he passed daily while delivering milk. The tablet stated that on this spot Lincoln and Douglas met for one of their historic joint debates.

Mr. Sandburg has had a many-sided experience. Perhaps therein lies his knowledge of and sympathy for his fellows. He saw active service in Porto Rico during the Spanish-American War. He worked at any and every kind of job that presented itself, and capitalized his experience. For a time he was a resident of Milwaukee; was secretary to Mayor Emil Seidel, 1910-1912, during which time he wrote for the *Milwaukee Leader*, then as now the organ of the Socialist party. While living in Wisconsin, he married Miss Lillian Steichen, a Milwaukee girl. In 1913 he became associate editor of *System Magazine*. For some years past he has been on the staff of the Chicago *Daily News*.

Sandburg first became known to the American public as a poet. Someone has called him the "Poet of the Commonplace." Perhaps that accounts for his popularity. The average reader sees far more, understands far more of the commonplace than of the exceptional. Sandburg's life, his work, radiate a sincere love for the masses whose problems he so well understands. Among his earlier works are *Chicago Poems*, *Cornhuskers*, *Smoke and Steel*, *Slabs of the Sunburnt West*, and *Rutabaga Stories*. Critics speak of him as a present-day Walt Whitman.

In his latest and undoubtedly his greatest work up to the present time, he enters a field hitherto foreign to him, the realm of biography. His *Abraham Lincoln, The Prairie Years*, is probably the most popular of all Lincoln biographies. He tells of the man, of his intimate everyday life, rather than writing a history of the period. For this type of life story of the great emancipator, Sandburg is especially fitted. He grew up in a region where the career of Lincoln still cast its spell; he mingled with the class of people that Lincoln knew and understood so well. Some day Sandburg will complete the story and show us the same Lincoln unchanged, but in a different environment, the man of the people transferred from the prairies to the White House.

From ABRAHAM LINCOLN, THE PRAIRIE YEARS, *by Carl Sandburg. Harcourt, Brace & Company, New York, Publishers. Reprinted by special permission of the publishers.*

Two men had spoken from platforms in Illinois to crowds of people in broiling summer sun and raw, sour northwest winds of fall—to audiences that stretched out beyond the reach of any but a well-trained, carrying voice. And farther than that the two men had given the nation a book. The main points of the Lincoln-Douglas debates reached millions of newspaper readers. Columns and pages of the speeches of the debates were published. Some newspapers in the larger cities printed the shorthand reports in full.

A book of passion, an almanac of American visions,

victories, defeats, a catechism of national thought and hope, was in the paragraphs of the debates between "the Tall Sucker and the Little Giant." A powerful fragment of America breathed in Douglas's saying at Quincy: "Let each state mind its own business and let its neighbors alone! If we will stand by that principle, then Mr. Lincoln will find that this great republic can exist forever divided into free and slave states. . . . Stand by that great principle, and we can go on as we have done, increasing in wealth, in population, in power, and in all the elements of greatness, until we shall be the admiration and terror of the world, . . . until we make this continent one ocean-bound republic. Under that principle we can receive that stream of intelligence which is constantly flowing from the Old World to the New, filling up our prairies, clearing our wilderness, and building cities, towns, railroads, and other internal improvements, and thus make this the asylum of the oppressed of the whole earth." It was the private belief of Douglas, though he would have lost blocks of votes by saying so, that a cordon of free states could be erected on the Great Plains, with railroads crossing them to the Pacific, and that after their settlement with towns and cities there would be peace and prosperity.

Those who wished quiet about the slavery question, and those who didn't, understood the searching examination for truth in Lincoln's inquiry: "You say slavery is wrong; but don't you constantly argue that this is not the right place to oppose it? You say it must not be opposed in the free states, because slavery is not there; it must not be opposed in the slave states because it is there; it must not be opposed in politics, because that will make a fuss; it must not be opposed in the pulpit, because it is not religion. Then where is the place to oppose it? There is no suitable place to oppose it."

So many could respond to the Lincoln view: "Judge

Douglas will have it that I want a negro wife. He can never be brought to understand that there is any middle ground on this subject. I have lived until my fiftieth year, and have never had a negro woman either for a slave or a wife, and I think I can live fifty centuries, for that matter, without having had one or either." Pointing to the Supreme Court decision that slaves as property could not be voted out of new territories, Lincoln said, "His Supreme Court, cooperating with him, has squatted his squatter sovereignty out." The argument had got down as thin as "soup made by boiling the shadow of a pigeon that had starved to death."

Lincoln was trying to stir up strife and rebellion, according to Douglas, and, "He who attempts to stir up odium and rebellion in this country against the constituted authorities, is stimulating the passions of men to resort to violence and to mobs, instead of to the law. Hence I tell you that I take the decisions of the Supreme Court as the law of the land, and I intend to obey them as such." He was the sincere spokesman of powerful men. "Suppose Mr. Lincoln succeeds in destroying public confidence in the Supreme Court, so that people will not respect its decisions, but will feel at liberty to disregard them, and resist the laws of the land, what will he have gained? He will have changed the government from one of laws into that of a mob, in which the strong arm of violence will be substituted for the decisions of the courts."

Douglas said he would not be brutal. "Humanity requires, and Christianity commands, that you shall extend to every inferior being, and every dependent being, all the privileges, immunities, and advantages which can be granted to them consistent with the safety of society." When he had sat at a table in Washington with Clay, Cass, Webster, what was their unified aim? "To devise means and measures by which we could defeat the mad and revolutionary schemes of the northern Abolitionists and southern disunionists." He wished the country to know: "They brought Fred Douglass to Freeport, when I was addressing a meeting there, in a carriage driven by the white owner, the negro sitting inside with the white lady and her daughter. I am told that one of Fred Douglass's kinsmen, another rich black negro, is now traveling in this state making speeches for his friend Lincoln as the champion of black men." America was a young and growing nation. "It swarms as often as a hive of bees. In less than fifteen years, if the same progress that has distinguished this country for the last fifteen years continues, every foot of vacant land between this and the Pacific Ocean, owned by the United States, will be occupied. And just as fast as our interests and our destiny require additional territory in the North, in the South, or on the islands of the ocean, I am for it, and when we acquire it I will leave the people free to do as they please on the subject of slavery and every other question."

Lincoln attacked a Supreme Court decision as "one of the thousand things constantly done to prepare the public mind to make property, and nothing but property, of the negro in all the states in this Union." In Kansas, the Douglas "self-government" proposed for all new western territories had been "nothing but a living, creeping lie." Why was slavery referred to in "covert language" and not mentioned plainly and openly in the United States Constitution? Why were the words "negro" and "slavery" left out? "It was hoped when it should be read by intelligent and patriotic men, after the institution of slavery had passed from among us, there should be nothing on the face of the great charter of liberty suggesting that such a thing as negro slavery had ever existed among us. They expected and intended that it should be put in the course of ultimate extinction."

Was it not always the single issue of quarrels? "Does

it not enter into the churches and rend them asunder? What divided the great Methodist Church into two parts, North and South? What has raised this constant disturbance in every Presbyterian general assembly that meets?" It was not politicians; this fact and issue somehow operated on the minds of men and divided them in every avenue of society, in politics, religion, literature, morals. "That is the issue that will continue in this country when these poor tongues of Judge Douglas and myself shall be silent. It is the eternal struggle between two principles. The one is the common right of humanity, and the other the divine right of kings. It is the same spirit that says, 'You toil and work and earn bread, and I'll eat it.' No matter in what shape it comes, whether from the mouth of a king who seeks to bestride the people of his own nation and live by the fruit of their labor, or from one race of men as an apology for enslaving another race, it is the same tyrannical principle."

The high point of the debates was in Douglas framing for Lincoln a series of questions at Ottawa. At Freeport Lincoln took up these questions one by one and replied. Then in his turn he put a series of questions to Douglas, one reading, "Can the people of a United States Territory, in any lawful way, against the wish of any citizen of the United States, exclude slavery from its limits, prior to the formation of a State constitution?" The answer of Douglas amounted to saying, "Yes." It raised a storm of opposition to him in the South, and lost him blocks of northern Democratic friends who wanted to maintain connections in the South.

Lincoln showed his questions to advisers beforehand; they told him to drop the main question. He answered, "I am after larger game; the battle of 1860 is worth a hundred of this." His guess was that Douglas's answer would split the Democratic party and make a three-cornered fight for the Presidency two years later.

From a cottage on the coast of Maine, where he was resting, Jefferson Davis let it be known that he wished that the two debaters would chew each other up till there was nothing left of either, after the way of the Kilkenny cats.

Sprinkled all through the speeches of Lincoln, as published, were stubby, homely words that reached out and made plain, quiet people feel that perhaps behind them was a heart that could understand them—the People—the listeners. His words won him hearts in unknown corners of far-off places.

The sentences of his arguments and prayers when published made the same impression on some people that his actual speaking did on one man, young Francis Grierson, who heard him at Alton, and wrote: "The instant he began to speak the ungainly mouth lost its heaviness, the half-listless eyes attained a wondrous power, and the people stood bewildered and breathless. Every movement of his long muscular frame denoted inflexible earnestness, and a something issued forth, elemental and mystical, that told what the man had been, what he was, and what he would do. There were moments when he seemed all legs and feet, and again he appeared all head and neck; yet every look of the deep-set eyes, every movement of the prominent jaw, every wave of the hard-gripping hand, produced an impression, and before he had spoken twenty minutes the conviction took possession of thousands that here was the prophetic man of the present.

"Lincoln had no genius for gesture and no desire to produce a sensation; from every feature of his face there radiated the calm, inherent strength that always accompanies power. He relied on no props. With a pride sufficient to protect his mind and a will sufficient to defend his body, he drank water when Douglas, with all his wit and rhetoric, could begin or end nothing without stimulants. Here, then, was one man out of all the millions who believed in himself. What thrilled the people who stood before Abraham Lincoln was the sight of a being who, in all his actions and habits, resembled themselves, gentle as he was strong, fearless as he was honest, who towered above them in that psychic radiance that penetrates in some mysterious way every fibre of the hearer's consciousness."

Stanzas from THE WINDY CITY, *by Carl Sandburg, Harcourt, Brace & Company, Publishers, New York. By permission of the publishers.*

Forgive us if the monotonous houses go mile on mile
Along monotonous streets out to the prairies—
If the faces of the houses mumble hard words
At the streets—and the street voices only say:
"Dust and a bitter wind shall come."

Forgive us if the lumber porches and doorsteps
Snarl at each other—
And the brick chimneys cough in a close-up of
Each other's faces—
And the ramshackle stairways watch each other
As thieves watch—
And dooryard lilacs near a malleable iron works
Long ago languished
In a short whispering purple.

And if the alley ash cans
Tell the garbage wagon drivers
The children that play the alley is Heaven
And the streets of Heaven shine
With a grand dazzle of stones of gold
And there are no policemen in Heaven—
Let the rag-tags have it their way.

And if the geraniums
In the tin cans of the window sills

Ask questions not worth answering—
And if a boy and a girl hunt the sun
With a sieve for sifting smoke—
Let it pass—let the answer be—
"Dust and a bitter wind shall come."

Forgive us if the jazz timebeats
Of these clumsy mass shadows
Moan in saxophone undertones,
And the footsteps of the jungle,
The fang cry, the rip claw hiss,
The sneak-up and the still watch,
The slant of the slit eyes waiting
If these bother respectable people
    with the right crimp in their napkins
    reading breakfast menu cards—
    forgive us—let it pass—let be.

If cripples sit on their stumps
And joke with the newsies bawling,
"Many lives lost! many lives lost!
Ter-ri-ble ac-ci-dent! many lives lost!"—
If again twelve men let a woman go,
"He done me wrong; I shot him"—
Or the blood of a child's head
Spatters on the hub of a motor truck—
Or a 44 gat cracks and lets the skylights
Into one more bank messenger—
Or if boys steal coal in a railroad yard
And run with humped gunnysacks
While a bull picks off one of the kids
And the kid wiggles with an ear in the cinders
And a mother comes to carry home
A bundle, a limp bundle,
To have his face washed, for the last time,
Forgive us if it happens—and happens again—
And happens again.

Forgive us if we work so hard
And the muscles bunch clumsy on us
And we never know why we work so hard—
If the big houses with little families
And the little houses with big families
Sneer at each other's bars of misunderstanding;
Pity us when we shackle and kill each other
And believe at first we understood
And later say we wonder why.

Alice Arnold Crawford

☼

ALICE ARNOLD was born in Fond du Lac in 1850 and there she lived her brief life except for the last two years. She was graduated from the Fond du Lac High School with the class of 1867. During her student years Miss Arnold attracted attention in her home city by the literary excellence of her school essays. After finishing her high school course she wrote regularly, both prose and poetry, and her work was accepted and published by some of the leading periodicals of the country. Among these were Harper's Weekly, The New York Independent, The Chicago Advance and The Christian Union. The young writer was deeply religious and her poems reflect her high character. In 1872 she married Charles A. Crawford and thereafter resided in Traverse City, Michigan, until her death in 1874 brought to its close a literary career of exceptional promise. Her collected poems were published the following year. *Blind Handel*, *Gates Ajar*, *After the Storm*, and *The Forest Easter* are excellent examples of the work of the girl poet. *The Forest Easter* was first published in Harper's Weekly at Easter-time. It was printed within the outline of a flower-twined cross and covered an entire page of Harper's. This poem in its artistic setting attracted attention throughout the country; the young writer became widely known and her contributions were sought eagerly by the leading magazines.

The Forest Easter and *Blind Handel* are reprinted on the following pages, together with several of her shorter poems.

From A FEW THOUGHTS FOR A FEW FRIENDS, *by Alice Arnold Crawford. Published by Jansen, McClurg & Company, Chicago, 1875.*

AFTER THE STORM

After the storm, a calm;
After the bruise, a balm;
For the ill brings good, in the Lord's own time,
And the sigh becomes the psalm.

After the drought, the dew;
After the cloud the blue,
For the sky will smile in the sun's good time,
And the earth grow glad and new.

Bloom is the heir of blight.
Dawn is the child of night,
And the rolling change of the busy world
Bids the Wrong yield back the Right.

Under the fount of ill,
Many a cup doth fill,
And the patient lip, tho' it drinketh oft,
Finds only the bitter still.

Truth seemeth oft to sleep,
Blessings so slow to reap,
Till the hours of waiting are weary to bear,
And the courage is hard to keep!

Nevertheless, I know,
Out of the dark must grow,
Sooner or later, whatever is fair,
Since the heavens have willed it so.

Life is the storm, and calm.
Life is the bruise, and balm.

But the peace and healing are surely to come,
    And the sigh is to be the psalm.

FAITH

Life hath full many a storm, whose waves
    Gleam fitfully, and surge and roll,—
Whose troubled waters beat and break
    Against the fortress of the soul.
And yet I fear not, though the sands
    Be slipping from my feet away;
I fear not, though my outstretched hands
    Grasp nothing but the dashing spray,
For Thou art with me—leading me
    On through the water's angry toss,
Till, through the blinding mists, I see
    My Rock, my Fortress, and thy Cross.

THE FOREST EASTER

In the forests of the North
Shines the Easter morning forth,
Shines and glimmers, flits and smiles
Down the winding woodland aisles.

See! the vapor's rising breath
Floats as life released from death,
Pure above the stainless snow.
Look! how shadows in the glow,
Melted from their icy keeping, out of hidden cells are creeping
Out of twilight niches leaping at the beck'ning of the light.
Has the spring remembered Easter, in the Northland still and white?
Have the symbols of the morning deck'd the dim cathedral wood?

Have they written "He is risen," in the snowy solitude?
Are the lilies incense breathing? Are the fair camillias
     wreathing
Carven birch and pillared pine?
Do the lustrous myrtles twine
With the roses waxen white?
Creeps the ivy's emerald vine
O'er the sky-built casement height?
Tell us sleeping, sluggish Spring!
Show us, living, waking Spring!
Where is laid thine off'ring for the Easter-tide.

"In the forests of the North,
O'er the snow hills peeping forth
Down the sunny side, through winter's frosted tear,
Through the mosses, cold and sere,
Pure and fair as lilies are,
Ope's the sweet arbutus star
Silken-petaled, rosy-tipped.
Never lovelier off'ring could tropic sunshine bring,
Offspring of an angel breath
Warmed to life through chill and death,
Never truer Easter sign
Robed a cross or strewed a shrine."

Ay, the Spring has chosen well—better than we understood.
Open star and budded bell best befit the cloister cell
     of the templed wood;
Best unfold the mystic story from the secret of its own;
Best proclaim the risen glory from the life itself has
     known.
Blossom of the wilderness! God-child of the snow's
     caress!
Heaven shall love thee not the less, blooming here alone.

ALICE ARNOLD CRAWFORD
BLIND HANDEL
He sat alone—the solemn service o'er;
No muffled footfall sounded on the floor;
The distant clangor of the closing door
From arch to arch leaped down the low octave
Of dying echoes, and within the nave
Dropped into silence.

                Calm, and sweetly grave,
As one in whom some joy and sorrow blend,
The blind old man, beside his time-worn friend,
Still lingered lovingly. Across the keys
He felt the warmth of sunshine, and the breeze
At play upon the silver of his hair.
And, down the aisles, he knew the list'ning air
In conscious emptiness hung dead and still,
But waiting for the soul of melody to thrill
Its silence into life.

                As one who loved them much
He sought the keys. They yielded to his touch,
And by some strange intelligence they caught
The thrilling impulse of their master's thought,
And followed softly, or in echoes rang
Their sweet response while he, trembling, sang
His life-song unto them.

                "We are alone
O voices of my soul! and joy, unknown
To those who know and love you less than I,
Is borne to me upon the melody
That wakens at my will. I feel no need of sight;
But, reaching forth, I draw my warmth and light
From out the world of sound. That fine and mystic sense
Vouchsafed to me, makes more than recompense
For outer darkness; since the shadowy line
That shuts me from the world wins the divine
To blest communion, until life grows sweet

From hidden springs, and makes itself complete
From sources of its own.

     "Men pity me;
And little eyes that mine shall never see
Turn tenderly to watch the groping feet
That, hesitating, tread the aisle and street.
They look on me as one whose night and day
Are wearily the same; and sadly say
My blindness is my prison, and no star
That, key-like, hangs without the dungeon bar,
Shall ever turn or open unto me
The royal dawn, or noon-tide majesty.

"And yet I sorrow not. No life is dark
Whose inner chambers hold the vital spark
Of heavenly happiness. I only stand
Within the shadow of my Father's hand,
And list, through all the ling'ring eventide,
For loving tones that, comforting, abide
Forever in the air. O perfect gift!
O blessing marvelous! By thee I lift
The upper windows of my charmed soul,
And let the harmonies of heaven roll
Full-voiced into mine ear.

     "And still I wait.
My groping fingers clasp the golden gate
That bounds the sweet hereafter, while the hymn
That trembles from the harps of seraphim
Floats out to me. These soft and mellow pipes
Awaked by me, are but th' imperfect types
Of what I hear,—the faint interpreters
Through which I speak to men,—sweet messengers
From me unto the world. I ask no more,
Since 'My Redeemer Liveth,' to restore,
In His own time, the fullness of my sight.
Then, for the loss of earth's imperfect light,

The crystal day shall evermore be given,
And Handel, 'blind and old,' shall see in heaven."

ARBUTUS

So I have found you, dainty, sweet,
Where life and death so strangely meet,—
Beside the dark pine's leaf-strewn feet,
        Arbutus mine!
Here, nestled in the rustling mound,
With tender cheek against the ground,
Though frozen dews have gemm'd you 'round,
        You smile and shine.
No summer sun has shed its gold
Upon you, slumb'ring in the mold;
Yet here, in darkness and in cold—
        Dear little flowers—
You bear, in every upturned face,
A subtle charm, a spotless grace,
That draws me to your dwelling place,
        In wintry hours.
O light and beauty, born of gloom!
What secret sunshine doth illume
And warm you into balmy bloom
        Among the snows?
What is the mystery of fear
That chills your life when we draw near,
Whose memory would hold so dear
        Your breath of rose?
"More heat than light!" Ay, they were wise
Who, through the many mysteries,
Did read this language in your eyes,
        So lowly bent.
O sweet Arbutus of the snow!
O meekest flow'ret! Be it so!
Thou lov'st us "more than thou durst show."—
        We are content.

Berton Braley

✧

BERTON BRALEY, author and newspaper correspondent, was born in Madison, Wisconsin, January 29, 1882. He was graduated from the University of Wisconsin in 1905. While a student in the university he wrote verses that attracted local attention. After completing his college course he spent several years in Montana as a newspaper reporter. In 1909 he was on the staff of the New York *Evening Mail;* in 1910 he was associate editor of *Puck*. For years his short poems have been familiar to readers of the daily newspapers. It is said that he has written and published more than eight thousand of these short poems, most of them humorous or dealing with everyday experiences. Some of his published volumes are: *Sonnets of a Freshman*, 1904; *Sonnets of a Suffragette*, 1913; *Songs of a Workaday World*, 1915; *Things as They Are*, 1916; *In Camp and Trench*, 1918; and *Buddy Ballads*, 1919. The last two were the outgrowth of his experience as a war correspondent from 1915 to 1919. Mr. Braley resides in New York City.

From A BANJO AT ARMAGEDDON *by Berton Braley, George H. Doran Company, Publishers, New York. Reprinted by special permission of the author.*

UP WITH THE FLAG!

Up with the flag! Up with the flag!
   Up with the flag we love!
Till its colors flutter from every roof
   And merge with the skies above.

And our eyes shall fill and our hearts shall thrill
   With the joy that is always new,
At the grand old sight of the red and white,
   And the stars in a field of blue.

Let our flag unfurled to a watching world
   Be proof that we keep our trust,
That we take our part with a valiant heart
   In a cause that we know is just!
Let it float on high, and if men must die
   To keep it from blot or stain,
They shall meet their fate with souls elate—
   And they shall not die in vain.

For the flag still holds in its ample folds
   The spell of its olden fame,
And our pulses leap, and we burn down deep
   With a wonderful, quenchless flame;
As the flag flings free for all to see
   In the sweep of the winds above,
Up with the flag! Up with the flag!
   Up with the flag we love!

OPPORTUNITY

With doubt and dismay you are smitten
   You think there's no chance for you, son?
Why, the best books haven't been written,
   The best race hasn't been run,
The best score hasn't been made yet,
   The best song hasn't been sung,
The best tune hasn't been played yet,
   Cheer up, for the world is young!

No chance? Why the world is just eager
   For things that you ought to create,
Its store of true wealth is still meagre—

Its needs are incessant and great,
It yearns for more power and beauty—
　More laughter and love and romance,
More loyalty, labor and duty,
　No chance—why there's nothing but chance!

For the best verse hasn't been rhymed yet,
　The best house hasn't been planned,
The highest peak hasn't been climbed yet,
　The mightiest rivers aren't spanned,
Don't worry and fret, faint hearted,
　The chances have just begun,
For the Best jobs haven't been started,
　The Best work hasn't been done.

THE JOY OF LIFE

I'd rather risk gamely
　And lose for my trying
Than grind around tamely
　—A cog in the mill.
I'd rather fail greatly
　With courage undying
Than plod on sedately
　With never a thrill!

The game's in the playing
　And, losing or winning,
The fun's in essaying
　Your bravest and best,
In taking your chances
　While Fate's wheel is spinning,
And backing your fancies
　With nerve and with zest!

Let stodgy folk censure
　And timid folk quaver,

But life sans adventure
  Is weary to bear,
The dangers we're sharing
  Give living its savour,
I'd rather die daring
  Than never to dare!

William Frederick Kirk

☼

WILLIAM F. KIRK, humorous writer, was born in Mankato, Minnesota, April 20, 1877. When he was four years of age the family moved to Chippewa Falls, Wisconsin, where, in due time, he was graduated from the high school. For some time thereafter he was employed by the *Milwaukee Sentinel* as writer of a daily column of humor. From 1905 to the time of his death he was connected with the Hearst Service. He has written much dialect and humorous verse and a few songs.

His published poems include *Fleeting Fancies*, 1904, *The Norsk Nightingale*, 1905, *Right off the Bat*, 1912, *Songs of Sergeant Swanson*, 1918, *The Harp of Fate*, 1925. Mr. Kirk spent most of his life in Chippwa Falls and there he died, March 25, 1927. Of all his published works, his own rating placed *The Norsk Nightingale* first. However, his verses are not all humorous as some of the following selections show. *The Visitor*, and *Getting By* display far more of life's philosophy than of humor or frivolity.

From OUT OF THE CURRENT, *by William F. Kirk. The Stratford Co., Publishers, Boston, Massachusetts, 1923. By permission of the publishers. All rights reserved.*

THE NEW STENOGRAPHER

I have a new stenographer. She came to work today.
She told me that she wrote the Graham System.
Two hundred words a minute seemed to her, she said,
    like play,

And word for word at that—she never missed 'em.
I gave her some dictation—a letter to a man—
And this, as I remember it, was how the letter ran:

"Dear sir: I have your favor, and in reply would state
That I accept the offer in yours of recent date.
I wish to say, however, that under no condition
Can I afford to think of your free lance proposition.
I shall begin tomorrow to turn the matter out.
The copy should be ready by August 10th, about.
Material of this nature should not be rushed unduly.
Thanking you for the favor, I am yours very truly."

She took it down in shorthand with apparent ease and grace—
She didn't call me back all in a flurry.
Thought I, "At last I have a girl worth keeping 'round the place!"
Then said, "Now write it out. You needn't hurry."
The Remington she tackled. Now and then she struck a key.
And after thirty minutes this is what she handed me:
"Dear sir, I have the feever and in a pile i sit
And I except the favor as you have reasoned it.
I wish to see, however, that under any condition
Can i for to think of a free lunch proposition.
I shall be in tomorrow to turn your mother out,
The cap will be red and will cost Ten, about.
Material of this nation should not rust. N. Dooley.
Thinking you have the feever, I am yours very truly!"

THE VISITOR

The rich man sat in his club one night;
  His hands were mottled, but deft.
A glass of brandy was in his right
  And a good cigar in his left.
His cheeks were heavy and violet-veined,

His eyes were two slits of gray.
Pendulous lipped, he puffed and sipped
  And idled the hours away.

The rich man dozed. Then he seem'd to wake—
  He stirred in his easy chair.
His fat old heart felt a sudden ache
  From a blow that had landed there.
He gazed at a youth with a fresh, strong face.
  "What are YOU doing here?" cried he.
Said the lad with a grin, "I just dropped in—
  I'm the boy that you used to be!

"Yes, I am the boy that you used to be
  When you captained them all at school,
The boy that protected the stupid lad
  Who sat on the dunce's stool;
The boy that forced the bully to whine
  While the rest looked on to laugh—
The boy that smashed through the football line
  And scattered them all like chaff!

"You were full of love for the battle then,
  You were sober and strong and lean.
You loved your God and your fellow men,
  Your hands and your heart were clean.
I hated to call on you here tonight—
  It's a sorrowful visit for me,
But I wanted to give you one more sight
  Of the boy that you used to be!"

* * * * *

The rich man rose from his easy chair;
  For a moment his gaze went far,
Then he gulped his drink with a weary air
  And lighted a fresh cigar.
"The boy that I used to be," he mused

As he called for his coat and hat.
"How real it seemed! But I must have dreamed!
There was never a boy like that!"

"GETTING BY"

This world is full of laddies
Who are acting as Fate's caddies
In the game that's known as "Living Out the String."
Though they seldom need a warning
And report for work each morning
To their notions of it all they fondly cling.
Dreaming of a life in clover,
Wishing that the day were over,
For a semblance of endeavor they will try.
And if you should ask them kindly
How it goes, they'd answer blindly
That it kept them good and busy "getting by!"

"Getting by!" Two words of meaning
Through this world of ours careening
On the tongue of every shirker in the land!
"Getting by!" And while they're skidding,
Thinking of the boss they're kidding
Who will fire them soon or later, out of hand!
Life is far too full of action
For this large and listless faction
And the years are taking payments as they fly.
In Life's discard ever growing,
Making but a sorry showing,
Lie the lads whose stock in trade is "getting by!"

From THE NORSK NIGHTINGALE, *by William F. Kirk.
Published by Small, Maynard & Co., 1905.*

A PSALM OF LIFE

Tal me not, yu knocking fallers,
  Life ban only empty dream;

Dar ban planty fun, ay tal yu,
   Ef yu try Yohn Yohnson's scheme.
Yohn ban yust a section foreman,
   Vorking hard vay up on Soo;
He ban yust so glad in morning
   As ven all his vork ban tru.

"Vork," says Yohn, "ban vat yu mak it.
   Ef yu tenk das vork ban hard,
Yu skol having planty headaches,—
   Yes, yu bet yure life, old pard;
But ay alvays yerk my coat off,
   Grab my shovel and my pick,
And dis yob ant seem lak hard von
   Ef ay du it purty qvick."

Yohn ban foreman over fallers.
   He ant have to vork, yu see;
But, yu bet, he ant no loafer,
   And he yust digs in, by yee!
"Listen, Olaf," he skol tal me,
   "Making living ant no trick,
And the hardest yob ban easy
   Ef yu only du it qvick!"

Let us den be op and yumping,
   Always glad to plow tru drift;
Ven our work ban done, den let us
   Give some oder faller lift.
Den, ay bet yu, old Saint Peter,
   He skol tenk ve're purty slick;
Ve can go tru gates, ay bet yu,
   Ef ve only du it qvick.

Eleanor Sawyer Chase

☼

ELEANOR S. CHASE (Mrs. Maurice Fatio) was born in Oshkosh, Wisconsin, March 3, 1903, the daughter of Mr. and Mrs. Charles Curry Chase, granddaughter of Edgar P. Sawyer, and great-granddaughter of Senator Philetus Sawyer. She received her early education in the Oshkosh Normal School and at Mt. Vernon Seminary, Washington, D. C. At the age of sixteen she entered the University of Wisconsin where her literary efforts attracted attention and where she wrote for the several college publications.

Through her childhood years Miss Chase showed a capacity for writing, both poetry and prose; as she grew older she contributed to various magazines. After leaving the University, she accepted a position with a publishing house in New York City, where she continued to write both poetry and short stories.

In the autumn of 1928 Miss Chase published her first extended work of fiction; *Pennagan Place*, a story of her native city, probably inspired by some local patriarchal family with whom she had come in contact. This work was a success from the beginning and one of the best sellers of the year.

In July, 1929 Miss Chase married Maurice Fatio, a well-known architect of New York City and Palm Beach, Florida. Mr. and Mrs. Fatio reside in Palm Beach, Florida where Mrs. Fatio is continuing her literary work.

SONG OF THE ROAD
By
Eleanor Sawyer Chase

At dawn your heart is too light for your load:
This is the song of the winding road.

    Up the road, where the mists hang low,
    And down the road, the people go,

    Whistling a bit when the road is blue.
    (Strange what a whistle will do for you!)

    Whistling, with darkness just ahead,
    Glad of the way that the road has led.

    All day long the feet pass by,
    Trampling the dust that rises high;

    Feet that bravely march to song;
    Wistful feet that trudge along;

    Feet that lag when the sun has set
    And the road is dark and the wind is wet;

    Vagabond feet that sadly still
    Must follow the night across the hill.

    (For the feet that keep to the hardest track
    Are the feet that never are coming back.)

    But when the orange lamps shine warm
    From roadside house and roadside farm,

    There are happy feet that cease to roam;
    Turn in at the gate—and stay at home.

For your heart grows heavy at night with your load:
This is the song of the winding road.

Bernard I. Durward

☼

BERNARD ISAAC DURWARD wrote a number of short poems which were collected and published as a centenary memorial in 1917. Mr. Durward was born in Montrose, Scotland in 1817, came to Milwaukee in 1845 and spent the remainder of his long life in Wisconsin. For some time he taught English in St. Francis Seminary. He wrote verses regularly, some of which attracted attention in their day. He was intensely religious, and theological and dogmatic references abound in his poems.

In 1861 during a row-boat trip down the Wisconsin river, Mr. Durward first saw the beautiful spot that was soon to become his home. Located in the scenic Devil's Lake region, it is still known to nature lovers as Durward's Glen. He brought his family to the glen in 1862 and there built a small cabin home. It is probable that he welcomed the opportunity to get away from Milwaukee. The Civil War was raging and the artist-poet seems to have been wholly out of sympathy with the Union cause. This he carried so far as to write verses very uncomplimentary to President Lincoln. This sympathy for the South and his intense religious enthusiasm very likely set him apart from his fellows in the Wisconsin metropolis. In his sylvan retreat he communed with nature and wrote more verses. With the help of a few neighbors he built a small stone chapel on his estate. Here came occasionally the dignitaries of the Catholic church to visit this strange man who, like the patriarchs of old, insisted on keeping his large family with him, even after they had reached adult years. He died in 1902 and was buried beside the stone chapel that his hands had helped to raise so many years before. The following selections from his poems will give the reader an idea of his style and expression.

JUNE

Ah! placid days of June!
You see the lilies of the valley born,
You see the dew-drops on the springing corn,
    And drink them all ere noon.
    For you the wilding rose
Opens her blushing bosom to the light;
For you, from clover fields of green and white,
    The honied fragrance flows.
    For you, yon stream glides on,
Bearing thy cloudless skies upon its breast;
The picture of a soul by love possessed,
    Gentle, and deep, and strong,
    That having wandered far,
Dashed over rocks, and sunk in pools of woe,
Is led at last through meadows green to flow
    By some blest guiding star.
    In the cool Indian trail
For you the small dove sits with lustrous eyes,
And seems naught less than bird from paradise
    Until we hear it wail,
    And then it speaks of earth,
A chastened echo, exquisite and low
To hollow voices of the heart, whose woe
    Finds words as rude as mirth.
    Oh, lady ever fair!
That I may sing of thee, I sing of June;
But weak the words, and harsh, alas, the tune
    That springs 'midst pain and care.

BERNARD I. DURWARD

TIME

Higher up on the banks of this stream
We have buried some friends that we love,
And have planted a cross on each newly-raised mound,
And a prayer in the heavens above.
They were beautiful, truthful or wise,
And their virtuous deeds to the last
Generations of men should be prized and proclaimed—
But this river is rushing so fast.

And the crosses will crumble to dust,
And the low narrow dwellings sink down,
And the prayer for their peace we may often forget,
And their beauty, or worth, or renown.
And we cannot return 'gainst the tide
Nor back o'er the rapids we've past,
Tho' we fain would return and their mem'ry renew—
But this river is rushing so fast.

EVENING

Purple, and crimson, and gold,
Fainting and fading away,
Calm, yet in haste, like a beautiful dream,
Or a swan on the stream,
The bright glories of day,
Ere the beauty is penciled or told,
Sinks into gray,
Fainting and fading in twilight away.

Linger! Oh, cease not to shine!
Leave me the light of her eyes!
Stay, till I gaze on her beautiful cheek,
And her forehead so meek,
And her lips where love lies,
And the passion of pity divine!
Vain are my sighs—
Loveliness fades into twilight, and dies.

Part III

HISTORY, SCIENCE AND ESSAYS

John Muir

☆

JOHN MUIR, writer, naturalist and explorer, was born at Dunbar, Scotland, April 21, 1838. When eleven years of age he came with his parents to Wisconsin, at that time the youngest member of the sisterhood of states. While yet in Scotland the boy had received an excellent education for one so young. It was fortunate that this training came to him in early life, and that he proved himself so apt a pupil; after his lot was cast in the Wisconsin forests there was no opportunity for further elementary school work. The family settled near the Fox river, twelve miles from Portage. On this wilderness farm the severest tasks occupied the daylight hours. The well is still shown that the future scientist excavated through solid granite to the depth of eighty feet. While he toiled he observed things that others did not see; in the absence of schools he became a student of nature. His books were his evening companions, and his investigations were often continued into the early morning hours. The young man came to be considered something of a genius by the country folk. Thus encouraged he entered the University of Wisconsin where he took special work but did not complete a regular course. Many traditions of John Muir's university days still linger within the walls of the venerable buildings on the hill. One of the contrivances in his room tilted his bed on end at a stated hour each morning and summarily aroused the inventor from his slumbers. This mechanism is now in possession of the State Historical Society.

Although his youth and young manhood were spent in

Wisconsin, John Muir became an adopted son of California and there his great work was accomplished. His publications gave to the world its first intimate and scientific knowledge of the Sierras, of the Yosemite Valley, and of the giant sequoia trees. There he spent the greater part of his life in patient investigation, the results of which he seemed in no hurry to publish. The fruits of this period came years later in his books: *The Mountains of California*, 1894, *Our National Parks*, 1901, *My First Summer in the Sierra*, 1911, and *The Yosemite*, 1912. Of an entirely different type is his *Story of my Boyhood and Youth* published in 1912. Of all his books, this last appeals most to Wisconsin readers; it is of this state that he writes. He died in Los Angeles, December 24, 1914.

John Muir was the first great American conservationist. For years by tongue and pen he urged the segregation and preservation of National Parks and Forest Reserves. For years the plea fell on ears that were more or less deaf to the appeal; it was not until Theodore Roosevelt came to the White House that the vision of the old explorer materialized in a Federal conservation policy.

Travelers to Alaska are shown the great Muir Glacier as one of the scenic wonders of the Territory. It was in 1879 that Muir made his first visit to Alaska and discovered Glacier Bay and the mammoth ice mass that bears his name. He explored portions of the Yukon and Mackenzie rivers, thus adding much to the world's knowledge of a region hitherto almost unknown.

A SUMMER PARADISE FOR SONG BIRDS

THE following is a brief review of the chapter entitled "A Paradise of Birds" in John Muir's "STORY OF MY BOYHOOD AND YOUTH." The entire story should be read by every lover of nature, young or old.

He begins with the emphatic statement that, in its pioneer period, Wisconsin was a summer paradise for song birds, and his narrative throughout indicates that, though only a lad, his powers of observation were highly developed, a trait on which was built his future fame. He tells of the birds that stayed throughout the year and of those that migrated with the coming of the chilling blasts. There are accurate records of when and how the migrating birds winged their way southward. Among those birds that braved the low winter temperatures, Muir mentions the nuthatch, chickadee, jay, owl, hawk, prairie chicken and quail.

The gifted naturalist takes the song birds one by one, and to each he pays such high tribute that the reader wonders which was his favorite. The bluebird, the robin, the brown thrush, the bobolink, the redwing blackbird, the meadowlark, the song sparrow,—each is described and praised in turn.

The game birds are described in an equally interesting manner. Ducks, wild geese, prairie chickens, quail, grouse, swans and loons are portrayed, not from the viewpoint of the hunter and killer, but from the attitude of a friendly and sympathetic admirer of the feathered species.

His description of the passenger pigeons, then the most numerous of all Wisconsin birds, and now entirely extinct, is especially vivid. By arrangement with the publishers, we are permitted to reprint the portion of the chapter that refers to these charming birds;—so familiar to the early pioneers.

THE PASSENGER PIGEONS*

It was a great memorable day when the first flock of passenger pigeons came to our farm, calling to mind the story we had read about them when we were at school in Scotland. Of all God's feathered people that sailed the Wisconsin sky, no other bird seemed to us so wonderful.

Reprinted by special permission of Houghton Mifflin Company, Publishers. All rights reserved.

The beautiful wanderers flew like the winds in flocks of millions from climate to climate in accord with the weather, finding their food—acorns, beechnuts, pinenuts, cranberries, strawberries, huckleberries, juniper berries, hackberries, buckwheat, rice, wheat, oats, corn—in fields and forests thousands of miles apart. I have seen flocks streaming south in the fall so large that they were flowing over from horizon to horizon in an almost continuous stream all day long, at the rate of forty or fifty miles an hour, like a mighty river in the sky, widening, contracting, descending like falls and cataracts, and rising suddenly here and there in huge ragged masses like high-plashing spray. How wonderful the distances they flew in a day—in a year—in a lifetime! They arrived in Wisconsin in the spring just after the sun had cleared away the snow, and alighted in the woods to feed on the fallen acorns that they had missed the previous autumn. A comparatively small flock swept thousands of acres perfectly clean of acorns in a few minutes, by moving straight ahead with a broad front. All got their share, for the rear constantly became the van by flying over the flock and alighting in front, the entire flock constantly changing from rear to front, revolving something like a wheel with a low buzzing wing roar that could be heard a long way off. In summer they feasted on wheat and oats and were easily approached as they rested on the trees along the sides of the field after a good full meal, displaying beautiful iridescent colors as they moved their necks backward and forward when we went very near them. Every shotgun was aimed at them and everybody feasted on pigeon pies, and not a few of the settlers feasted also on the beauty of the wonderful birds. The breast of the male is a fine rosy red, the lower part of the neck behind and along the sides changing from the red of the breast to gold, emerald green and rich crimson. The general color of the upper parts is grayish blue, the under parts white.

The extreme length of the bird is about seventeen inches; the finely modeled slender tail about eight inches, and extent of wings twenty-four inches. The females are scarcely less beautiful. "Oh, what bonnie, bonnie birds!" we exclaimed over the first that fell into our hands. "Oh, what colors! Look at their breasts, bonnie as roses, and at their necks aglow wi' every color juist like the wonderfu' wood ducks. Oh, the bonnie, bonnie creatures, they beat a'! Where did they a' come fra, and where are they a' gan? It's awfu' like a sin to kill them!" To this some smug, practical old sinner would remark: "Aye, it's a peety, as ye say, to kill the bonnie things, but they were made to be killed, and sent for us to eat as the quails were sent to God's chosen people, the Israelites, when they were starving in the desert ayont the Red Sea." And I must confess that meat was never put up in neater, handsomer-painted packages.

In the New England and Canada woods beechnuts were their best and most abundant food, farther north, cranberries and huckleberries. After everything was cleaned up in the north and winter was coming on, they went south for rice, corn, acorns, haws, wild grapes, crab-apples, sparkle-berries, etc. They seemed to require more than half of the continent for feeding-grounds, moving from one table to another, field to field, forest to forest, finding something ripe and wholesome all the year round. In going south in the fine Indian-summer weather they flew high and followed one another, though the head of the flock might be hundreds of miles in advance. But against head winds they took advantage of the inequalities of the ground, flying comparatively low. All followed the leader's ups and downs over hill and dale though far out of sight, never hesitating at any turn of the way, vertical or horizontal that the leaders had taken, though the largest flocks stretched across several States, and belts of different kinds of weather.

There were no roosting- or breeding-places near our farm, and I never saw any of them until long after the great flocks were exterminated. I therefore quote, from Audubon's and Pokagon's vivid descriptions:

"Toward evening," Audubon says, "they depart for the roosting place, which may be hundreds of miles distant. One on the banks of Green River, Kentucky, was over three miles wide and forty long."

"My first view of it," says the great naturalist, "was about a fortnight after it had been chosen by the birds, and I arrived there nearly two hours before sunset. Few pigeons were then to be seen, but a great many persons with horses and wagons and armed with guns, long poles, sulphur pots, pine pitch torches, etc., had already established encampments on the borders. Two farmers had driven upwards of three hundred hogs a distance of more than a hundred miles to be fattened on slaughtered pigeons. Here and there the people employed in plucking and salting what had already been secured were sitting in the midst of piles of birds. Dung several inches thick covered the ground. Many trees two feet in diameter were broken off at no great distance from the ground, and the branches of many of the tallest and largest had given way, as if the forest had been swept by a tornado.

"Not a pigeon had arrived at sundown. Suddenly a general cry arose—'Here they come!' The noise they made, though still distant, reminded me of a hard gale at sea passing through the rigging of a close-reefed ship. Thousands were soon knocked down by the pole-men. The birds continued to pour in. The fires were lighted and a magnificent as well as terrifying sight presented itself. The pigeons pouring in alighted everywhere, one above another, until solid masses were formed on the branches all around. Here and there the perches gave way with a crash, and falling destroyed hundreds beneath, forcing down the dense groups with which every stick was loaded; a scene of uproar and conflict. I found it useless to speak or even to shout to those persons nearest me. Even the reports of the guns were seldom heard, and I was made aware of the firing only by seeing the shooters reloading. None dared venture within the line of devastation. The hogs had been penned up in due time, the picking up of the dead and wounded being left for the next morning's employment. The pigeons were constantly coming in and it was after midnight before I perceived a decrease in the number of those that arrived. The uproar continued all night, and anxious to know how far the sound reached I sent off a man who, returning two hours later, informed me that he had heard it distinctly three miles distant.

"Toward daylight the noise in some measure subsided; long before objects were distinguishable the pigeons began to move off in a direction quite different from that in which they had arrived the evening before, and at sunrise all that were able to fly had disappeared. The howling of the wolves now reached our ears, and the foxes, lynxes, cougars, bears, coons, opossums, and polecats were seen sneaking off, while eagles and hawks of different species, accompanied by a crowd of vultures, came to supplant them and enjoy a share of the spoil.

"Then the authors of all this devastation began their entry among the dead, the dying and the mangled. The pigeons were picked up and piled in heaps until each had as many as they could possibly dispose of, when the hogs were loosed to feed on the remainder.

"The breeding places are selected with reference to abundance of food, and countless myriads resort to them. At this period the note of the pigeon is coo coo coo, like that of the domestic species but much shorter. They caress by billing, and during the incubation the male supplies the female with food. As the young grow, the tyrant of creation appears to disturb the peaceful scene, armed with axes to chop down the squab-laden trees, and the abomination of desolation and destruction produced far surpasses even that of the roosting places."

Pokagon, an educated Indian writer, says: "I saw one nesting place in Wisconsin one hundred miles long and from three to ten miles wide. Every tree, some of them quite low and scrubby, had from one to fifty nests on each. Some of the nests overflow from the oaks to the hemlock and pine woods. When the pigeon hunters attack the breeding-places they sometimes cut the timber from thousands of acres. Millions are caught in nets with salt or grain for bait, and schooners, sometimes loaded down with the birds, are taken to New York where they are sold for a cent apiece."

Carl Schurz

☼

ALTHOUGH born in a foreign land and somewhat nomadic in the matter of residence after coming to America, it is safe to say that Carl Schurz began his colorful career as writer and statesman while a resident of Wisconsin. He was born at Liblar, Prussia, March 2, 1829; was educated at the University of Bonn where he identified himself with the student liberals who advocated rebellion against the monarchical form of government. After the failure of a revolutionary movement, he was forced to flee from his native land. He spent several years in Switzerland, Scotland and France, and in 1852 came to the United States. After residing in Philadelphia three years, Schurz came to Watertown, Wis. in 1855. On a beautiful knoll overlooking the Rock river he built a comfortable home where he resided until the outbreak of the Civil War, and where his family continued to live while he was in the military service of his adopted country. This eminence on the northern edge of Watertown is still one of the beauty spots of the neighborhood, but the old Schurz home was destroyed by fire several years ago, and a modern house now occupies the site. During the time he resided in Watertown he was active in politics; he was a candidate for lieutenant governor, but was defeated. In 1860 Schurz did much to carry Wisconsin for Lincoln. He was a forceful, convincing speaker and appealed to his German neighbors in their native language. After Lincoln was inaugurated, Schurz was appointed minister to Spain, but resigned within a few months to enter the Union Army. He was promoted rapidly until he reached the rank of Major General in 1863. He especially distinguished himself in the battles of Manassas, Chancellorsville, Gettysburg, and Chattanooga.

Carl Schurz was at different times a resident of Pennsylvania, Wisconsin, Missouri, Michigan and New York. In 1869 he was elected United States Senator from Missouri. When Hayes became President, Schurz entered the cabinet as Secretary of the Interior. With the close of the Hayes administration, he became editor of the New York Evening Post, 1881-1884. He died in New York City, May 14, 1906.

Among his published works are *Speeches*, 1861, *Life of Henry Clay*, 1887, and *Abraham Lincoln*, 1891. His *Reminiscences*, the story of his active life, is his most voluminous work.

From THE REMINISCENCES OF CARL SCHURZ, *Volume Three. The McClure Company, New York, Publishers. 1908.*

CHAPTER III

THE leisure hours of camp life during the winter and spring of 1864 had permitted me to plod through several volumes of Herbert Spencer, and to carry on a somewhat active correspondence with friends in Washington and various parts of the Northern States. The political intelligence brought by letters and newspapers was by no means cheering. To the army mind—that is, to those in the field looking at political happenings from afar, and having nothing in view but to bring the struggle against the rebellion and for the restoration of the Union under the new conditions to a successful issue—the requirements of the situation appeared to be simple and clear. The one thing needed first of all seemed to be that the administration be supported in its efforts to rally the whole force of the Union sentiment of the country against the common enemy. No doubt, there might be differences of opinion as to how this should be done in detail. No doubt, some things had been done by, or under, the auspices of the administration that were open to criticism. No doubt, our government had not been as successful in the field as it should have been. No doubt, there were different theories as to the actual status of the rebel States in or out of the Union, and as to the methods of accomplishing their reconstruction when the rebellion should have been overcome. But in point of fact, the rebellion was not yet overcome, and it was questionable whether it would ever be overcome if the Union forces acted at cross purposes in directing their efforts. And if the rebellion was not overcome, all these disputes would appear to have been vain and idle. But the criticism of the government—legitimate in itself if it were designed only to enlighten the administration and lead to a correction of its errors—had assumed a virulent temper, and had been turned into attempts to prevent the renomination of Mr. Lincoln.

The most alarming feature of this commotion was that many men were active in it whose patriotism was above question, and whose character stood so high in public estimation that their example might exercise a wide influence. There was much impatience at the slow progress of the war for the Union, and the administration was largely held responsible for it. The most impetuous of the impatient urged that a President must be chosen who would carry on the war with more energy. Not a few serious patriots, especially in the East, were displeased with Mr. Lincoln's somewhat loose ways of conducting the public business, with his rustic manners, and with the robust character of his humor, and concluded that the Republic must have a President more mindful of the dignity of his office. In some of the States fierce factional fights were raging among the Union men, and one faction would demand the election of another President if Mr.

Lincoln seemed to favor the other faction. It was publicly said, and believed by many, that Mr. Lincoln had only one steadfast friend in the lower House of Congress, and few more in the Senate, the disaffection being due partly to the fact that Mr. Lincoln had not been able to gratify the wishes of the Senators and Representatives as to appointments; and partly to differences of opinion as to the reconstruction policy to be adopted. These various elements of discontent combined, would possibly have constituted a formidable force, had they been able to unite upon an opposition candidate who would have satisfied the country that he was better fitted for the presidency in this crisis than Mr. Lincoln. But the only statesman of high standing who in any degree appeared available for such a purpose was Mr. Chase, who, with all his great qualities, seemed unable to call forth any popular enthusiasm. Neither could the candidacy of General Fremont, brought forward by the radicals of Missouri, highly respectable and patriotic men, who were embittered by the countenance given by Mr. Lincoln to the "conservative" faction in that State, command much confidence and support.

These distracting movements inside the Union party could therefore only serve to encourage and strengthen the Democrats. With great skill and energy, they worked upon the desire for peace naturally existing and growing among the people as the war dragged on without any distinct prospect of its early termination, and hoped to ride into power on the strength of the peace-cry, and on the charge that the policy of the Republican administration had resulted in utter failure.

Would not the rejection of Mr. Lincoln by the Republican National Convention be tantamount to an open confession of such failure, and thus put a terrible weapon in the hands of the opposition? Was not, quite aside from his exceptional hold upon the esteem and affection of the masses of the people, Lincoln's renomination so natural, indeed, so necessary, that it was difficult to understand how any unprejudiced Union man could oppose it? That, in spite of all this, such opposition should find the support of estimable Union men, was indeed an alarming symptom.

This aspect of the situation disquieted me profoundly. I did not, indeed, seriously apprehend that Mr. Lincoln's nomination could be prevented. But the question was, whether the efforts made to prevent it would not have a demoralizing effect upon the party, and put his success at the election in jeopardy. And in case of the government falling into the hands of the Democratic party, in whose councils such men as Vallandigham and Fernando Wood wielded much—perhaps decisive—influence, the probability was that either the dissolution of the Union would be acquiesced in, or the Union would be patched up again by means of a compromise involving the preservation of slavery.

In the troubled contemplation of this appalling possibility, it occurred to me that I might perhaps render better service by entering the political campaign as a speaker, than by superintending the training of new troops in my camp near Nashville, for the uncertain contingency of their ever firing a cartridge. I received various letters suggesting the same thing, among them a very urgent one from Mr. Elihu B. Washburne, a prominent member of Congress from Illinois, and another from Thaddeus Stevens of Pennsylvania, who painted to me in strong colors the dangers of the situation, and insisted that I must "go on the stump," as I had done in the campaign of 1860. Finally I concluded that I ought to do so. I wrote to Mr. Lincoln, informing him of my purpose. In his reply he observed that if I did so, it would be at the risk of my active employment in the army. I was willing to take the risk unconditionally, and asked, through the regular military channels, to be relieved of my present duties. This relief was granted, and I promptly gave up my command of the camp and journeyed to Bethlehem, Pennsylvania, where my family were at that time, and asked for permission to visit Washington—military officers being at that time forbidden to visit Washington without special permission from the War Department. I wished to confer with Mr. Lincoln on the political situation, and more particularly to get his view of the exigencies of the campaign. The official permit for a visit to Washington arrived promptly.

Although Lincoln, to the astonishment of his Republican opponents, who would not recognize any popular force behind him, had been renominated with substantial unanimity by the National Convention, the hostile movements in the Republican ranks did not cease. Senator Benjamin F. Wade, from Ohio, one of the oldest, most courageous, and most highly respected of the anti-slavery champions, and Henry Winter Davis, a member of the National House of Representatives from Maryland, a man of high character and an orator of rare brilliancy, rose in open revolt against Lincoln's reconstruction ideas, and issued a formal manifesto, in which, in language of startling vehemence, they assailed the integrity of his motives as those of an usurper carried away by lust of power. And then cries arose in the most unexpected quarters that Lincoln could not possibly be elected. Such men as Horace Greely and Thurlow Weed, usually hostile to one another in Republican factional fights, united in the gloomy prediction that Lincoln would most surely be defeated; and men of similar importance, severally and as members of committees, plied Lincoln himself with urgent entreaties that he should withdraw from the contest and make room for another more promising candidate. Neither was there much encouragement in the popular temper as it manifested itself during the first two months after Lincoln's renomination. The people seemed to be utterly spiritless. They would hardly attend a massmeeting, much less inspire the speaker with enthusiastic acclamations. This may have been partly owing to the fact that the Democrats had not yet held their National Convention, and there was, therefore, neither a candidate nor a declared policy of the opposite party to attack. But, surely, the administration party could not have been in a more lethargic and spiritless condition. Its atmosphere was thoroughly depressing.

I called upon Mr. Lincoln on a hot afternoon late in July. He greeted me cordially, and asked me to wait in his office until he should be through with the current business of the day, and then to spend the evening with him at the cottage on the grounds of the Soldiers' Home, which he occupied during the summer. In the carriage on the way thither he made various inquiries concerning the attitude of this and that public man, and this and that group of people, and we discussed the question whether it would be good policy to attempt an active campaign before the Democrats should have "shown their hand" in their National Convention. He argued that such an attempt would be unwise unless some unforeseen change in the situation called for it. Arrived at the cottage, he asked me to sit down with him on a lounge in a sort of parlor which was rather scantily furnished, and began to speak about the attacks made upon him by party friends, and their efforts to force his withdrawal from the candidacy. The substance of what he said I can recount from a letter written at the time to an intimate friend.

He spoke as if he felt a pressing need to ease his heart by giving voice to the sorrowful thoughts distressing him. He would not complain of the fearful burden and care and responsibility put upon his shoulders. Nobody knew the weight of that burden save himself. But was it necessary, was it generous, was it right, to impeach even the rectitude of his motives? "They urge me with almost violent language," he said, "to withdraw from the contest, although I have been unanimously nominated, in order to make room for a better man. I wish I could. Perhaps some other man might do this business better than I. That is possible. I do not deny it. But I am here, and that better man is not here. And if I should step aside to make room for him, it is not at all sure—perhaps not even probable—that he would get here. It is much more likely that the factions opposed to me would fall to fighting among themselves, and that those who want me to make room for a better man would get a man whom most of them would not want in at all. My withdrawal, therefore, might, and probably would, bring on a confusion worse confounded. God knows, I have at least tried very hard to do my duty—to do right to everybody and wrong to nobody. And now to have it said by men who have been my friends and who ought to know me better, that I have been seduced by what they call the lust of power, and that I have been doing this and that unscrupulous thing hurtful to the common cause, only to keep myself in office! Have they thought of that common cause when trying to break me down? I hope they have."

So he went on as if speaking to himself, now pausing for a second, then uttering a sentence or two with vehement emphasis. Meanwhile the dusk of evening had set in, and when the room was lighted I thought I saw his sad eyes moist and his rugged features working strangely, as if under a very strong and painful emotion. At length he stopped, as if waiting for me to say something, and, touched as I was, I only expressed as well as I could, my confident assurance that the people, undisturbed by the bickerings of his critics, believed in him and would faithfully stand by him. The conversation, then turning upon things to be done, became more cheerful, and in the course of the evening he explained to me various acts of the administration which in the campaign might be questioned and call for defense. As to his differences with members of Congress concerning reconstruction, he laid particular stress upon the fact that, looked at from a constitutional standpoint, the Executive could do many things by virtue of the war power, which Congress could not do in the way of ordinary legislation. When I took my leave that night he was in a calm mood, indulged himself in a few humorous remarks, shook my hand heartily, and said: "Well, things might look better, and they might look worse. Go in, and let us all do the best we can."

The campaign did not become spirited until after the Democratic National Convention. But then it started in good earnest, and the prospects brightened at once. The Democrats, made overconfident by the apparent lethargy of the popular mind and the acrimonious wrangling inside of the Union party, had recklessly overshot the mark. They declared in their platform that the war against the rebellion was a failure, and that immediate efforts should be made for a cessation of hostilities, with a view to an ultimate convention of all the States for a peaceable settlement on the basis of reunion. Considering the fact that the leaders of the rebellion vociferously, defiantly insisted upon the independence of the Southern Confederacy as a condition *sine qua non* of any settlement, this proposition looked like a complete surrender. It was too much, not only for the malcontents within the Union party, but also for many Democrats. Even the candidate of their own party, General McClellan, who had been nominated for the purpose of conciliating the patriotic war-spirit still alive in the Democratic ranks, found it necessary to repudiate that part of the platform—first, in justice to his own feelings, and secondly, to save the last chance of success in the election. Then came the inspiring tidings of Sherman's victorious march into the heart of Georgia and the capture of Atlanta, kindling all over the North a blaze of jubilant enthusiasm, and covering the declaration that the war was a failure, with contemptuous derision. And, finally, more potent perhaps than all else, the tender affection of the popular heart for Abraham Lincoln burst forth with all its warmth. This tender affection, cherished among the plain people of the land, among the soldiers in the field, and their "folks at home" was a sentimental element of strength which Lincoln's critical opponents in the Union party had wholly ignored. Now they became aware of it, not without surprise. I believe that, had the Democratic Convention been more prudent, and had no victories happened to cheer the masses, even then "Father Abraham's" personal popularity alone would have been sufficient to give him the victory in the election of 1864. I made many speeches in New York, Pennsylvania, and the Western States as far as Wisconsin, three of which were printed in the collection which was published in 1865. While writing these reminiscences I read them over—let me confess it—with much satisfaction. But that they contributed much to Lincoln's success, I candidly do not believe. They were well-meant, but, although they had a wide circulation and much praise at the time, they were really superfluous. In fact, during its last two months, the presidential campaign of 1864 seemed to run itself. With a thoroughly united Union party, it became more and more a popular jubilee as the election approached. However, the size of his majority did not come up to the expectation of Lincoln's friends.

A few days after the election I read in the papers the report of a speech delivered by Lincoln in response to a serenade, in which he offered the hand of friendship to those who had opposed him in these words: "Now that the election is over, may not all, having a common interest, reunite in a common effort to save our common community? For my own part, I have striven, and will strive, to place no obstacle in the way. So long as I have been here, I have not willingly planted a thorn in any man's bosom. While I am deeply sensible of the high compliment of a re-election, it adds nothing to my satisfaction that any other man may be pained or disappointed by the result. May I ask those who were with me to join with me in the same spirit towards those who were against me?" When I read those noble words, which so touchingly revealed the whole tender generosity of Lincoln's great soul, the haggard face I had seen that evening in the cottage at the Soldiers' Home rose up vividly in my memory.

Rasmus B. Anderson

☼

RASMUS B. ANDERSON, foremost Scandinavian scholar in Wisconsin, writer and translator of Scandinavian literature, was born in Albion, Dane County, Wisconsin, January 12, 1846. He was graduated from Luther College in 1866. From 1875 to 1883 he was professor of Scandinavian language and literature in the University of Wisconsin. He was appointed United States Minister to Denmark in 1885 and filled the position with honor and ability during the succeeding four years.

His literary work has been almost entirely in the field of Scandinavian history and story. Among his best known works are: *America Not Discovered by Columbus*, 1874, *Norse Mythology*, 1875, *Viking Tales of the North*, 1877, *The Younger Edda*, 1880, *Norwegian Immigration*, 1895, and the *Life Story of Rasmus B. Anderson*, 1915. Of the above works, the translations from the Scandinavian are an especial contribution to readers who have no knowledge of the originals. Professor Anderson resides in Madison and is, at the present time, a curator of the State Historical Society.

VIKING TALES OF THE NORTH, *translated from the Icelandic by Rasmus B. Anderson. S. C. Griggs and Company, Chicago, Publishers. 1877. By permission of the author.*

THE SAGA OF FRIDTHJOF THE BOLD

I

THE beginning of this saga is, that king Bele ruled over the Sogn fylke. He had three children: a son, who hight

Helge, another by name Halfdan, and a daughter called Ingeborg, a fair looking woman, of great wisdom, and the foremost of the king's children. On the coast bordering the fjord on the west side there was a large byre, called Baldershage (Balder's Meads). There was a Place of Peace and a great temple inclosed with high wooden pales. Many gods were there, yet none of them was such a favorite as Balder; and so jealous were the heathen people of this place, that no harm should be done therein, either to beasts or to men; and no dealings must there take place between men and women. The place where the king dwelt hight Syrstrand, but on the other side of the fjord was a byre called Framness. There dwelt a man who hight Thorstein, the son of Viking. His byre was over against the dwelling of the king. With his wife, Thorstein had a son, by name Fridthjof, a man taller and stronger than anybody else, and even from his youth furnished with very unusual prowess. He was called Fridthjof the Bold, and so much was he beloved that all men prayed for his welfare. The children of the king were still young when their mother died. Hilding was the name of a good bonde in Sogn. He offered to foster the king's daughter, and so she was brought up in his house well and carefully. She was called Ingeborg the Fair. Fridthjof was also fostered by the bonde Hilding, and thus Ingeborg was his foster-sister, and both of them were peerless among children. King Bele growing old, his personal property began to ebb away from his hands. Thorstein ruled over the third part of his kingdom, and from that man Bele got more aid than from any other source. Every third year Thorstein invited the king to a very costly banquet, while the king, on the other hand, gave a feast to Thorstein the other two years. At an early age Helge, Bele's son, turned to offering to the gods, and yet neither he nor his brother was much beloved. Thorstein had a ship called Ellide, rowed on each side by fifteen oars, furnished with bow-shaped stem and stern, and strong-built like an ocean-going vessel, and its sides were clamped with iron. So strong was Fridthjof, that he, at the bow of the ship, rowed with two oars thirteen ells long, while everywhere else there were two men at each oar. Fridthjof was considered peerless among young men of that time, and the sons of the king were jealous, because he was praised more than themselves. Now king Bele was taken ill, and when he was rapidly approaching death he sent for his sons and said to them: This illness will be my bane, but this I bid you, that you keep friendship with the friends that I have had, for it seems to me that you are inferior to Thorstein and his son Fridthjof in all things, both in good counsel and bravery. You shall raise a mound over me. Hereupon Bele died. Soon afterward Thorstein also was taken sick, and then he said to Fridthjof: This will I bid you, my son, that you govern your temper and yield to the sons of the king, for this is fitting on account of their dignity, and besides it seems to me that your future promises much good. I wish to be buried in a how opposite the how of king Bele, on this side of the fjord, close by the sea, so that it may be an easy thing to shout to one another about things that are about to happen. Bjorn and Asmund hight the foster-brothers of Fridthjof; both of them were large and strong men. Shortly after this Thorstein died. He was buried in a how according to his request, but Fridthjof took his land and all his personal property after him.

II

Fridthjof became the most famous man, and the bravest in all dangers. His foster-brother, Bjorn, he valued most, but Asmund served both of them. The best thing he got of his father's heritage was the ship Ellide, and another costly thing was a gold ring, and a dearer one was not to be found in all Norway. So bounteous a man was Fridthjof that he was commonly said to be no less honorable than the sons of the king, excepting their royal dignity. On account of this they showed great coldness and enmity toward Fridthjof, and they could not easily bear to hear him spoken of as superior to themselves; and, furthermore, they seemed to have seen that their sister, Ingeborg, and Fridthjof had fallen into mutual love. Now the time came when the kings had to attend a banquet at Fridthjof's, at Framness, and, as usual, he entertained everybody more splendidly than they were wont to be entertained. Ingeborg was also present at this feast, and Fridthjof frequently talked with her. Said the king's daughter to him: you have a good gold ring. Said Fridthjof: That is true. Hereupon, the brothers went home, and their envy of Fridthjof grew. Shortly afterward Fridthjof became very sad. Bjorn, his foster-brother, asked him what the matter was. Fridthjof answered that he had in mind to woo Ingeborg; for, said he, though my title is less than that of her brothers, still I am not inferior to them in personal worth. Says Bjorn: Let us do so. Then Fridthjof, in company with a few men, went to see the brothers. The kings were sitting on their father's how, when Fridthjof greeted them courteously. Thereupon, he presented his request, saying that he prayed for their sister, Ingeborg, Bele's daughter. Said the kings: You do not show great wisdom in making this request, thinking that we will give her in marriage to a man who is without dignity. We therefore most positively refuse to give our consent. Said Fridthjof: Then my errand is quickly done; but this shall be given in return, that hereafter I shall never give you my help, though you may be in want of it. They said they did not care about it at all. Then Fridthjof returned home, and got back his cheerful mind.

III

There was a king, by name Ring, who ruled over Ringric, which also is a part of Norway. He was a mighty fylke-king, of great ability, but at this time somewhat advanced in age. Spoke he to his men: I have heard that the sons of Bele have broken off their friendship with Fridthjof, a man of quite uncommon excellence. Now I will send some men to the kings, and offer them this choice,—either they must become subject and tributary to me, or I will equip an army against them; and I think it will be easy to capture their kingdom, for they are not my peers either in forces or in wisdom, and yet it would be a great honor to me in my old age to put them to death. Hereupon king Ring's messengers left, and, meeting the brothers, Helge and Halfdan, in Sogn, they spoke to them as follows: This message does king Ring send you, that you must either pay a tribute to him, or he will come and harry your kingdom. They made answer that they were unwilling to learn in their youth that which they had no mind to know in their old age, namely, to serve him with shame; and now, said they, we shall gather all the army that we may be able to get together. And so they did; but, as it seemed to them that their army would be small, they sent Hilding's foster-father to Fridthjof, asking him to come and help the kings. Fridthjof was sitting at the knave-play when Hilding came. Said Hilding: Our kings send you their greetings, and request your help for the battle with king Ring, who is going to invade their kingdom with arrogance and wrong. Fridthjof answered nothing, but said to Bjorn, with whom he was playing: There is an open place there, foster-brother, and you will not be able to mend it; but I will attack the red piece, and see whether it can be saved. Said Hilding then again: King Helge bade me say this to you, Fridthjof, that you should go into this warfare together with them, or you might look for a severe treatment from them when they come back. Said Bjorn then: There is a choice between two, foster-brother, and there are two moves by which you may escape. Says Fridthjof: Then I think it advisable to attack the knave first; and yet the double game is sure to be doubtful. No other answer to his errand did Hilding get, and so, without delay, he went back and told the kings what Fridthjof had said. They asked Hilding what meaning he could make out of those words. Answered he: When he spoke of the open place, he thought, in my opinion, of leaving his place in your expedition open; but when he pretended to attack the red piece, I think he by this meant your sister, Ingeborg; watch her, therefore, as well as you can. But when I threatened him with severe treatment from you, Bjorn considered it a choice between two, but Fridthjof said the knave must be attacked first, and by this he meant king Ring. Then the kings busked themselves for departure, but before they went they brought Ingeborg to Baldershage, and eight maidens with her. Said they that Fridthjof would not be so daring that he would go thither to meet her, for nobody is so rash as to injure anybody there. But the brothers went south to Jadar, and met king Ring in Sokn-Sound. What most of all made king Ring angry was that the brothers had said that they thought it a shame to fight with a man so old that he was unable to mount his horse without help.

IV

When the kings had gone away Fridthjof took his robes of state, and put his good gold ring on his hand; then the foster-brothers went down to the sea and launched Ellide. Said Bjorn: Whither shall we now turn the prow, foster-brother? Answered Fridthjof: To Baldershage, and amuse ourselves with Ingeborg. Said Bjorn: It is not a proper thing to do, to provoke the gods. Said Fridthjof: Yet that risk shall now be run; besides, I rate the favor of Ingeborg of more account than that of Balder. Hereupon they rowed over the fjord, walked up to Baldershage and entered Ingeborg's bower, where she sat, together with eight maidens, and they, too, were eight. But when they came there all the place was covered with cloth of pall and other fine woven stuff. Then Ingeborg arose and said: Why are you so overbold, Fridthjof, that you have come here without the consent of my brothers, and thus provoke the wrath of the gods? Made answer Fridthjof: However this may be, I consider your love of more account than the wrath of the gods. Answered Ingeborg: You shall be welcome here, and all your men. Then she made room for him to sit at her side, and drank his toast of the best wine, and they sat and were merry together. Then Ingeborg, seeing the gold ring on his hand, asked whether he was the owner of that precious thing. Fridthjof said it was his. She praised the ring very much. Said Fridthjof: I will give you the ring if you promise not to part with it, and will send it to me when you no longer care to keep it, and with it we pledge our troth and love to each other. With this pledging of troth they exchanged rings. Fridthjof spent many nights at Baldershage, and every day he went over there now and then to be merry with Ingeborg.

V

Now it is to be told of the brothers, that they met king Ring, who had more forces than they; then some people went between them, trying to bring about an agreement, so that there should be no battle. King Ring said he was willing to settle with them, on the condition that the brothers submit to him and give him their sister, Ingeborg the Fair, in marriage, together with the third part of all their possessions. The kings consented to this, for they saw that they had to do with a force far superior to their own. This peace was firmly established by oaths, and the wedding was to be in Sogn, when king Ring came to meet his betrothed. The brothers fared home again with their troops, right ill content with the result. When Fridthjof thought the time had come when the brothers might be expected home, he said to the daughter of the king: Well and handsomely you have treated us, nor has the bonde Balder been angry with us. But as soon as you know that your kings have come home, then spread your bed-sheets on the hall of the goddesses, for that is the highest of all the houses in this place, and we can easily see it from our byre. Said the king's daughter: You have not followed the example of other men in this matter, but we certainly must welcome our friends when you come to us.

Frederic L. Paxson

☼

FREDERIC L. PAXSON was born in Philadelphia, Pennsylvania, February 23, 1877 of Quaker parentage. He was graduated from the University of Pennsylvania in 1898. In 1910 he came to the University of Wisconsin as professor of American History, and has since resided in Madison.

F. L. Paxson is not only a popular class-room and platform lecturer; he is a widely known writer as well. His books on American History have a national and even international reputation. Among his contributions to historical literature are: *The Last American Frontier*, 1910; *The Civil War*, 1911; *The New Nation*, 1915; *Recent History of the United States*, 1921; and *History of the American Frontier*, 1924. This last work received the Pulitzer Prize as the best work on American history published in 1924. Mr. Paxson is a curator of the State Historical Society of Wisconsin.

HISTORY OF THE AMERICAN FRONTIER, 1763-1893, *by Frederic L. Paxson. Published by Houghton Mifflin Company, Boston and New York, 1924. Reprinted by permission of the publishers. All rights reserved.*

CHAPTER XVI

PROBLEMS OF THE SOUTHWEST BORDER

NAPOLEON BONAPARTE refused to go on record as to the boundaries of Louisiana, but we know to-day that it was his intention, had he completed his colonial experiment, to seize the Gulf of Mexico shore between the Mississippi and the Rio Grande, and claim it all. When the province that he discarded into Jefferson's hands became the southwest border of the United States, its western limits were uncertain. And Spain, who had watched with apprehension the advance of both England and France, viewed with renewed alarm the presence at New Orleans of an American frontier force. The settlements in Texas had been planted in the eighteenth century to be a buffer for New Spain, the Internal Provinces had been organized, and Upper California had been colonized with the same intent. The Spanish officers who from New Orleans had watched the leaders of opinion in Kentucky and Tennessee with nervous fear since 1785, now took their station along the trail that ran from the head of the Sabine River to San Antonio, and determined to maintain an outpost here. In Louisiana, James Wilkinson was an unfit leader of the American army, for no one had illicit relations more than he with these Spanish officials. He was an unstable foundation for the cornerstone of empire.

After the delivery of New Orleans to Wilkinson and Claiborne in December, 1803, the latter became temporary governor, exercising in the name of the President full military power, and all the functions possessed by all the Spanish officials whom he displaced. Congress authorized such autocratic rule until it should have time to give further consideration to the government of the province. There were in Louisiana perhaps eight thousand whites in the vicinity of New Orleans, and fifty thousand south of the Red River. In Upper Louisiana, between New Madrid and St. Louis, there may have been six thousand more. Most of these were French or Spanish, though there was among them a new admixture of Americans, tempted across the Mississippi by easy naturalization and generous land grants. The people spoke French, lived under the civil rather than the common law, and were in general devout followers of the communion of the Catholic Church. They contained little of the element that made American westerners clamor for self-government before they were ripe for it. Instead, the creoles of Louisiana, with the numerous half-breed mixtures, accepted what government came to them with tranquil indifference. Their normal indolent politeness did not conceal their contempt for the American representatives of a rough and ready civilization, but they made no resistance to their sale as chattels by France to the United States.

In March, 1804, Congress divided the province of Louisiana by the line of the thirty-third parallel running west from the Mississippi. South of this line, the Territory of New Orleans was left in Claiborne's hands, as a territory of the lowest grade. North of the line, the District of Louisiana was attached for purposes of government to Indiana Territory, where William Henry Harrison had been in command since 1801. This latter combination was unsuccessful, and popular neither at Vincennes nor at St. Louis. In 1805, accordingly, Indiana was cut down. Michigan Territory was launched, with the seat of government at Detroit, under William Hull; and Louisiana District was allowed to be a Territory, with its government at St. Louis. Both Indiana and Orleans at this time were raised to the second territorial status, and allowed a legislature.

The exploration of the tract that thus became the two territories of Orleans and Louisiana went on apace. Between 1804 and 1806 the northern and western limits were visited, without discovering anything that called for or received immediate attention. But at the south and west each year revealed increasing difficulty and uncertainty. Pike, on his return from the Upper Mississippi was transferred at once to this scene, and played there a part whose meaning is as uncertain to the historian as it may have been to him.

Under orders from Wilkinson, he left St. Louis July 15, 1806, to escort a group of Indians to their homes in the Osage and Pawnee villages, and then to proceed to the headwaters of the Arkansas and Red rivers. The internal topography was as cloudy at the border of New Spain as it was at that of Oregon. There would have been good reason for an investigation of the region for the simple purpose of ascertaining the facts, but the connection of Wilkinson with it makes such explanation of motive hard to accept. Somewhere to the southwest lay the frontier of Spain. It was fairly clear that on the Gulf Shore there would be established an equilibrium not far from the Sabine River; but inland neither Spain nor the United States knew what the limits ought to be. Pike was ordered to disguise his military identity, which would not have been necessary had his purpose been simply to explore the Territory of Louisiana; and he was given careful instructions and an untruthful story to be used in case he should fall in with troops of Spain. Like a good soldier he accepted his orders without question, and he does not seem to have suspected that anything but a proper military purpose was behind his mission. When he returned to the United States in 1807, and found that he was connected in the public mind with the plot of Aaron Burr, his indignation was so pronounced as to appear genuine.

Leaving the St. Louis border with his Indian charges, Pike visited their villages, and then struck off across what is now the eastern end of Kansas for the great northern bend of the Arkansas River. He followed the river to the Rocky Mountains, where it emerges through the front range at the Royal Gorge, where Pueblo now stands. From an examination of such maps as he could have seen, there was reason to believe that south of the Arkansas was the basin of the Red River. Certainly in their lower reaches these rivers lay parallel. The Sangre de Cristo range that Pike now crossed may have appeared to him to be the northern ridge of the Red River basin; but when he struck the stream beyond the range, which was the Rio Grande in San Luis Park, he built himself a fortified post on it. If he thought it to be the Red River, there was no occasion for a fort. If he knew it was the Rio Grande, he must have been conscious of a trespass, for his fort was on a western branch of the main stream. But he also knew that on the border, people were talking of a probable war with Spain. His commander, Wilkinson, had proceeded during the summer first to Natchez and then to the head of Red River navigation at Natchitoches, where he went through the motions of making a truce with the Spanish leaders who were in the vicinity of Nacogdoches. Between them they held the international boundary near the point where it was fixed by treaty in 1819. But while they were doing this downstream, Pike was building his fort upon the Rio Grande, and claiming that he thought himself upon the Red.

In February, 1807, Pike was visited at his camp by a courteous Spanish officer, with a detachment of soldiers and militia, and was invited to accompany him to his commander at Chihuahua. The force was so great that compliance could not be avoided. The Spanish relieved Pike of all his notes and papers, which were forwarded through military channels to headquarters at Mexico City (though no one seems ever to have read them). The Americans were escorted as guests down the road that ascends the upper Rio Grande. They passed through Santa Fe, where New Spain had a civilization as ancient as that of New England. They continued to El Paso, where the river leaves the mountain trough that has become New Mexico; and thence they crossed the desert of Chihuahua. Spain had no use for Pike, though it desired to check his reconnoissance; and the impending war failed to come about. From Chihuahua, therefore, Pike was escorted to the eastern road that led, and still leads, from Durango to Laredo, and thence across the Rio Grande to San Antonio. In the summer of 1807 he was passed along the whole length of the Texas road to Nacogdoches, and was delivered across the neutral ground to Wilkinson at Natchitoches.

By the time of Pike's arrival at the American border post, whatever may have been the original intention of Wilkinson in dispatching him had changed to patriotism and peace. Aaron Burr had been arrested, and the word treason had been noisily shouted at his followers. Pike found himself misjudged and minus the notes which might have made a valuable book upon his trip. However his reputation was not permanently destroyed and he died a brigadier-general under fire at York in 1813. He had meantime brought out in 1810 a volume whose chief contribution lies in establishing the topographical data respecting the sources of the Arkansas and Red and in describing the remote civilization of New Mexico. The picturesque life that Pike was taken through upon his enforced pilgrimage was new to him and interesting to his fellows. The scarcity of merchandise in New Mexico suggested a profitable field for border trade. But the time was not yet ripe for this. Santa Fe was a thousand miles away from St. Louis across the southern plains, whose inhospitality impressed Pike, as the northern plains had similarly impressed Lewis and Clark.

The mystery connected with the aims of Aaron Burr, and the devious course of James Wilkinson respecting them, is involved with the genuine tenseness of Spanish-American relations, and the old habit of the Mississippi Valley lightly to undertake ventures inconsistent with Federal law and duty. The arrest of Burr in January, 1807, brought his enterprise to an end, and was followed by peace and reaction in the West. He serves as a convenient scale upon which to measure frontier potentialities.

Aaron Burr was still in middle life and a national figure, when his career was suddenly terminated in 1804. He rose to power and repute through his skill in walking the shady paths of New York politics. Here as an organizer of Jeffersonian principles he became a democratic leader whose practical grip upon the vote gave him as much influence as Jefferson possessed with his power over the minds of men. He could not attain this position without brushing more than once against the sterner side of Alexander Hamilton, who as Federalist leader of the State and confidant of Washington, held a national position superior to his own. There have been times when the rival bosses of New York politics have at heart been friends, and in collusion against the public, but between Hamilton and Burr there was deep distrust and a genuine contempt.

The prominence of Burr led to his downfall. In 1800 by agreement among the Jeffersonian leaders, he became Jefferson's mate upon the party ticket. Under the Constitution the electors would ballot for two names, and the one receiving the largest number of votes would become President. But when the Democratic-Republicans determined upon their candidates it was clear to all that Jefferson was the party choice for President. The victory of 1800 was sweeping. Jefferson and Burr received more votes than their Federalist opponents, but the party organization was so effective that every Jeffersonian elector voted for both Jefferson and Burr, with the result that there was a tie that could be settled only by an election in the House of Representatives. This defect in the Constitution was corrected by the Twelfth Amendment; but in 1800 the contest produced a stubborn fight whose sole foundation was the lack of principle of Burr. He knew that morally no one had voted for him for President and that the course of honor was to procure the immediate election of Jefferson by the House. He nevertheless allowed his friends, and he had many, to try to secure the coveted post for him. The House was divided, with the Federalist minority holding the balance of power, and with the personal enemy of Burr, Alexander Hamilton, holding the confidence of the Federalists. In the end, and through the efforts of Hamilton, Jefferson was seated; and to Hamilton is attributed the profound remark that though Jefferson had bad principles, Burr had none. Burr became Vice President, with his party turned against him because of his treachery, and with the personal antipathy to Hamilton deep and implacable.

On July 11, 1804, Burr killed Hamilton in a duel fought near the heights at Weehawken where there was a long established habit of settling such New York disputes. These contests were frequent enough in American life in the eighteenth century, and the accident of killing an opponent was one that might easily happen to any gentleman. It was inconvenient, but not incurable. But Aaron Burr was already notorious, and Hamilton was a great national figure. Instead of easy forgiveness, Burr found indictment for murder in both New York and New Jersey. After his disaster, dueling rapidly gave way before adverse public opinion, and he became a victim of a suddenly shifted standard of manners and ethics. He returned to Washington where as Vice President he was secure from actual molestation, but as his term of office reached completion, March 4, 1805, he was a man without a party or a home. He became a man without a country.

In prospecting for a field in which to spend his later years (Burr was just forty-nine when he left office), his attention turned toward the West, which was natural because of two reasons. Federalism and Alexander Hamilton were so unpopular there that the killing of Hamilton was no affront; and personal encounters lasted much longer on the frontier than in the East. McMaster records that a traveling showman, passed through Tennessee "exhibiting a wax figure of Burr as he appeared when he slew the leviathan of Federalism." There was here abundant opportunity for a man of resource and charm, and the affairs of Spain were so upset that almost anything might be made to happen.

Within a few days of the death of Hamilton it was suggested to Anthony Merry, the British minister in Washington, that measures for the rupture of the Union were under way. And in the ensuing months, Merry was led to believe that for a relatively small investment, £110,000 and the loan of a small fleet at New Orleans, England might procure this. A picture of a Mississippi Valley federation dazzled his eyes, and his dispatches to the British Foreign Office show how fully he desired authority to encourage Burr. The British Government was not to be caught in such behavior. There was no allusion in its instructions to Merry that the Burr dispatches had ever been received. And in the summer of 1806 Merry was mystified and chagrined to learn that he was to be allowed to come home on account of an ill health of which he was unaware.

The Spanish minister in Washington, the Marquis of Casa Yrujo, heard a different story. He thought he learned through an emmisary supposed to be from Burr that the long-expected attack upon New Spain was about to take place; and that for a consideration Burr would prevent the expedition from succeeding:—would sell it out, in short. Yrujo heard wild talk of kidnapping Jefferson as part of the performance.

It is hardly to be believed that Merry and Yrujo could have been right, and Burr honest either with them or the United States. But the uncertainties that follow from a perusal of the correspondence of the English and Spanish governments are made worse by the tales that appear to have been told by Burr or his friends to the leaders of the West. In the summer of 1805 Burr, now a private citizen made a trip to New Orleans by the river route. Ostensibly he was looking for a place to settle down, practice law, and start a western political career. He was received everywhere, and everywhere his personal magnetism overcame what doubts there were as to the legality or patriotism of his intentions. He found one western man of fortune who placed money at his disposal, Harmon Blennerhassett who lived in semi-feudal state on an island near Marietta in the Upper Ohio. Blennerhassett was dazzled by the idea of a career of conquest and a kingdom for Burr that should include the spoils of Spain, Louisiana and Mexico. And he saw himself ambassador at a European court.

What Burr said to the western politicians like Andrew Jackson, and Henry Clay, William Henry Harrison, and James Wilkinson can only be surmised. They may have thought it only a filibustering expedition at the expense of Spain, or a speculation in land titles on the Red River. They were not likely to have been interested in making a new king or emperor or in splitting the United States, now that the purchase of Louisiana had insured a western outlet to the sea. The evidence that exists is not enough to prove what Burr's intention was; but it is sufficient to establish the fact that to every hearer he told the story that he thought would interest. It has been common enough to speak of the Burr conspiracy and call it treason. Adams and McMaster, in their great histories, have leaned this way. McCaleb, who has made the most exhaustive study of the plot, holds that whatever was in Burr's concealed intent, it was not treason in the West. The looseness of the federal bond there had endangered the Union since the beginning, and it is doubtful whether many Americans had as yet taught themselves to believe that the Union must last forever. The natural lawlessness of the border regions and the old habit for intrigue for advantage at New Orleans made the West ripe for illicit ventures. But as soon as the leaders of opinion heard that Jefferson called it treason they backed out.

After his trip of 1805, Burr returned by sea to New

York and organized an expedition. He sent agents, some of whom talked too much, to arrange for building flatboats on the Ohio and to enlist adventurers to follow him down the Mississippi. The West in 1806 was filled with gossip about him, but if he was only proceeding against Spain there was no local feeling to block him. In the autumn he joined his parties, and in Kentucky was taken into court to explain himself. Henry Clay was his counsel, and convinced not only himself but the court that Burr had no evil intent. At Nashville it had to be explained again to Andrew Jackson; and Jackson, satisfied, continued to recruit for Burr. By December the party was again afloat, while Jefferson, now aroused by both his dislike of Burr and the rumors of military expeditions against Spain, issued a proclamation directing the conspirators to disband. The proclamation followed Burr down the Mississippi. In January, 1807, Burr abandoned his men and took to flight. James Wilkinson, who had been in his confidence and had appeared to be a part of the conspiracy, turned loyal. As commander of the army in the West, Wilkinson established a *modus vivendi* with Spain in November, 1806. He returned to New Orleans, warned Jefferson of danger, proclaimed martial law, and wrecked the effort. What he had promised Burr to do is not known; but what he did was to take the pose of savior of his country. The Spanish minister, Yrujo, commenting on the affair after the arrest of Burr, accused Wilkinson of treasonable desire, but loyalty to the Spanish Government that so long had pensioned him. Wilkinson would now, he prophesied, make application for special compensation for extraordinary service, "he has sacrificed Burr in order to obtain—advantages."

The Burr conspiracy collapsed, and neither the United States nor Spain suffered from it. But the ease with which Burr obtained Western aid for what was at best a shady venture, gives emphasis to the importance of the purchase of Louisiana as a means of holding the Union together. The separatist western spirit was dying, but by no means dead. The flame of national zeal, that in the next decade was to make a war with England unavoidable, was unlighted in 1803 and only beginning to burn in 1806.

With Burr arrested and on trial before John Marshall on charge of treason, the Mississippi Valley forgot this episode, and continued on its normal growth. The border territories, Mississippi, Orleans, Louisiana, Indiana, and Michigan, were increased by the creation of Illinois in 1809; and Louisiana, with some self-government after 1805, took the final steps towards the statehood guaranteed by the treaty of 1803.

The State of Louisiana was added to the Union April 30, 1812. From 1805 to 1811 Governor Claiborne and his subjects were in almost continuous open breach, there being few points at which the creole and the frontiersman could act in unison. The precedent established in the case of Ohio was followed by Congress, which passed an enabling act early in 1811, under which a convention met at New Orleans on November 4. The constitution of Louisiana was frankly based upon the second Kentucky constitution, framed in 1799. Although the French law that had prevailed in the former province was continued as the legal basis for the new State, the influences that were most vocal and effective were not French. The newly arrived immigrants from the southwest seized control of the new establishment. The convention met on the day upon which, at Washington, the new Congress convened to force war upon an unwilling President. Louisiana was an outpost in that war, and among the earliest measures preliminary to war was an enlargement of its territory to the northeast in the direction of Spanish Florida.

At the time of the Louisiana Purchase the United States raised the question whether the province included West Florida, but received no satisfaction from France.

The Gulf Shore was so important to the development of the Southwest, whose rivers crossed the Spanish strip, that the United States was bound to search for a theory that would include West Florida in Louisiana. The fact was that in 1762-1763 when France ceded Louisiana to Spain and England, the eastern boundary of the province extended to the region of the Perdido River, which now forms part of the eastern boundary of Alabama. England received from Spain in 1763 both Spanish Florida and the strip that Spain had just received from France. This became West Florida and was an administrative unit under England until 1783 and under Spain thereafter. The language of the treaty of 1803 referred to Louisiana as it was in 1800 in the hands of Spain, and as it had been in 1762 in the hands of France. By insisting upon the old French boundary, the United States made the point that West Florida ought to be included. By emphasizing the Louisiana that existed in 1800, Spain argued that West Florida was a thing apart.

The western end of West Florida reached the Mississippi between the thirty-first parallel and the River Iberville. Here American adventurers squatted before 1810, declared their independence of Spain, and invited annexation by the United States. Madison issued a proclamation in October, 1810, declaring that by purchase the United States extended as far east as the Perdido and directed Governor Claiborne to seize the territory as far as the Pearl River. On April 14, 1812, Congress added this tract to Louisiana; while that State entered the Union on April 30. A few days later, the rest of the strip, from the Pearl to the Perdido, was added to Mississippi Territory, thus bringing Mobile within American claim. General Wilkinson gave the claim reality a little later by occupying Mobile by force. The region that England might use as a military base against the United States was thereby somewhat reduced.

Jenkin Lloyd Jones

☼

ALTHOUGH Jenkin Lloyd Jones was born in a foreign land and died in a neighboring state, Wisconsin was his home much of the time during the years of his long life. He was born in Cardiganshire, Wales, November 14, 1843, and came to Wisconsin with his parents while an infant. He has said that he celebrated his first birthday anniversary by landing at Castle Garden which was then the receiving station for immigrants.

In 1845 the family came to Wisconsin and settled on a heavily timbered tract of land near Ixonia for which was paid $1.20 an acre. Many of the early settlers avoided the rich prairie lands because of a feeling that land that did not grow timber would not produce anything else. For ten years the Jones family battled with giant trees and massive boulders in an effort to clear the land; then with a conviction that their lot had not been cast in easy places, the Ixonia farm was sold and a tract of 400 acres was bought near the present village of Spring Green in Sauk county. On this farm Jenkin Lloyd Jones grew to young manhood, working on the farm summers and going to school during the winters. In 1862 he enlisted as an artilleryman in the Sixth Wisconsin Battery, and served until the end of the war. During the entire period of his military service, Mr. Jones kept a diary which survived the vicissitudes of war and time and was finally published in 1914 by the Wisconsin History Commission, under the title of *An Artilleryman's Diary*.

After the war ended Mr. Jones spent another year on the Spring Green farm; then entered Meadville (Pa.)

Theological Seminary from which he was graduated in 1870. For a year after his graduation he ministered to a church in Winnetka, Illinois, and then accepted the pastorate of All Souls Unitarian Church in Janesville, Wisconsin, where he remained until 1883. He then became pastor of All Souls Church in Chicago where he continued his ministry for thirty-two years. In 1909 the University of Wisconsin recognized the untiring service of the great preacher and writer by investing him with the degree of LL.D.

In 1890 Dr. Jones purchased the site of the once prosperous village of Helena which included the abandoned shot tower. Tower Hill became a summer seminary where Dr. Jones gathered around him tired teachers and preachers from all over the country who with him found rest and intellectual recreation. His death occurred September 12, 1918; his Tower Hill estate was given to the state and became a public park.

In addition to *An Artilleryman's Diary*, Dr. Jones wrote: *The Faith that Makes Faithful*, 1886; *Practical Piety*, 1890; *Bits of Wayside Gospel*, 1899; *Love and Loyalty*, 1907, and *On the Firing Line in the Battle for Sobriety*, 1910.

From AN ARTILLERYMAN'S DIARY, *by Jenkin Lloyd Jones. Published by the Wisconsin History Commission, 1914.*

CHATTANOOGA, Tuesday, May 2. (1865) The sun rose in all its majesty, promising a splendid day. After breakfast Landen and George Spencer were going on top of Lookout. They had a pass for three and invited me to go along. Having a great desire to visit, I was soon before the officer of the day, thence to Captain Hood, and the request was granted. With a loaf of bread and tin cup in my haversack, we started.

Delayed till 8 A. M. waiting for pass to go through

picket lines. Two miles brisk walking brought us to the base of the mountain which looked much more formidable there than from camp. We made the ascent on the military road which has been blasted and macadamized by Uncle Sam. It ran zigzag along the east slope of the hill, and not too steep to drive a team quite readily. Patiently we trudged along around massive piles of eternal rocks and past beautiful rustic springs of pure cold water, gushing from solid rocks, partly fixed by the hand of man for the accommodation of man and beast. The road was lined on both sides with heavy foliage of living green, with an occasional opening, through which we could look back on the map-like plat of Chattanooga, with its well-laid camps, and cool our heated brows with the cool refreshing breezes.

Up and up we go, ever and anon we pass a notice by the engineer, giving the elevation above the Tennessee and the distance up to the top. For over two hours we tugged upwards, our enthusiasm somewhat abated by the fatigue, but finally we reached the summit. A sentinel with white gloves and glistening brass, a "true regular" demanded to see our pass. We are now two miles or more from the point which overlooks the town. Here was quite a town called Summer Town with a large tavern, stables, etc. Evidently this was once a great pleasure resort in the summer season for the aristocracy. Here were also extensive hospital buildings erected by the U. S., accommodating I should judge, over 5000 sick. Also the camp of the Regular Brigade quartered here for over a year.

But time was precious and we pushed on toward the west side of the mountain which is about a mile and a half across, through a heavy growth of timber with a beautiful variety of wild flowers. Before noon we stood on the grounds where Hooker and his men won immortal fame in November, 1863. Directly beneath us we could see the remains of the camp in Lookout Valley. On the further side of the valley was a train of cars leaving Sequatchie Station, looking very diminutive like a child's plaything. On the parapet we walked around the craggy points towards the Point, passing several heavy lines of rebel earthworks. 'Tis astounding how men could ever fight on such precipitous rocks. By a most lovely spring gushing over the very brink we seated ourselves in the refreshing shade of a sycamore, and ate our dinner with keen relish.

Now we stood on the veritable point, 1600 feet above high water mark of the Tennessee, 200 feet straight down the rocks. The scene from this place was the grandest I have ever seen, and may be the most extensive I may ever see again. Chattanooga looked very regular and flat, Mission Ridge dwindled down to an apparent flat, and miles beyond it was but one flat ocean of green timber. Off to the east the eye could distinguish four distinct ranges of mountains beyond the Mission Ridge, the last being the obscure Smoky Mountains of North Carolina, undoubtedly sixty miles distant. To the northeast the view was much further, nothing to intercept the vision as far as the naked eye could reach. We could look over into Western Virginia and East Tennessee, and imagine all kinds of things of the human beings scattered along. To the west and north the eye had not as wide a range, the Cumberland Mountains being as high, if not higher, but could easily see Alabama in that way. Five different states of our now almost happy Union from one place. Watered by the creek-like Tennessee River, which made a double slant to the foot of the mountain, leaving the point of land on the opposite side in the exact shape of a huge foot, hence the name "Moccasin Point," where Thomas's batteries were so hotly engaged with Lookout during Bragg's siege.

Here we found a photograph gallery erected on the jut of a rock—takes pictures of objects on an adjoining point, $6.00 per dozen. He has many very beautiful plates of the mountain scenery, prominent among them is the Lula Falls and Lake about six miles south of the summit; but one day's furlough would not grant us the pleasure of visiting it, so we commenced the descent in the nearest direction, which appeared but a short distance. For awhile we went directly downward through the seam in the rock, then by aid of trees and shrubs we kept up with ourselves. Down, down we went, but yet no bottom, often obliged to rest. An hour's walk brought us to the bottom, and thankful for it. We wended our way to camp, tired but well satisfied with our excursion.

We reached camp by 5 P.M. Found everything quiet. Nobody mustered out as yet but much talk of it. 18th Ohio Battery and brigade of infantry taken to Dalton today by Steedman. I understand he has made several attempts at negotiations with rebel General Wofford, but failed. He is now to resort to strenuous measures.

Chattanooga, Wednesday, May 3. Went on guard last night at sunset, acting as corporal of the guard. Was on duty from 12 P.M. to 12 M. more fatiguing I think than to stand on post. Went to town this afternoon. Found the town guarded exclusively by negro troops, white troops retired this morning. They must intend to dispense with some of us soon. My health is good. News is sought with great eagerness. There are but few cents of money in the camp, and one paper often goes into every shanty.

Chattanooga, Thursday, May 4. A very hot, sultry day. Another battery drill this morning under Lieutenant Sweet. Still the excitement runs high. Grape-vine telegraph is very productive. Every hour through the day has its "special items." Bets run high, with stakes mostly "something good to eat" after the "muster out." The situation is yet unclouded, and I can see nothing to prevent us from being sent home soon. Bathed in the Tennessee River in the evening, drilled on the gun after supper. Looks like rain, hope it will and cool the air.

Chattanooga, Friday, May 5. No rain to cool the terrible air or lay the dust, which flies in heavy clouds, reminding one very vividly of old Spring Green prairie. Have been very busy all day, could not find time to write a letter. 7 A.M. went out for brigade drill by Major Mendenhall, but he did not come, so we had an interesting drill of our own. A. Sweet is bringing the Company up to its old Rienzi standard in drilling. Great strife among the detachments, both trying to come into battery first. Second piece is ready first every time. Returned to camp by 11, another hour in column to water and back.

After dinner went out to Mission Ridge after wood, two wagons and four men. At the picket post our gallant driver took up two of the fair ones, who after enjoying their quid of tobacco silently for a mile or so, said the ride "holped 'em right smart." Drilled two hours after supper. Ration day. Drew two day's rations of bread and three of hardtack, no more soft bread to be issued. They want us to eat the surplus hard-tack. This is considered significant.

* * * * *

(Jenkin Lloyd Jones wrote his diary, of which the above is an extract, while almost a boy. He was seventeen years of age when he enlisted and twenty-one when he was mustered out.)

Increase A. Lapham

☼

I. A. LAPHAM, naturalist and archaeologist, was born at Palmyra, New York, March 7, 1811. He came to Milwaukee in 1836 where he became a real estate dealer. He seems not to have given all his time to business, for he made an exhaustive study of the resources of Wisconsin, possibly as an aid to his sales of land. Nothing seemed to escape his attention; the flora, the fauna, the geography and topography, the soil values of the new territory, all were carefully noted, and in 1844 were published under the title of *Geographical and Topographical Description of Wisconsin*. This little book, now so rare that a copy is a curiosity, was instrumental in bringing to Wisconsin many settlers from New York and New England; it was the only published guide to the translake region. Later Dr. Lapham devoted much time to Wisconsin archaeology, and especially to the mapping and description of Indian earthworks. The result of this investigation appeared in 1855 as *Antiquities of Wisconsin*. He was chief geologist of the state from 1873 to 1875. He died at Oconomowoc, September 14, 1875.

From "GEOGRAPHICAL AND TOPOGRAPHICAL DESCRIPTION OF WISCONSIN," *by I. A. Lapham. Published by P. C. Hale, Milwaukee, Wisconsin, 1844.*

THE Territory of Wisconsin, as established at present, is bounded as follows: commencing in the middle of Lake Michigan, in north latitude forty-two degrees and thirty minutes; thence north along the middle of the Lake to a point opposite the main channel or entrance of Green

Bay; thence through said channel and Green Bay to the mouth of the Menomonee river; thence through the middle of the main channel of said river to that head nearest the Lake of the Desert; thence in a direct line to the middle of said Lake; thence through the middle of the main channel of the Montreal river to its mouth; thence with a direct line across Lake Superior to where the Territorial line of the United States last touches said Lake northwest; thence along said Territorial line to a point due north of the head waters or source of the Mississippi river, supposed to be in longitude ninety-six degrees and two minutes west from Greenwich; thence due south to the head waters of the Mississippi; thence along the middle or center of the main channel of said river to latitude forty-two degrees and thirty minutes north; thence due east to the place of beginning. It therefore embraces all that portion of the United States lying between the State of Michigan on the east, and the Mississippi on the west, which separates it from the Territory of Iowa; and between the State of Illinois on the south and the British possessions on the north; extending from forty-two and a half, to the forty-ninth degree of north latitude, and embracing about ten degrees of longitude. Taking the length of a degree of latitude and longitude in this part of the globe, it is ascertained that Wisconsin is about five hundred and fifteen miles from east to west, and four hundred and forty-nine miles from north to south, measuring from the extreme points. But the average or mean extent of the Territory in longitude is only about four and one third degrees, or two hundred and six or seven miles, showing a superficial area of about ninety-three thousand square miles or sections, or nearly twenty-six hundred townships of six miles square each. Wisconsin is, therefore, more than one half larger than Virginia, (the largest state in the Union), and more than twice as large as the State of New York. This calculation, however, is only an approximation to the truth, for so little is accurately known of the course of the Menomonee, Montreal, and a part of the Mississippi rivers, that no accurate estimate can be made of the extent of territory embraced within the limits of Wisconsin. The Menomonee has been ascertained to have a course very different from what was supposed, at the time it was selected as a part of the boundary; and a revision of that portion of the boundary between Michigan and Wisconsin which lies between Green Bay and Lake Superior becomes necessary, and will probably soon receive the action of Congress. A survey was made in 1840 and 1841 by Captain Cram, and it now only remains for Congress to decide upon the exact boundary. The Wasecota, a branch of the Menomonee, is ascertained to have its source nearest the Lake of the Desert, and will therefore probably be established as part of the boundary.

Wisconsin being a part of the "Territory of the United States northwest of the Ohio river," claims, and indeed, Congress has by direct action, confirmed to her all the rights and privileges secured by the ordinance of Congress of July 13, 1787, one of which is, "that Congress shall have the authority to form one or two States in that part of said territory which lies north of an east and west line drawn through the southerly end or extreme of Lake Michigan"; thereby fixing unalterably (without common consent) the southern boundaries of Michigan and Wisconsin. Notwithstanding this plain provision of the ordinance, which is declared to be "articles of compact between the original States, and the people and States in the said territory, and forever to remain unalterable unless by common consent," yet Congress in establishing the boundaries of the State of Illinois, extended that State about sixty miles north of the line thus unalterably established by the ordinance. This is claimed to be obviously unjust and contrary to the spirit and letter of the compact with the original States. The subject of reclaiming this portion of our territory has been agitated in the Legislative Assembly, and it is probable that Wisconsin will insist upon her rights when she is admitted into the Union as an independent State. Michigan was compelled by superior influence to submit to a compromise by which she obtained, besides other valuable considerations, a much larger portion of territory than that in dispute; and Wisconsin may from the same cause be obliged to submit to wrong for want of ability to enforce her rights.

It is also contended by many that the portion of country set off to Michigan on Lake Superior, between the straits of Mackina and the Montreal river, as a compensation in part, for the strip of land given to Ohio from her southern border, should also have constituted a portion of Wisconsin; and especially as Michigan never made the least claim to it, and as the convenience of the inhabitants (when it becomes inhabited) will be best consulted by uniting them with Wisconsin. The validity of our claim to this territory however, may be questioned; for it cannot be made out as clearly as in the case of territory given to Illinois.

The difficulties which it has been apprehended might at some future time arise between the United States and Great Britain relative to that portion of our northern boundary lying between Lake Superior and the Lake of the Woods, have been prevented by the settlement of that question in the treaty of 1842, usually known as "Webster's Treaty." Great Britain claimed all that portion of our Territory lying north of the St. Louis river, while we claimed that the Kamanistaquia, or Dog river should be the boundary. By the treaty, an intermediate route was agreed upon; and here again it is contended that the general government has given away a portion of the territory which should properly have belonged to Wisconsin.

It is not probable that Illinois, Michigan, and Great Britain will be very ready to surrender the territory now claimed by them, and hence it becomes an important question to determine in what manner these disputes shall be settled. As in all cases of a similar nature, we may expect some difficulties to arise. It has been proposed in the Legislature to abandon all claims of this kind, upon condition that Congress shall construct certain works of internal improvement which are at present very much needed; and if the whole subject can be thus easily disposed of, it is undoubtedly the best policy for the United States to accept of this very reasonable compromise.

It is to be hoped that these questions of boundary may be settled to the satisfaction of all concerned, before they become of such importance as to create much excitement, trouble or difficulty in their adjustment.

There are no mountains, properly speaking, in Wisconsin; the whole being one vast plain, varied only by river hills, and the gentle swells or undulations of country usually denominated "rolling." This plain lies at an elevation of from six to fifteen hundred feet above the level of the ocean. The highest lands are those forming the dividing ridge between the waters of Lake Superior and the Mississippi. From this ridge there is a gradual descent toward the south and southwest. This inclination is interrupted in the region of the lower Wisconsin and Neenah rivers, where we find another ridge extending across the Territory, from which proceeds another gently descending slope, drained mostly by the waters of Rock river and its branches. These slopes indicate, and are occasioned by the dip or inclination of the rocky strata beneath the soil. The Wisconsin hills and many of the bluffs along the Mississippi river, often attain the height of three hundred feet above their base, and the Blue Mound was ascertained by Dr. Locke, by barometrical observations, to be one thousand feet above the Wisconsin river at Helena. The surface is further diversified by the Platte and Sinsinawa Mounds, but these prominent elevations are so rare that they form very marked objects in the landscape, and serve the traveller in the unsettled portions of the country, as guides by which to direct his course. The country immediately bordering on Lake Superior has a very abrupt descent toward the lake; hence the streams entering that lake are full of rapids and waterfalls, being comparatively worthless for all purposes of navigation, but affording a vast superabundance of water power, which may at some future time be brought into requisition to manufacture lumber from the immense quantities of pine trees with which this part of the Territory abounds.

There is another ridge of very broken land running from the entrance of Green Bay in a southwesterly direction, forming the "divide" between the waters of Lake Michigan and those running into the Bay and Neenah, and continuing thence through the western part of Washington county, crossing Bark river near the Nagowicka lake, and thence passing in the same general direction, through Walworth county into the State of Illinois. The very irregular and broken appearance of this ridge is probably owing to the soft and easily decomposed limestone rock of which it is composed.

On our northern border is Lake Superior, the largest body of fresh water in the world, and on the east is Lake Michigan, second only to Lake Superior in magnitude, forming links in the great chain of inland seas by which we are connected with the "lower country" by a navigation as important for all purposes of commerce as the ocean itself. Besides these immense lakes, Wisconsin abounds in those of smaller size, scattered profusely over her whole surface. They are from one to twenty or thirty miles in extent. Many of them are the most beautiful that can be imagined—the water deep and of crystal clearness and purity, surrounded by sloping hills and promontories covered with scattered groves and clumps of trees. Some are of a more picturesque kind, being more rugged in their appearance, with steep, rocky bluffs, crowned with cedar, hemlock, spruce and other evergreen trees of a similar character. Perhaps a small rocky island will vary the scene, covered with a conical mass of vegetation, the low shrubs and bushes being arranged around the margin, and the tall trees in the center. These lakes usually abound in fish of various kinds, affording food for the pioneer settler; and among the pebbles on their shores may occasionally be found fine specimens of agate, carnelian, and other precious stones. In the bays where the water is shallow and but little affected by the winds, the wild rice (*Zizania aquatica*) grows in abundance, affording subsistence for the Indian, and attracting innumerable water birds to these lakes. The rice has never been made use of by the settlers in Wisconsin as an article of food, although at some places it affords one of the principal means of support for the red men. It is said to be about equal to oat-meal in its qualities, and resembles it in some degree in taste. The difficulty of collecting it, and its inferior quality, will always prevent its use by white men, except in cases of extreme necessity. The Lake of the Woods, and Rainy Lake, near our north boundary, have been so often described as to need only to be mentioned here. Their thousand small wooded islands give them a peculiarly interesting and picturesque character not to be found in any other scenery in the world. Among the small lakes may be mentioned Lake Winnebago, St. Croix (upper and lower), Cass Lake, Lake Pepin, The Four Lakes, the Mille Lac, Ottawa, Pewaugan, Pewaukee, Geneva, Green, Koshkonong, and many others, all more fully described in another part of this work.

The Mississippi, the great river of rivers, forms, as before remarked, the western boundary of Wisconsin. It is augmented in this Territory by the waters of the Wisconsin, Black, Chippewa, St. Croix and St. Francis rivers, which alone would be sufficient to form a very respectable "Father of Waters," but which do not perceptably swell the mighty flood of the Mississippi; these with Rock river, which empties into the Mississippi in Illinois, and the St. Louis, Bois Brule, Mauvaise and Montreal rivers, tributaries of Lake Superior; and the Menomonee, Fox or Neenah, Wolf and Milwaukee rivers, tributaries of Lake Michigan, are the principal rivers in Wisconsin. Innumerable smaller streams and branches run through the whole extent of the Territory, so that no portion of it is without an abundant supply of good, and generally pure water. The Mississippi is navigable as far up as the Falls of St. Anthony. The Wisconsin is navigable as far up as the Portage by small steamboats, at certain seasons of the year; and they have been up Rock river as far as Aztalan, in Jefferson County, but these streams are comparatively of little value for purposes of navigation. All the principal rivers are, however, navigable for canoes. Their waters usually originate in springs and lakes of pure and cold water. Many of them, especially in the northern or primitive region, are precipitated over rocky barriers, forming beautiful cascades or rapids, and affording valuable sites for mills and manufactures of all kinds. The Falls of St. Anthony, on the Mississippi, seven miles above the mouth of the St. Peters, are only surpassed by the great Niagara, in picturesque beauty and grandeur; and are now becoming a place of fashionable resort for summer tourists.

The rivers running into the Mississippi take their rise in the vicinity of the sources of those running into the lakes, and they often originate in the same lake or swamp, so that the communication from the Mississippi to the lakes is rendered comparatively easy at various points.

The greatest depression in the dividing ridge in the Territory is supposed to be at Fort Winnebago, where the Wisconsin river approaches within half a mile of the Neenah, and where, at times of high water, canoes have actually passed across from one stream to the other. Some of the rivers are supplied from the tamarack swamps, from which the water takes a dark color.

Eliza R. Scidmore

☼

ELIZA R. SCIDMORE, writer and traveler, was born in Madison, Wisconsin, October 14, 1856, died in Geneva, Switzerland, November 3, 1928. She wrote a number of books descriptive of the Far East. For many years she lived in Japan where her brother, George H. Scidmore, was in the consular service. Miss Scidmore was at the time of her death, foreign secretary of the National Geographic Society with which she became associated in 1890.

Among her published books are: *Alaska, The Southern Coast and the Sitkan Archipelago*, 1885; *Jinrikisha Days in Japan*, 1890; *Guide to Alaska and the Northwest Coast*, 1890; *Westward to the Far East; From East to West; Java, the Garden of the East*, 1897; *China, the Long Lived Empire*, 1900; *Winter India*, 1903; and *As the Hague Ordains*, 1907.

JAVA, THE GARDEN OF THE EAST, *by Eliza Ruhamah Scidmore, Published by The Century Co., New York, 1898. By permission of the publishers.*

IN "JAVA MAJOR"

IN the earliest morning a clean white lighthouse on an islet was seen ahead, and as the sun rose, bluish mountains came up from the sea, grew in height, outlined themselves, and then stood out, detached volcanic peaks of most lovely lines, against the purest, pale-blue sky; soft clouds floated up and clung to the summits; the blue and green at the water's edge resolved itself into groves and lines of palms;

and over sea and sky and the wonderland before us was all the dewy freshness of dawn in Eden. It looked very truly the "gem" and the "pearl of the East," this "Java Major" of the ancients, and the Djawa of the native people, which has called forth more extravagant praise and had more adjectives expended on it than any other one island in the world. Yet this little continent is only 666 miles long and from 56 to 135 miles wide, and on an area of 49,197 square miles (nearly the same as that of the State of New York) supports a population of 24,000,000, greater than that of all the other islands of the Indian Ocean put together. With 1600 miles of coast-line, it has few harbors, the north shore being swampy and flat, with shallows extending far out, while the southern coast is steep and bold, and the one harbor of Tjilatjap breaks the long line of surf where the Indian Ocean beats against the southern cliffs. Fortunately, hurricanes and typhoons are unknown in the waters around this "summer land of the world," and the seasons have but an even, regular change from wet to dry in Java. From April to October the dry monsoon blows from the southeast, and brings the best weather of the year—dry, hot days and the coolest nights. From October to April the southwest or wet monsoon blows. Then every day has its afternoon shower, the air is heavy and stifling, all the tropic world is asteam and astew and afloat, vegetation is magnificent, insect life triumphant, and the mountains are hidden in nearly perpetual mist. There are heavy thunder-storms at the turn of the monsoon, and the one we had watched from the sea the Hallowe'en night before our arrival had washed earth and air until the foliage glistened, the air fairly sparkled, nature wore her most radiant smiles, and the tropics were ideal.

It was more workaday and prosaic when the ship, steaming in between long breakwaters, made fast to the stone quays of Tandjon Priok, facing a long line of corrugated-iron warehouses, behind which was the railway connecting the port with the city of Batavia. The gradual silting up of Batavia harbor after an eruption of Mount Salak in 1699, which first dammed and then sent torrents of mud and sand down the Tjiliwong River, finally obliged commerce to remove to this deep bay six miles farther east, where the colonials have made a model modern harbor, at a cost of twenty-six and a half million gulden, all paid from current revenues, without the island's ceasing to pay its regular tribute to the crown of Holland. The customs officers at Tandjon Priok were courteous and lenient, passing our tourist luggage with the briefest formality, and kindly explaining how our steamer-chairs could be stored in the railway rooms until our return to port. It is but nine miles from the Tandjon Priok wharf to the main station in the heart of the original city of Batavia—a stretch of swampy ground dotted and lined with palm-groves and banana-patches, with tiny woven baskets of houses perched on stilts clustered at the foot of tall cocoa-trees that are the staff and source of life and of every economical blessing of native existence. We leaped excitedly from one side of the little car to the other, to see each more and more tropical picture; groups of bare brown children frolicking in the road, and mothers with babies astride of their hips, or swinging comfortably in a scarf knotted across one shoulder, and every-day life going on under the palms most naturally, although to our eyes it was so strange and theatrical.

* * * * *

No Europeans live at Tandjon Priok, nor in the old city of Batavia, which from the frightful mortality during two centuries was known as "the graveyard of Europeans." The banks and business houses, the Chinese and Arab towns, are in the "old town"; but Europeans desert that quarter before sundown, and betake themselves to the "new town" suburbs, where every house is in a park of its own, and the avenues are broad and straight, and all the distances are magnificent. The city of Batavia, literally "fair meadows," grandiloquently "the queen of the East," and without exaggeration "the gridiron of the East," dates from 1621, when the Dutch removed from Bantam, where quarrels between Portuguese, Javanese, and the East India Company had been disturbing trade for fifteen years, and built Fort Jacatra at the mouth of a river off which a cluster of islands sheltered a fine harbor. Its position in the midst of swamps was unhealthy, and the mortality was so appalling as to seem incredible. Dutch records tell of 87,000 soldiers and sailors dying in the government hospital between 1714 and 1776, and of 1,119,375 dying at Batavia between 1730 and August, 1752—a period of twenty-two years and eight months. The deadly Java fever occasioning this seemingly incredible mortality was worst between the years 1733 and 1738, during which time 2000 of the Dutch East India Company's servants and free Christians died annually. Staunton, who visited Batavia with Lord Macartney's embassy in 1793, called it the "most unwholesome place in the universe," and "the pestilential climate" was considered a sufficient defense against attack from any European power.

The people were long in learning that those who went to the higher suburbs to sleep, and built houses of the most open construction to admit of the fullest sweep of air, were free from the fever of the walled town, surrounded by swamps, cut by stagnant canals, and facing a harbor whose mud-banks were exposed at low tide. The city walls were destroyed at the beginning of this century by the energetic Marshal Daendels, who began building the new town. The quaint old air-tight Dutch buildings were torn down, and streets were widened; and there is now a great out-spread town of red-roofed, whitewashed houses, with no special features or picturesqueness to make its street-scenes either distinctly Dutch or tropical. Modern Batavia had 111,763 inhabitants on December 31, 1894, less than a tenth of whom are Europeans, with 26,776 Chinese and 72,934 natives. While the eighteenth-century Stadhuis might have been brought from Holland entire, a steam tramway starts from its door and thence shrieks its way to the farthest suburb, the telephone "hellos" from center to suburb, and modern inventions make tropical living possible.

The Dutch do not welcome tourists, nor encourage one to visit their paradise of the Indies. Too many travelers have come, seen, and gone away to tell disagreeable truths about Dutch methods and rule; to expose the source and means of the profitable returns of twenty million dollars and more for each of so many years of the last and the preceding century—all from islands whose whole area only equals that of the State of New York. Although the tyrannic rule and the "culture system," or forced labor, are things of the dark past, the Dutch brain is slow and suspicious, and the idea being fixed fast that no stranger comes to Java on kindly or hospitable errands, the colonial authorities must know within twenty-four hours why one visits the Indies. They demand one's name, age, religion, nationality, place of nativity, and occupation, the name of the ship that brought the suspect to Java, and the name of its captain —a dim threat lurking in this latter query of holding the unlucky mariner responsible should his importation prove an expense or embarrassment to the island. Still another permit—a *toelatings-kaart*, or "admission ticket"—must be obtained if one wishes to travel farther than Buitenzorg, the cooler capital, forty miles away in the hills. The tourist pure and simple, the sight-seer and pleasure traveler, is not yet quite comprehended, and his passports usually accredit him as traveling in the interior for "scientific purposes." Guides or efficient couriers in the real sense do not exist yet. The English-speaking servant is rare and delusive, yet a necessity unless one speaks Dutch or Low Malay. Of all the countries one may ever travel in, none equals Java in the difficulty of being understood; and it is a question, too, whether the Malays who do not know any English are harder to get along with than the Dutch who know a little.

Thirty years ago Alfred Russel Wallace inveighed against the unnecessary discomforts, annoyances, and expense of travel in Java, and every tourist since has repeated his plaint. The philippics of returned travelers furnish steady amusement for Singapore residents; and no one brings back the same enthusiasm that embarked with him. It is not the Java of the Javanese that these returned ones berate so vehemently, but the Netherlands India, and the state created and brought about by the merciless, cold-blooded, rapacious Hollanders who came half-way round the world and down to the equator, nine thousand miles away from their homes, to acquire an empire and enslave a race, and who impose their hampering customs and restrictions upon even alien visitors. Java undoubtedly is "the very finest and most interesting tropical island in the world," and the Javanese the most gentle, attractive, and innately refined people of the East, after the Japanese; but the Dutch in Java "beat the Dutch" in Europe ten points to one, and there is nothing so surprising and amazing, in all man's proper study of mankind, as this equatorial Hollander transplanted from the cold fens of Europe; nor is anything so strange as the effect of a high temperature on Low-Country temperament. The most rigid, conventional, narrow, thrifty, prudish, and Protestant people in Europe bloom out in the forcing-house of the tropics into strange laxity, and one does not know the Hollanders until one sees them in this "summer land of the world," whither they threatened to emigrate in a body during the time of the Spanish Inquisition.

Edward Alsworth Ross

☼

EDWARD A. ROSS, widely known as a sociologist, educator and writer, was born at Virden, Illinois, December 12, 1866. After completing his undergraduate work at Coe College in 1886, Mr. Ross studied at Johns Hopkins and at Berlin. Prior to his association with the University of Wisconsin in 1906, he had been professor of sociology at Leland Stanford Jr. University, 1893-1900, and at the University of Nebraska, 1901-1906. Since 1906 Professor Ross has been a resident of Wisconsin except for the periods spent in foreign countries while accumulating first-hand the materials for his books. Among his best known works are: *Honest Dollars*, 1896; *Social Control*, 1901; *The Changing Chinese*, 1915; *The Old World in the New*, 1914; *South of Panama*, 1915; and *Russia in Upheaval*, 1918.

From SOUTH OF PANAMA, *by Edward Alsworth Ross, Ph.D., LL.D. Published by The Century Co., New York, 1915. By permission of the publishers.*

CHAPTER VIII
MORALS

"WE are thinking of having our telephone taken out," remarked an American in Buenos Aires. "When the operator is tired she will ignore your call or else report '*ocupado*' when, in fact, the number you want is free. She finds it easier to lie than to connect you." "And incivility," I asked, "much complaint on that score?" "No," he replied; "central is never impertinent."

This brings out one aspect of Spanish-American manners; the other appears in the creole station agent of an English railway in Argentina. Owing to a closed switch two trains had collided at his station with great loss of life. Questioned as to why the switch had not been opened after he had received notice of the meeting of the trains at his station, he replied, "The switchman was sick abed and there were no other peons about." "But why didn't you throw the switch yourself?" "I? Why I am the station agent. How should I do it? One has his dignity to consider."

The old social order of the colonial era fostered courtesy; and now that privileged classes are gone and good manners have been generalized, society is the richer for the vanished régime. In the manner of muleteer, of field peon, even of negro longshoreman there is something of the old time deference. Yet underneath it there is no servility but rather a democratic sense of personal worth which will stand abuse from no one.

The Peruvians, being nearest to Lima, the chief radiant point of Spanish influence, have probably been more affected by Old World *cortesia* than any other South Americans. One happy result is their comparative freedom from brawls. In five months Harry Franck, the traveler, had seen but one fracas. Even in their cups men do not quarrel. Since each knows the right thing to do and say in every situation, there is little friction. Among Americans how many brawls arise from misunderstandings! But when peaceful intent is made known in conventional forms misunderstandings are rare.

There are probably two reasons why ordinary Americans are so lacking in manners. One is the continuous westward movement causing the perpetual recurrence of rude frontier conditions. The other is the sudden growth of a feeling of independence in multitudes of immigrants from the humbler strata of Europe. The old American, as you find him in the South, knows that there is a politeness for equals as well as a feudal politeness. But the immigrants soon drop their native manners as servile and think by roughness and surliness to express the spirit of the true democrat.

The courtesy of the South Americans of the upper class warms the heart of the stranger. Lie overnight in a village and next morning the gobernador and his friends will ride with you a couple of miles. After you have stopped a few days in a town several persons you have met will be at the station to see you off. If you are ill the faithfulness of your friends of a day or two in calling and inquiring about you is a real solace. On shipboard the South American passengers are the most approachable, the quickest to reach a footing of good fellowship. Friends embrace on meeting or parting and one soon ceases to object to it. Even business communications are not pared down to bare utility. An Ecuador merchant wants the steamer to pick up his coffee, so he wires up the coast:

Senor Capitan del Vapor Manavi—

I salute you most affectionately. I have five hundred sacks afloat and ready.

Your affectionate friend,

Concha.

An American would wire:
Five hundred sacks afloat.

Smith.

It is easy to belittle such demonstrativeness as empty form but I believe such depreciation is unjust. These people are affectionate in the family, and seem to carry out some of this warm-heartedness to their relatives and friends. In tropical South America people are good to their friends, and their warmth of manner is not a mask.

An American lady in Lima probably hit the bull's eye with the shrewd remark, "The Peruvian women being so *simpatica* and affectionate in manner are charming friends, though of course you *can't depend upon them in a tight place*."

Generous these people are but their generosity is for family and friends, not often for a cause or for the common good. "Altruism," said a minister, as we surveyed the glorious scenery from a peak above Quito, "scarcely exists here. I have never known of more than two or three Ecuadoreans working for the public interest. Rich men do not consider ways of serving their fellows. In an emergency everybody looks to government to provide relief. The recent bequest by a woman of $60,000.00 for the benefit of superannuated Indian female servants is the only philanthropic gift I have heard of in five years."

"Ordinary Peruvians," declared a Lima sociologist, "are affectionate and generous in disposition but care nothing for the general welfare. Theirs is a life of egoism tempered by affection." Nor is the Bolivian any better. "In my thirty years here," said a German merchant, "not once have I known a rich man to give five *centavos* for education although they do leave money for hospitals and orphanages,"—which tallies with the statement of an educator, "I have never known a rich Bolivian to give a penny to a public utility, such as a school."

A Chilean of American ancestry illustrated the egoism of the Chileans by the fact that when, as not infrequently happens, a country house is attacked by bandits, the neighbors do not rush to the aid of the beleaguered but each barricades himself in his own house. Nor does it occur to them to form a *posse* to pursue the bandits. They leave that to the police.

* * * * *

The South Europeans are proverbially sober, so wherever in South America the Spanish element predominates there is little hard drinking. The poens of the pampas gamble recklessly but drink little. Wassail is by no means as rife among the students of the University of Buenos Aires as it is in our own universities. Said a young Argentine, "When we are planning a banquet it makes a great difference to us whether or not there are to be foreigners among the guests. The presence of foreigners obliges us to add from a third to a half to the cost of the banquet in order to provide liquors." Still, even Iberic sobriety is not fool-proof. In the ports the native born are affected by the customs of the foreign element. In Guayaquil there are twenty bars where there was one forty years ago and within the last ten years the consumption of spirits has increased fifty per cent, chiefly owing to the spread of the brandy-and-soda habit. In the University Club at Lima the outstanding feature is not the two or three pieces of gymnastic apparatus, the baths—which are noticeable by their absence—or the locked and unused library, but the large and varied display of bottled goods at the bar.

The victims of alcohol on the West Coast are chiefly the natives and mestizos, who crave it as the North American Indians craved firewater. Drinking makes the holiday or feast for the natives and is becoming worse as rum from the sugar plantations displaces their ancient *chicha*. The Peruvians of the interior drink to a serious extent. In every little town is a *bodega* or two stocked to the ceiling with bottles of many colors. Aside from hard goods there is nothing to slake thirst but ditch water. The lack of soft drink is a misfortune, for I am sure a thousand soda fountains well placed would work a moral revolution in Peru.

* * * * *

It is impossible to exaggerate the ravages of alcohol among the half-Indian masses. Often the husband drinks up all he earns and the woman by her labor supports the children. Encina declares, "With few exceptions the Chilean laborer gambles away or drinks up most of his wages." Fortunately, the women almost never drink. There is no instruction of school children in temperance and, so far, moral suasion has had little effect. The lack of diversions in the rural districts makes it very hard to wean the country folk from their liquor. Compulsive social action is needed but the great vineyardists are politically powerful enough to prevent it. The law forbidding the sale of liquor within 650 feet of a school is often ignored. The employers are against alcohol so far as it lowers the efficiency of labor, but they set no example of temperance.

Paul Samuel Reinsch

☆

PAUL S. REINSCH is another of Wisconsin's writers and educators who never had a permanent residence outside his native state. He was born in Milwaukee, June 10, 1870, was graduated from the University of Wisconsin, 1892, and from the law department of the university, 1894. For some time thereafter, he studied abroad. In 1899 Mr. Reinsch became assistant professor of political science at the University of Wisconsin, and was elected full professor in 1901, a position he filled with distinction until 1913. At this time, Dr. Reinsch, an ardent admirer of President Woodrow Wilson, was appointed United States Minister to China. His diplomatic services in this Far Eastern field continued until 1919 when he tendered his resignation, returned to the United States and engaged in law practice. The next year he became counsellor to the Chinese government. He died in Shanghai, China, January 24, 1923. Dr. Reinsch was one of the foremost authorities in the United States on Oriental affairs. His published works include: *The Common Law in the Early American Colonies*, 1899; *World Politics at the End of the Nineteenth Century as Influenced by the Oriental Situation*, 1900; *Colonial Government*, 1902; *Colonial Administration*, 1905; *American Legislatures and Legislative Methods*, 1907; *Intellectual Currents in the Far East*, 1911; *International Unions*, 1911; *An American Diplomat in China*, 1913-19, 1922; and *Secret Diplomacy*, 1922.

In the untimely death of Dr. Reinsch, Wisconsin lost one of its most eminent sons; while the world of diplomacy and letters joined with his native state in mourning the loss of an international character.

From AMERICAN LEGISLATURES AND LEGISLATIVE METHODS, *by Paul S. Reinsch. Published by The Century Company, New York, 1907. By permission of the publishers.*

CHAPTER VI

Procedure in State Legislatures

LEGISLATIVE procedure among our many commonwealths, while subject to infinite modification and diversity of detail, most generally follows along the line of a certain recognized practice common in substance to almost all our state legislatures. The first step in the process of actual lawmaking occurs when the bill is presented to the house, endorsed with the title and the name of its sponsor. In usual procedure, the introduction of bills takes place at the time appointed in the order of business for the day. A member rising in his place and obtaining recognition, begs leave to introduce a bill. This being tacitly granted, the bill is sent by a page to the clerk who reads the bill by title, upon which the officer presiding announces the first reading of the bill. In most legislative bodies a second reading and announcement immediately follow. However the constitution and usage in some states call for separate readings on different days. Upon the second reading of the bill, it is assigned to such committee as may seem appropriate, in the House of Representatives or Assembly by the speaker, in the Upper House by the lieutenant-governor or president of the Senate. At times reference to some particular committee is made at the request or suggestion of the member introducing the bill. After due consideration, if a favorable view is taken, the committee reports the bill back to the house, together with its recommendations thereon. If unfavorable the committee rarely reports.* Sometimes the committee reports a recommendation simply for passage, indefinite postponement, reference to some other committee, etc.; or, in other instances, it may report various amendments or make a detailed statement. In case of the report failing to satisfy the house, a motion may be passed to recommit, with or without instructions. A bill may be recommitted at any time previous to its passage. The local legislatures have not to any great extent followed their national prototype in a frequent use of the Committee of the Whole. While it may be convened upon the request of a certain portion of the members present (usually one-sixth), its use is of comparatively rare occurence.

The bill, once reported, is usually placed upon the calendar for the succeeding legislative day under the title of "Bills ready for engrossment and third reading." At this stage the bill is subject to general discussion and amendment on the floor. If the bill is by the house ordered to be engrossed and read a third time, the clerk passes it over to the proper officials for engrossment. This function is ordinarily performed by the engrossing and comparing clerks, whose duty it is carefully to prepare the engrossment and make certain that it is correct in phraseology and exactly similar to the original bill as amended. Their work is usually checked and supervised by a Committee on Engrossed Bills. The usage in many states permits that whenever a bill, fairly written or printed without interlineation or erasure, is without amendment ordered to be engrossed for a third reading, it may be reported to the house as the engrossed bill. The neglect of enforcing the provisions for careful examination and supervision of engrossment and enrolment, at

---

*In the Wisconsin legislature all bills referred to a committee must be reported back to the house in which they originated. This prevents bills from being "smothered" by hostile committees.

times permits the creeping in of error and misconstruction, through careless or unscrupulous action of subordinates. After engrossment the bill goes to its third reading, on which occasion it receives the final test in the house prior to passage. The progress of the bill may be hastened by its being made a special order for a certain day. This object is also facilitated by the widespread use of the suspension of the rules, particularly in the final days of the session. Once having successfully accomplished its passage through one house, the bill is taken to the other chamber together with a special message announcing its passage. Here, having been read twice by title, it is referred to the appropriate committee, and treated in a fashion similar to that of bills originating in this house. Upon decisive action being taken, a message is sent to the originating house announcing the fact of concurrence or amendment.

Should the bill receive favorable action in both houses, the concurring body returns the bill to that in which it originated, where it is given into the charge of the enrolling clerk, who makes a proper copy of the same. It is the function of the Committee on Enrolled Bills to supervise the making of the new copy and the comparing of it with the engrossed bill. When the copy has been made in a satisfactory manner, the members of this committee report the bill back to their house. The engrossed bill remains filed with the clerk of the originating house; while the enrolled bill receives his endorsement, as well as the signatures of the presiding officer of each body. Then the clerk sends the enrolled bill to the governor for his approval or veto. In some states, the bill may by joint resolution of the two houses be recalled from the governor for reconsideration. The approval of the Executive is commonly expressed by his signature, and is followed by a message to the originating house announcing the signing of the bill and its deposit with the secretary of state. Dissent ordinarily takes the form of the governor's returning the bill to the originating house with a message giving his reasons for disapproval. The veto may in a number of states also be exercised at the close of the session by allowing the undesirable bills passed during the final days to expire by the withholding of the Executive signature.

The methods of financial legislation in the state legislatures are full of confusion and are indeed in urgent need of systematization. The unity of a budget in which the resources and necessary expenditures of a state are summarized and balanced is entirely lacking; and in general the members do not at any stage of the session enjoy a fair opportunity to understand the exact nature and mutual relations of the various financial proposals of legislation. While a general appropriation bill, covering the regular needs of the departments of government, is usually prepared by the financial committee, any member has of course the right to introduce bills directly or incidentally carrying an appropriation. Such measures are generally referred, not to the committee dealing with appropriations, but to that which has jurisdiction over the special subject matter of the bill.* The difficulty of forming a clear conception of the scope of pending financial legislation is augmented by the fact that in many states there are large permanent appropriations which do not need special reenactment at every session, and whose relation to temporary and annual appropriations it is not easy for the ordinary member to gage. While most appropriations are made in fixed amounts, indefinite appropriations are found in states where no strict constitutional provisions on this matter exist; and even where the latter is the case, the appropriations are often so general and so liberal that, though for a fixed amount, they

*In some states all bills involving appropriations must be referred to the financial committee.

are very indefinite as to the manner in which the money is to be expended. The last days of the session are usually so crowded with appropriation bills, that it is not possible even for the chairman of the Finance Committee and other leaders to enjoy a complete survey of such legislation. The bills that are passed are then submitted to the governor, who is thus enabled to fix the final character of the financial legislation, although his discretion is very much hampered in the states which do not permit the veto of individual items in an appropriation bill. At no stage of the session and not even for a long time thereafter can it be determined with accuracy how much money has actually been appropriated. That such a condition of affairs does not result in careful administration of state finances is not surprising. Upon the legislature itself it has a most demoralizing effect, especially since so many members are predisposed, on the principle of "do unto others," to vote for almost any appropriation that may come up.

It is a general practice for some state official, the auditor, or controller, or secretary of state, to prepare a statement of the financial condition of the state, to which in most cases is added an estimate of the appropriations necessary for the various departments. This statement is printed and placed in the hands of the legislators. But as most of the latter are inexperienced in dealing with financial and statistical matters, and as there is no financial minister in the legislature, whose duty it is by lucid explanation to give life to dead statistics, these estimates do not have a very enlightening effect upon the average member. In some cases other means have been provided for the purpose of furnishing estimates. The new constitution of Alabama provides that the state officers shall, before the opening of the legislature, prepare a general appropriation bill covering the needs of the various departments and institutions of the state, within the limits of its probable revenue. This bill gives the legislature something definite to work on. In Indiana, the governor, immediately after the November election, appoints a committee from the state legislature, whose duty it is to examine the various state institutions and to make a report upon their condition and their financial needs. In most states, the preparation of the general appropriation bill is left to the Committee on Appropriations, which is called in some legislatures Committee on Ways and Means, or on Finance.

* * * * *

There is a growing tendency to make permanent appropriations for certain administrative and educational activities of the state. Though the freedom of legislatures is limited by this practice, it is of course not in itself harmful as long as the appropriations are originally made with sufficient care and surrounded with proper safeguards. In fact, some of the activities in which the states are now engaged could hardly be carried on with the best of success were it not possible to assure the agents and representatives of the state of a reasonably permanent income to be used for such purposes. Permanent appropriations are used most commonly to provide for salaries of offices created by law, for the work of special departments or commissions, and for the maintenance of educational and charitable institutions. They are permanent in the sense that a new statute is not needed at every session to keep them in force, and that actual expenses incurred under them will be paid out of the treasury without annual appropriations. A very common example of this kind of appropriation is a law granting the proceeds of a certain tax (*e. g.*, a two-fifth mill tax) to a state institution. Such a law may of course be repealed by any subsequent legislature, but the amount accruing to the fund, prior to its repeal, will be paid by the state treasurer to the beneficiary institution, and may be expended for its purposes. In a number of states, however, the constitution provides that the appropriations can be made only for a certain time, this period in no case exceeding two years. In these states it is thus impossible to make permanent or continuing appropriations; but even in their case, though appropriations must be renewed annually or biennially, the fact that certain offices and institutions have to be maintained does itself tend to make a large number of appropriations continuous in fact, though not in form. The New York general appropriation bill is composed largely of appropriations which are permanent in fact. In the states in which no such constitutional restrictions exist, the legislature can of course legally appropriate money for an indefinite period. It is held in these states that such a general law is sufficient authority for all payments under it. In Ohio, where permanent appropriations are forbidden, the Supreme Court has held that if expenses have been authorized without an appropriation being made to pay them, and if expenses are actually incurred, they create a debt against the state, for the payment of which, however, a proper appropriation is necessary. The states in which permanent appropriations have been most freely used are the following: Colorado, Connecticut, Iowa, Minnesota, New Hampshire, North Dakota, South Carolina, Vermont, West Virginia, and Wisconsin.

It is a provision found quite generally in state constitutions that appropriations shall be fixed and specific. In practice, however, while the specific amount of the grant must be given in the law, the manner in which it is to be spent is frequently left to the discretion of officials. * * * Governor Lanman of Texas, in a recent message severely criticizes the practice of appropriating lump sums to be spent at the discretion of officials, and urges the desirability of itemized and specified appropriations. It must be said, on the other hand, that effective itemizing could, after all, come only from the expert officials who alone have the necessary practical knowledge of the activities and works contemplated in any appropriation bill. Many constitutions impose limitations on the power of legislatures to make appropriations for private or local purposes. In Illinois such appropriations are entirely forbidden. In New York, Michigan, and Virginia they necessitate a two-thirds vote of each house. In a large number of states the legislature cannot authorize the payment of any claim under a contract the subject matter of which is not provided for by an existing law.

Reuben Gold Thwaites

※

TO REUBEN GOLD THWAITES Wisconsin people are indebted for a mass of historical information pertaining to their state and to the old Northwest. Born in Dorchester, Mass., in 1853, he came to Oshkosh, Wis., in 1866 where he resided for several years. In 1872 he was a reporter for the Oshkosh *Times* and covered the National Democratic Convention at Baltimore that year. In 1874 he entered Yale College for special work in English Literature. Returning to Wisconsin in 1876 he became managing editor of the Wisconsin *State Journal* at Madison. In 1885 he formed his connection with the State Historical Society which continued until his death in 1913. This position gave him ample opportunity to pursue his investigations in the field of history. Volume after volume came from his busy pen. Among his best known works are *Historic Waterways*, *The Story of Wisconsin*, *The Storied Ohio*, and *Original Journals of Lewis and Clark*. His monumental work, the translation and editing of the *Jesuit Relations* in seventy-three volumes, is better known to scholars than to the reading public. So well was this work done by Dr. Thwaites and his able assistants that no attempt to improve the work has since been made. On the whole it is safe to say that no other writer of the history of the Northwest has approached Dr. Thwaites, either in the quantity or the quality of the work produced.

From THE STORY OF WISCONSIN, *by Reuben Gold Thwaites. Published by D. Lothrop Company, Boston, Mass. Reprinted by permission of the publisher.*

THE BLACK HAWK WAR

THE BLACK HAWK WAR, in 1832, was an epoch-making event. The opening of the lead mines was one great incentive to the rapid development of Territorial Wisconsin; the Black Hawk insurrection was the other. This uprising of the natives, so potent in its consequences, was the outgrowth of a protracted series of events, which can be but inadequately set forth in this limited space. It is perhaps sufficient for our purpose to say that when in 1804, certain of the Sac and Fox chiefs purporting to be representatives of their united tribes, sold their title in the lead mines to the general government, certain other head-men not present at the council, claimed that the sale was not authorized. Among the opponents of the treaty was Black Hawk, a Sac leader, then twenty-seven years of age, who lived with his followers at the junction of the Rock River with the Mississippi, the site of the present city of Rock Island, Illinois. Black Hawk was a fine specimen of savage humanity. He was not a chief, he was but the leader by sufferance of a band of Sacs who were opposed to the constituted authorities. These malcontents were so friendly to the English marplots who had long tempted our Northwestern savages, that the party was always popularly known as "The British band," to distinguish it from the majority, which was generally on friendly terms with the Americans.

There was in the treaty of 1804 an unfortunate clause, to the effect that, "As long as the lands which are now ceded to the United States remain their (the general government's) property, the Indians belonging to the said tribes shall enjoy the privilege of living or hunting upon them." In other words, until the lands were pre-empted by actual settlers the Indians might remain upon them. All of the Sacs and Foxes except the British band at Rock Island removed at an early day to the west side of the Mississippi, but Black Hawk continued to hold his village on the east side. He was born there. The oldtime Sac burying-ground was in the neighborhood; the soil was rich and the Hawk appears to have become attached, with all the sentimental ardor of an unusually patriotic nature, to this beautiful resting-place of his ancestors. He was, too, restless and ambitious, and not disposed to bend to the will of the tribal chiefs—Keokuk, Wapello, Morgan and the rest—and his followers were ever arrayed against them in council. He was a warm admirer of his British "father," and yearly his blanketed band would proceed by the old, deeply-worn Sac trail across Northern Illinois and Southern Michigan to the English Indian agency at Malden, Canada, to return laden with gifts and flattery. He passionately hated the Americans because they annoyed him, because marauders of our nationality had stolen his property, because he had once been beaten by one of them, because they were intruders on the domains of his people, because his English father hated them, because his rivals were their friends.

In 1823, although the line of settlement was still fifty or sixty miles to the east, the whites evinced a covetous desire for his fertile fields along the Mississippi and began to squat there. The newcomers, year by year, robbed their Indian neighbors, destroyed their crops and burned their permanent bark lodges every time the villagers were absent upon the chase. The tribal chiefs advised Black Hawk to leave and take up his lot with them across the river. But the obstinate patriot indignantly declined and proposed to stay at all hazards. Black Hawk, like Tecumseh, had a prophet friend and adviser—a shrewd, crafty fellow, half Winnebago and half Sac, chief of a village some thirty-five miles up the Rock, where Prophetstown, Illinois, now is. This rascally wizard cultivated the vanity of the Hawk and made him believe that the latter's power could not be overcome by the Americans, and that in due time the Pottawatomies of Northeastern Illinois and Southeastern Wisconsin, and the Winnebagoes of the Rock River valley and the lead mines, would come to his assistance.

When the British band returned from their hunt in the spring of 1830, they found their town shattered, the cemetery plowed over and the whites more abundant than ever. Several squatters, who had illegally been upon the land for seven years and caused the Indians much trouble, had finally preëmpted the village site, the burial place and Black Hawk's favorite planting ground. This was a trick to accord with the letter, but to violate the spirit of the treaty of 1804, for a belt of practically unoccupied territory, forty miles wide, still lay to the eastward. The Indians, howling with rage, at once took the trail to Malden, where they were liberally treated and encouraged to rise in arms against the acquisitive Americans.

In the spring of 1831, when the natives had returned to their old home after a gloomy and profitless winter's hunt, they were warned away by the whites. Black Hawk firmly declined to go and threatened the settlers with force if they did not themselves remove from his village. This was construed into a "bloody menace," and the Illinois militia were at once called out by a flaming executive proclamation, to "repel the invasion of the British band." Sixteen hundred volunteers, with ten companies of United States troops, made a demonstration before Black Hawk's camp, the twenty-fifth of June, and during that night the unhappy savages paddled across the river, where they signed an agreement never to return to the east side without the express permission of the United States government.

Unfortunately for them, they failed to keep this covenant. The intrigues of the British, aided by the mischievous prophet and by unauthorized overtures from some of the Winnebago and Pottawatomie hot-heads, resulted in Black Hawk casting prudence to the winds. His people had lost their chance of putting in a crop, and the succeeding winter's hunt proved a failure. Starvation stared them in the face, and a desperate sally was decided upon, in the vain hope that the United States would not dare to persist in driving them away from their beloved village.

On the sixth of April, Black Hawk, with five hundred warriors, mostly Sacs, with all their women, children and domestic belongings, recrossed the Mississippi and passed up the Rock to the prophet's town. Their intention was to there raise a crop of corn and, if practicable, to take the war-path in the fall. The news of the "invasion" spread like wildfire throughout the Illinois and Wisconsin settlements. The governor of Illinois issued another fiery proclamation, summoning the people to arms, and the United States was called on to send an army to help quell the uprising. Some of the settlers fled from the country, others hastily threw up rude log forts, and everywhere was intense excitement and preparation for bloody strife.

In an incredibly short time three hundred regular troops under General Atkinson, and sixteen hundred horse and two hundred foot volunteers, were on the march. Black Hawk, after sending a defiant message to Atkinson, retreated up Rock River, making a stand at Stillman's Creek. Here he would have surrendered, but on the fourteenth of May the drunken pickets of the advance party of whites killed his messengers of peace. Smarting for revenge, he turned and swiftly routed Stillman's two hundred and seventy-five horsemen, with a mere handful of thirty-five braves to assist him. The cowardly rangers who fled at the first volley of the savages, without returning it, were haunted by the genius of fear, and, dashing madly through swamps and creeks, did not stop until they reached Dixon, twenty-five miles away; while many kept on at a keen gallop till they reached their own firesides, fifty or more miles farther, carrying the absurd report that Black Hawk and two thousand blood-thirsty warriors were sweeping Northern Illinois with the besom of destruction.

The war having now begun in earnest, Black Hawk, greatly encouraged and rich in supplies captured in Stillman's camp, felt impelled to carry it forward with vigor. Removing his women and children to the swampy fastnesses of Lake Koshkonong, near the headwaters of the Rock River, in Wisconsin, he thence descended with his braves into Northern Illinois. The people flew like chickens to cover, on warning of the Hawk's foray. There was consternation throughout the entire West. Exaggerated reports of his forces and the nature of his expedition were spread throughout the land. His name became coupled with stories of savage cunning and cruelty, and served as a household bugaboo, the country over. The effect on the Illinois militia was singular enough, considering the haste they had made to take the field: they instantly disbanded.

A fresh levy was soon raised, but during the hiatus there were irregular hostilities all along the Illinois-Wisconsin border, in which Black Hawk and a few Winnebago and Pottawatomie allies, succeeded in making life miserable enough for the settlers and miners. The most notable skirmishes were at Pecatonica, Blue Mounds, and Sinsiniwa Mound, in Wisconsin; and Apple River, Plum River, Burr Oak Grove, Kellogg's Grove and Davis's Farm (near Ottawa), in Illinois. At Davis's Farm, a party of Pottawatomies and Sacs, under the notorious renegade, Mike Girty, captured two white girls, Sylvia and Rachael Hall, and it cost the Government two thousand dollars to redeem them from the Wisconsin Winnebagoes, in whose keeping they had been placed. In these border strifes, fully two hundred whites and nearly as many Indians lost their lives, and there were numerous instances of romantic heroism on the part of the settlers, men and women alike.

In about three weeks after Stillman's defeat the reorganized militia took the field, reinforced by the regulars under Atkinson. Black Hawk was forced to fly to Lake Koshkonong, and when the pursuit became too warm he hastily withdrew westward to the Wisconsin River. Closely following him were a brigade of Illinois troopers under General James D. Henry and a battalion of Wisconsin lead-mine rangers under Major Henry Dodge, afterwards governor of the Territory.

The pursuers came up with the natives at Prairie du Sac. Here the south bank of the Wisconsin consists of steep, grassy bluffs, of three hundred feet altitude, hence the encounter which ensued is known in history as the Battle of Wisconsin Heights. With consummate skill, Black Hawk made a stand on the summit of the heights, and with a small party of warriors held the whites in check until the non-combatants had crossed the broad river bottoms below and gained shelter upon the willow-grown shore opposite. The loss on either side was slight, the action being notable only for the Sac leader's superior management.

During the night the passage of the river was fully accomplished by the fugitives. A large party was sent down stream upon a raft and in canoes begged from the Winnebagoes; but those who took this method of escape were brutally fired upon near the mouth of the river by a detachment from the garrison at Prairie du Chien, and fifteen killed in cold blood. The rest of the pursued, headed by Black Hawk—who had again made an attempt to surrender his forces to the white army, but failed for want of a competent interpreter—pushed across country, guided by Winnebagoes, to the mouth of the Bad Ax, where, it will be remembered, Red Bird had attacked the keel-boats five years before.

They were followed, three days behind, by the united army of regulars, who steadily gained on them. The country between the Wisconsin and the Mississippi is rough and forbidding in character; swamps and turbulent rivers are freely interspersed between the steep, thickly-wooded hills. The uneven pathway was strewn with the corpses of Sacs who had died of wounds and starvation, and there were frequent evidences that the fleeing wretches were sustaining life on the bark of trees and the sparse flesh of their fagged-out ponies.

On Wednesday, the first of August, Black Hawk and his now sadly depleted and almost famished band reached the Mississippi, near where the picturesque Bad Ax contributes its mite to the rolling flood. There were only two or three canoes to be had, and the crossing progressed slowly and with frequent loss of life. That afternoon a government supply steamer, the Warrior, from Prairie du Chien, appeared on the scene. The Indians a third time tried to surrender, but their white flag was fired at, and round after round of canister swept the camp. The next day the troops arrived on the heights above the river bench, the Warrior again opened its attack, and thus, caught between two galling fires, the poor savages soon succumbed. But fifty remained alive on the spot to be taken prisoners. Some three hundred weaklings had reached the opposite shore through the hail of iron and lead. Of these three hundred helpless, half-starved, unarmed non-combatants, over one half were slaughtered by Wabashaw's Sioux who had been sent out to waylay them. So that out of the band of one thousand Indians who had crossed the Mississippi in April, not more than one hundred and fifty, all told, lived to tell the tragic story of the Black Hawk War—a tale fraught with dishonor to the American name.

The rest can soon be told. The Winnebago guerrillas, who had played fast and loose during the campaign, delivered to the whites at Prairie du Chien, the unfortunate Black Hawk, who had fled from the Bad Ax to seek an asylum with his false friends. The proud old man, shorn of all his strength, was presented to the President at Washington, forced to sign articles of perpetual peace and then turned over for safe keeping to Keokuk, his hated and hating rival. Black Hawk, with all his racial limitations, had in his character a strength and manliness of fiber that was most remarkable, and displayed throughout his brief campaign a positive genius for military evolutions. He may be safely ranked as one of the most interesting specimens of the North American savage to be met with in history.

The immediate and lasting results of the Black Hawk War were not only the humbling of the Indians of Wisconsin and Illinois, but the wide advertising of the country through which the contest had been waged. During and soon after the war, the newspapers of the Eastern States were filled with descriptions, more or less florid, of the scenic charms of the Rock River Valley, the groves and prairies on every hand, the park-like district of the Four Lakes, the Wisconsin River highlands and the picturesque hills and almost impenetrable forests of Western Wisconsin. Books and pamphlets were issued from the press by the score, giving accounts of the newly-discovered paradise, and soon a tide of immigration set in toward Northern Illinois and Southern Wisconsin. Then necessarily followed, in short season, the survey and opening to sale of public lands heretofore reserved, and the purchase of what hunting grounds were still in possession of the Indian tribes. The development of Wisconsin thus received a sudden and enormous impetus, so that when it was divorced from Michigan, in 1836, and reared into an independent Territory, there were about twelve thousand whites within the borders of the nascent commonwealth, and many of the sites of future cities of the State were occupied by permanent agricultural settlers.

Louise Phelps Kellogg

✧

LOUISE PHELPS KELLOGG, historical writer, was born in Milwaukee, and all her work has been done in Wisconsin. She was graduated from the University of Wisconsin in 1897 and received her Ph.D. degree from the same institution in 1901. Dr. Kellogg taught history at the university, 1899-1900, joined the staff of the State Historical Society of Wisconsin in 1901, and is now senior research associate. She collaborated with Dr. Reuben Gold Thwaites in producing a number of publications dealing with the early settlement of the Upper Ohio, later turning her attention to the documentary history of Wisconsin and the Northwest during the period of French domination. Her *French Régime in Wisconsin and the Northwest*, published in 1925, is a masterpiece of patient research and well stated facts. It is doubtful if any other book so concisely and yet so fully and accurately covers the ground. Perhaps it is not too much to say that Dr. Kellogg is the greatest living authority on Wisconsin's pre-territorial history. Many of her shorter contributions appear in the Wisconsin Magazine of History.

From THE FRENCH RÉGIME IN WISCONSIN AND THE NORTHWEST *by Louise Phelps Kellogg. Published by the State Historical Society of Wisconsin, Madison, 1925.*

EXPLORATION OF THE MISSISSIPPI VALLEY

WHILE Frontenac was occupied in overawing the Iroquois and regulating the fur trade, which was again in danger of slipping from the French grasp, Talon's projected expedition set out to discover the Mississippi. Jolliet probably knew the western country as well as any living Frenchman; it would seem that he had already been as far as the Mascouten village on the upper Fox, then the farthest west of French exploration in Wisconsin. The choice of Marquette to accompany this expedition of discovery seems to have given umbrage to some of his colleagues in the western missions. Allouez had long desired to be the apostle to the Illinois; Marquette was young and comparatively untried, why might his opportunity not wait until a later time? Nevertheless his youthful ardor was one element that determined his choice—that and his skill in map-making and his knowledge of Indian languages.

For his own part Marquette was overjoyed at the opportunity. At his mission on Chequamegon Bay he had met some visiting Illinois, had heard of the great river which they had crossed in their journey, and had made some progress in learning the Illinois language. Now at St. Ignace he welcomed Jolliet with enthusiasm on his arrival, December 8, 1672, with their commission. The winter was spent in preparations, among which was the drawing of a map from the knowledge acquired from the Indians. "We were not long in preparing all our equipment," Marquette wrote in his journal; "Indian corn, with some smoked meat, constituted all our provisions; with these we embarked—Monsieur Jollyet and myself, with five men—in two bark canoes, fully resolved to do and suffer everything for so glorious an undertaking." We know the names of only two of the *voyageurs* who accompanied the expedition; these were Pierre Porteret and Jacques Largilliers, who were present in 1671 at the pageant at the Sault, and later accompanied Marquette on his final journey, and cared for him at his death.

It was the seventeenth of May when the little flotilla

left St. Ignace, freighted with so many hopes, discarding so many fears—since the Indians sought to dissuade the explorers from their enterprise by stories of dangers that would be encountered, monsters which lurked along the stream, rapids that would swallow their frail barks, and heat that would roast them alive. Jolliet knew enough of interior North America to discount the natives' exaggerated reports, and the discoverers set forth with light hearts. As far as the Mascouten village all was familiar; this was reached without hazard on the seventh of June.

While these young Frenchmen were thus adventuring for king and country in the wilds of North America, their king in person was leading a vast army toward the border of the Netherlands. Contrast the two expeditions—the tiny canoes of the *voyageurs* slipping swiftly along the Wisconsin waterways; the great state coach of Louis XIV and all the royal family lumbering on to the siege of Maestricht, accompanied by the paraphernalia of a royal progress and the equipment of a mighty army. Yet the world has well nigh forgotten that in June, 1673, Louis XIV captured the Dutch fortress; it will never forget that in that month Jolliet and Marquette first saw the Mississippi River.

Marquette was delighted with their reception by the villagers on the upper Fox. The Miami he found "the most civil, the most liberal, and the most shapely. . . . The Maskoutens and Kikabous are ruder and seem peasants in comparison with the others." Guides were furnished by the Miami to lead the explorers through the wild-rice mazes of the upper Fox. When the portage was reached the guides carried the canoes across, and left the travelers to go on alone. The expedition had now "left the waters flowing to Quebeq, four or five hundred leagues from here, to float on those that would henceforth take us through strange lands." Now was disproved the theory that rivers ran from the Great Lakes toward the western sea, while at the same time the most convenient portage route from the basin of the Great Lakes to the waters of the Mississippi was found.

The westward-flowing stream on which they embarked Marquette was told by his guides was named the Meskousing or the Miskous. His description gives the characteristic features of our central river. "It is very wide; it has a sandy bottom, which forms various shoals that render the navigation difficult. It is full of islands covered with vines. . . . After navigating about thirty leagues, we saw a spot presenting all the appearances of an iron mine."

It was the seventeenth of June when the mouth of the Wisconsin was reached and their canoes entered the long-sought river. "Here we are then," writes Marquette, "on this so renowned River. . . . The Mississippi." A pleasant month had been spent on the Fox-Wisconsin portage route; another month on the great river brought them to the southern limit of their voyage. After leaving the Mascouten village, they saw no vestiges of inhabitants until June 25; then at the water's western edge they descried human tracks, and landing with the peace calumet in hand they found a village of the Peoria tribesmen, where they were graciously entertained with feasts and dances. The explorers setting out the last of June, their canoes soon came abreast of the cliffs near Alton, on which were painted the Piasa monsters. Soon they were involved in the swift currents where the Missouri enters, the only rapids they mention on their route. The Missouri River Marquette called the Pekitanoui, and hoped "by its means to discover the Vermillion or California Sea."

Twenty leagues below the Missouri came in an eastern stream, on which the explorers understood the Shawnee lived. This they no doubt learned from the Monsoupelia tribe, whose village they found on the east bank some distance below the Ohio. Marquette left with the latter tribe a Latin letter for whom it might concern, which ultimately found its way to Virginia. Somewhat farther south on the western bank were met the Michigamea, some of whom understood the Illinois language. From them they heard of the Quapaw at the mouth of the Arkansas River, at whose village they reached the southern limit of their voyage. They were now convinced both by Indian reports and by the course of the stream that they had traversed, that the Mississippi discharged its waters into the Gulf of Mexico. Between the Arkansas and the Mississippi's mouth they might meet Spaniards, with whom the French were then at war. They decided to turn northward, which they did on July 17, one month from the day they first saw the great river, and two months from that of their departure from St. Ignace.

Frederick J. Turner

☼

WITH the exception of fourteen years spent as professor in Harvard College, Frederick J. Turner has lived continuously in Wisconsin. Born in Portage, Wisconsin, November 14, 1861, he had the opportunity to observe his native state during the period of its transition from frontier to populous commonwealth. After completing his preparatory school work he entered the University of Wisconsin from which institution he was graduated in 1884. Mr. Turner was professor of American History in the University of Wisconsin from 1889 to 1910. In 1910 he was elected professor of history in Harvard College and remained there until 1924 when he retired from active college work. He has written: *Rise of the New West*, 1906, *The Frontier in American History*, 1920, beside other historical sketches and textbooks. Mr. Turner now resides in Madison.

The following selection from the *Rise of the New West*, dealing with the period of the Missouri Compromise, is of peculiar interest to the people of Wisconsin. Senator Rufus King, who made the outstanding argument against the extension of slavery, was the great-grandfather of General Charles King of Milwaukee, included in this series of sketches as an eminent Wisconsin writer. Senator King of New York was one of the group of American statesmen who, during the first half of the nineteenth century, made the Congress of the United States one of the greatest parliamentary bodies in history.

RISE OF THE NEW WEST, *by Frederick Jackson Turner, Ph.D. Harper & Brothers, Publishers, New York and London, 1906. Reprinted by permission of the author and of the publishers. All rights reserved.*

In Maryland, Virginia, and North Carolina, ever since the decline of the tobacco culture, a strong opposition to slavery had existed, shown in the votes of those states on the Ordinance of 1787, and in the fact that as late as 1827 the great majority of the abolition societies of the United States were to be found in this region. But the problem of dealing with the free negro weighed upon the south. Even in the north these people were unwelcome. They frequently became a charge upon the community, and they were placed under numerous disabilities.

The idea of deporting freedmen from the United States found support both among the humanitarians, who saw in it a step towards general emancipation, and among the slave-holders who viewed the increase of the free negroes with apprehension. To promote this solution of the problem, the Colonization Society was incorporated in 1816, and it found support, not only from antislavery agitators like Lundy, who edited the *Genius of Universal Emancipation* at Baltimore, but also from slave-holders like Jefferson, Clay, and Randolph. It was the design of this society to found on the coast of Africa a colony of free blacks, brought from the United States. Although, after unsuccessful efforts, Liberia was finally established in the twenties, with the assistance of the general government (but not under its jurisdiction), it never promoted state emancipation. Nevertheless, at first it met with much sympathy in Virginia, where in 1820 the governor proposed to the legislature the use of one-third of the state revenue as a fund to promote the emancipation and deportation of the negroes.

The unprofitableness of slavery in the border states,

where outworn fields, the decline of tobacco culture, and the competition of western lands bore hard on the planter, now became an argument in favor of permitting slavery to pass freely into the new country of the west. Any limitation of the area of slavery would diminish the value of the slaves and would leave the old south to support, under increasingly hard conditions, the redundant and unwelcome slave population in its midst. The hard times from 1817 to 1820 rendered slave property a still greater burden to Virginia. Moreover, the increase of the proportion of slaves to whites, if slavery were confined to the region east of the Mississippi, might eventually make possible a servile insurrection, particularly if foreign war should break out. All of these difficulties would be met, in the opinion of the south, by scattering the existing slaves and thus mitigating the evil without increasing the number of those in bondage.

It was seen that the struggle was not simply one of morals and of rival social and industrial institutions, but was a question of political power between the two great and opposing sections, interested, on the one side, in manufacturing and in the raising of food products under a system of free labor; and on the other, in the production of the great staples, cotton, tobacco, and sugar, by the use of slave labor. Already the southern section had shown its opposition to tariff and internal improvements, which the majority of the northern states vehemently favored. In other words, the slavery issue was seen to be a struggle for sectional domination.

At the beginning of the nation in 1790, the population of the north and the south were almost exactly balanced. Steadily, however, the free states drew ahead, until in 1820 they possessed a population of 5,152,000 against 4,485,000 for the slave-holding states and territories; and in the House of Representatives, by the operation of the three-fifths ratio, the free states could muster 105 votes to but 81 for the slave states. Thus power had passed definitely to the north in the House of Representatives. The instinct for self-preservation that led the planters to stand out against an apportionment in their legislatures which would throw power into the hands of non-slaveholders now led them to seek for some means to protect the interests of their minority section in the nation as a whole. The Senate offered such an opportunity: by the alternate admission of free and slave states from 1802 to 1818, out of the twenty-two states of the nation eleven were slave-holding and eleven free. If the south retained this balance, the Senate could block the action of the majority which controlled the lower House.

Such was the situation when the application of Missouri for admission as a state in 1819 presented to Congress the whole question of slavery beyond the Mississippi, where freedom and slavery had found a new fighting-ground. East of the Mississippi the Ohio was a natural dividing-line; farther west there appeared no obvious boundary between slavery and freedom. By a natural process of selection, the valleys of the western tributaries of the Mississippi, as far north as the Arkansas and Missouri, in which slaves had been allowed while it was a part of French and Spanish Louisiana (no restraints having been imposed by Congress), received an increasing proportion of the slave-holding planters. It would, in the ordinary course of events, become the area of slave states.

The struggle began in the House of Representatives, when the application of Missouri for statehood was met by an amendment, introduced by Tallmadge of New York, February 13, 1819, providing that further introduction of slavery be prohibited, and that all children born within the state after admission should be free at the age of twenty-five years. Tallmadge had already shown his attitude on this question when in 1818 he opposed the admission of Illinois under its constitution, which seemed to him to make insufficient barriers to slavery. Brief as was the first Missouri debate, the whole subject was opened up by arguments to which later discussion added but little. The speaker, Henry Clay, in spite of the fact that early in his political career he had favored gradual emancipation in Kentucky, led the opposition to restriction. His principal reliance was upon the arguments that the evils of slavery would be mitigated by diffusion, and that the proposed restriction was unconstitutional. Tallmadge and Taylor, of New York, combated these arguments so vigorously and with such bold challenge of the whole system of slavery in new territories, that Cobb, of Georgia declared, "You have kindled a fire which all the waters of the ocean cannot put out, which seas of blood can only extinguish."

* * * * *

No argument in the debate in 1819 was more effective than the speech of Rufus King in the Senate, which was widely circulated as a campaign document expressing the northern view. King's antislavery attitude, shown as early as 1785, when he made an earnest fight to secure the exclusion of slavery from the territories, was clearly stated in his constitutional argument in favor of restriction on Missouri, and his speech may be accepted as typical. But it was also the speech of an old-time Federalist, apprehensive of the growth of western power under southern leadership.

He held that, under the power of making all needful rules and regulations respecting the territory and other property of the United States, Congress had the right to prohibit slavery in the Louisiana purchase, which belonged to the United States in full dominion. Congress was further empowered, but not required, to admit new states into the Union. Since the Constitution contained no express provision respecting slavery in a new state, Congress could make the perpetual prohibition of slavery a condition of admission. In support of this argument, King appealed to the precedent of the Ordinance of 1787, and of the states of Ohio, Indiana, and Illinois, all admitted on the conditions expressed in that ordinance. In admitting the state of Louisiana in 1812, a different group of conditions had been attached, such as the requirement of the use of the English language in judicial and legislative proceedings.

The next question was the effect of the Louisiana treaty, by which the United States had made this promise: "The inhabitants of the ceded territory shall be incorporated in the Union of the United States, and admitted as soon as possible, according to the principles of the Federal constitution, to the enjoyment of all the rights, advantages and immunities of citizens of the United States; and in the meantime they shall be maintained and protected in the free enjoyment of their liberty, property and the religion which they profess." King contended that, by the admission of Missouri to the Union, its inhabitants would obtain all of the "federal" rights which citizens of the United States derived from its Constitution, though not the rights derived from the constitutions and laws of the various states. In his opinion, the term *property* did not describe slaves, inasmuch as the terms of the treaty should be construed according to diplomatic usage, and not all nations permitted slavery. In any case, property acquired since the territory was occupied by the United States was not included in the treaty, and, therefore, the prohibition of the future introduction of slaves into Missouri would not affect its guarantees.

Could Missouri, after admission, revoke the consent to the exclusion of slavery under its powers as a sovereign state? Such action, King declared, would be contrary to the obligations of good faith, for even sovereigns were bound by their engagements. Moreover, the judicial power of the United States would deliver from bondage any person detained as a slave in a state which had agreed, as a condition of admission, that slavery should be excluded.

Having thus set forth the constitutional principles, King next took up the expediency of the exclusion of slavery from new states. He struck with firm hand the chord of sectional rivalry in his argument against the injustice to the north of creating new slave-holding states, which would have a political representation, under the "federal ratio," not possessed by the north. Under this provision for counting three-fifths of the slaves, five free persons in Virginia (so he argued) had as much power in the choice of representatives to Congress and in the appointment of presidential electors as seven free persons in any of the states in which slavery did not exist. The disproportionate power and influence allowed to the original slave-holding states was a necessary sacrifice to the establishment of the Constitution; but the arrangement was limited to the old thirteen states, and was not applicable to the states made out of territory since acquired. This argument had been familiar to New England ever since the purchase of Louisiana. Finally, he argued that the safety of the Union demanded the exclusion of slavery west of the Mississippi, where the exposed and important frontier needed a barrier of free citizens against the attacks of future assailants.

To the southern mind, King's sectional appeal unblushingly raised the prospect of the rule of a free majority over a slave-holding minority, the downfall of the ascendency so long held by the south, and the creation of a new Union, in which the western states should be admitted on terms of subordination to the will of the majority, whose power would thus become perpetual.

When the next Congress met, in December, 1819, the

admission of Alabama was quickly completed; and the House also passed a bill admitting Maine to the Union, Massachusetts having agreed to this division of the ancient commonwealth, on condition that consent of Congress should be obtained prior to March 4, 1820. The Senate, quick to see the opportunity afforded by the situation, combined the bill for the admission of Maine with that for the unrestricted admission of Missouri, a proposition carried (February 16, 1820) by a vote of 23 to 21. Senator Thomas, who represented Illinois, which, as we have seen, was divided in its interests on the question of slavery, and who, as the vote showed, could produce a tie in the Senate, moved a compromise amendment, providing for the admission of Missouri as a slave state and for the prohibition of slavery north of 36° 30′ in the rest of the Louisiana purchase; and on the next day his amendment passed the Senate by a vote of 34 to 10.

The debate in the Senate was marked by another speech of Rufus King, just re-elected a senator from New York by an almost unanimous vote. With this prestige, and the knowledge that the states of Pennsylvania and New York stood behind him, he reiterated his arguments with such power, that John Quincy Adams, who listened to the debate, wrote in his diary that "the great slave-holders in the House gnawed their lips and clenched their fists as they heard him."

Milo M. Quaife

☆

MILO M. QUAIFE was born in Nashua, Iowa, October 6, 1880. He received his early education in Iowa and was graduated from Iowa College at Grinnell in 1903. He was superintendent of the State Historical Society of Wisconsin from 1914 to 1920.

He is the author of a number of books and innumerable shorter articles. Among his books are: *The Doctrine of Non-Intervention with Slavery in the Territories*, 1910, and *Wisconsin, Its History and Its People*, 1924. His present home is near Detroit, Michigan.

From WISCONSIN, ITS HISTORY AND ITS PEOPLE, *by Milo Milton Quaife, The S. J. Clarke Publishing Co., Chicago, 1924.*

THE RED MEN OF WISCONSIN

WHEN the white man first came to America he found the New World occupied by a race of people to whom the mistaken geographical ideas of Columbus attached the name of "Indian." In addition to a new world, Columbus had made known to Europeans a new division of the human race. The culture and mode of life of the Indians varied greatly in different portions of America, the chief cause of the variations being, apparently, the differing geographical conditions to which the several tribes and racial groups were subject. The three most forward centers of culture were those of the Aztecs in Mexico, the Iroquoian Confederacy, which had its center in Western New York; and the Haida culture on the coast of British Columbia. So respectable were the attainments of the

Aztecs, that some have been inclined to question whether they were not the cultural superiors of their Spanish conquerors. Between them and some of the more backward tribes of the continent, such as the Utes of the Great Basin, was fixed a great gulf.

The tribesmen of Wisconsin, at the coming of the whites, occupied a cultural position midway between these extremes. They were a stationary people, so far as the exigencies of war permitted. Although they relied largely on hunting for subsistence, they also gave considerable attention to agriculture, and to a greater extent than men today commonly realize, were the first farmers of Wisconsin. Corn, (still commonly known as Indian) was their most important crop, but in addition to this, great quantities of beans, squashes, pumpkins, and melons were raised. Another cereal of exceeding value to the natives of Wisconsin was the wild rice which grew so abundantly in the marshes bordering the lake shores. The wild rice plant provided a never-failing food crop, and the grain could easily be stored and preserved for a long period of time. Aside from its value to the native as a direct source of food supply, it supported the vast flocks of wild fowl which swarmed the waters and darkened the air of primitive Wisconsin.

If the soil of Wisconsin rewarded liberally the crude agricultural efforts of the Indian, her forests, rivers, and lakes offered equal attractions in game and fish. Buffalo, elk, and deer were everywhere to be found; while the conical huts of the muskrat dotted all the marshes. Finally, the waters teemed with game fish as fine as could be found in all the world. To the savage red man, in short, Wisconsin afforded a rarely attractive home.

* * * * *

Freedom, indeed, the red man enjoyed in high degree, but for it he paid a huge price. If at certain seasons he reveled in abundance, at others stark famine beset him.

He was inured to a life of physical activity and exposure, yet he knew nothing of the laws of sanitation, and could only resort to jugglery and necromancy for relief from the diseases and epidemics which menaced him. So great were the perils of infancy and childhood that only the hardiest survived them. Although the Indian women became mothers early and often, comparatively few of their offspring survived to maturity. Instances of longevity were not uncommon, yet the lot of the aged and infirm was one of unalloyed privation and misery, which terminated all too commonly in death at the hands of one's relatives, or in the still more dreadful fate of being abandoned by them to die of exposure and starvation.

It followed as a necessary consequence of the Indian mode of life that the native population of Wisconsin was exceedingly sparse. There could, of course, be no such thing as cities, or even considerable towns, since there was no economic organization capable either of evoking or supporting such aggregations of population. Since the Indians were fond of society they commonly dwelt together in villages. These were located with great shrewdness from the viewpoint of utilizing to the utmost the natural advantages of the country. Significant evidence is afforded by the fact that practically every city of any considerable importance in Wisconsin is built on the site of an earlier Indian town. A final factor which added its weight to those of pestilence and famine in limiting the Indian population was the incessant warfare carried on. Upon the slaying of an enemy in war depended the recognition of the youth as a man, and but few failed to win the coveted distinction at a comparatively early age. The entire Indian population of the state, probably, never equalled the population of Madison today. Primitive Wisconsin was but a magnificent wilderness wherein a few thousand savages resided, gathered for the most part along certain great natural highways of travel. Small as this population was it played a vital part in shaping the occupation and development of the state by the white race. Some 10,000 red men still reside in the state, and during most of the three-hundred-year period which our narrative traverses, the red race has had much to do with shaping its course. The reader will be enabled to understand the story better, therefore, if we devote some attention at this point to sketching the history of the several tribes identified with Wisconsin.

The Indians left no written records, and for all that lies back of the advent of the white man we must resort, for the reconstruction of their story, to the testimony of such other sources of evidence as can be found. When the French first came into the Northwest they encountered the Winnebago tribe living on the shore of Green Bay and in the lower valley of Fox River. Nor could the French learn, apparently, of any previous residence of the tribe, for in the *Jesuit Relation* of 1671 it is stated that the Winnebago had always dwelt in the Green Bay region. The Winnebago belong to the Siouan family, which was widely distributed over North America, and various theories have been advanced concerning their origin and place of residence before coming into the upper Mississippi Valley. Into the discussion of these we have no present occasion to enter. Sufficient is it for our present purpose to note that for some time prior to the year 1600 northern and eastern Wisconsin seems to have been occupied by Siouan tribes, while the southern portion of the state belonged to the Illinois, who were members of the great Algonquian family. The Sioux and the Illinois, therefore, may be regarded as the aboriginal inhabitants of Wisconsin.

The first half of the seventeenth century, which witnessed the establishment along the Atlantic coast of the first permanent French, Dutch, and English settlements in America, was marked by important changes among the denizens of forest-clad Wisconsin. For one thing, the Winnebago engaged in disastrous wars with the Huron, who dwelt to the east of the lake which still bears their name, and with their southern neighbors, the Illinois. How the tribe was weakened by the losses it sustained is graphicly revealed in an ancient narrative, lying on the borderland between history and tradition, which records with Homeric simplicity and candor one phase of the conflict. The "Puants," it relates, were in former times a proud and haughty race, who tyrannized over all their neighbors and "cooked in their kettles" any strangers who came among them. When the Ottawa sent an embassy to them they cooked and ate the unfortunate envoys. This crime so incensed all the nations that they joined with the Ottawa in a league for the destruction of the Winnebago. The latter, harassed by frequent raids, fell into dissension among themselves, reproaching one another over the misfortunes which had been brought upon them by the perfidy of those who slew the envoys.

"When they found they were vigorously attacked," continues the chronicle, "they were compelled to unite all their forces in one village, where they numbered four or five thousand men; but maladies wrought among them more devastation than even the war did, and the exhalations from the rotting corpses caused great mortality. They could not bury their dead, and were soon reduced to 1,500 men. Despite all these misfortunes they sent a party of 500 warriors against the Outagamies (or Foxes), who dwelt on the other shore of the lake; but all these men perished while making that journey, by a tempest which arose. Their enemies were moved by this disaster, and said the gods ought to be satisfied with so many punishments; so they ceased making war on those who remained."

Glenn Frank

☼

GLENN FRANK, writer and university president, was born at Queen City, Missouri, October 1, 1887. He was graduated from Northwestern University in 1912. From 1919 to 1921 he was associate editor of *Century Magazine*, and editor-in-chief from 1921 to 1925. Since 1925 he has been president of the University of Wisconsin.

He is the author of *The Politics of Industry*, 1919; *An American Looks at His World*, and shorter articles that have appeared from time to time in magazines. He is best known to the reading public from his short pithy essays which appear regularly in the daily newspapers.

The following PRAYER FOR THOSE IN GOVERNMENT *delivered by President Glenn Frank before the Fifty-eighth Wisconsin Senate at its opening session, Wednesday, January 12, 1927 is an example of his beauty of style and depth of thought.*

ALMIGHTY GOD, Lord of all Governments, help us, in the opening hours of this legislative session, to realize the sanctity of politics.

Help us to know that the call to office that has brought us here is nothing less than a call to co-operation with Thee in the wise direction of life in this commonwealth.

Give us the insight and grant us the power to lift this business of government into an adventure that we may with reverence call the Politics of God, because by it we shall seek to fashion the life of this commonwealth in the likeness of that City of God which has been the dream of saints and seers for unnumbered centuries.

Save us from the sins to which we shall be subtly tempted as the calls of parties and the cries of interest beat upon this seat of government.

Save us from thinking about the next election when we should be thinking about the next generation.

Save us from dealing in personalities when we should be dealing in principles.

Save us from thinking too much about the vote of majorities when we should be thinking about the virtue of measures.

Save us, in crucial hours of debate, from saying the things that will take when we should be saying the things that are true.

Save us from indulging in catch-words when we should be searching for facts.

Save us from making party an end in itself when we should be making it a means to an end.

We do not ask mere protection from these temptations that will surround us in these legislative halls; we ask also for an ever finer insight into the meaning of government that we may be better servants of the men and women who have committed the government of this commonwealth into our hands.

Help us to realize that the unborn are part of our constituency, although they have no vote at the polls.

May we have greater reverence for the truth than for the past.

Help us to make party our servant rather than our master.

May we know that it profits us nothing to win elections if we lose our courage.

Help us to be independent alike of tyrannical majorities and tirading minorities when the truth abides in neither.

May sincerity inspire our motives and science inform our methods.

Help us to serve the crowd without flattering it and believe in it without bowing to its idolatries.

Almighty God, Lord of all Governments, to whom all hearts are open, and from whom no secrets are hid, may the words of our mouths, the meditations of our hearts, and the intent of our measures be acceptable in Thy sight.

May we come with clear minds, clean hands, and courageous hearts to the sacrament of public service.

May we be worthy of the high calling of government. Amen.

THE QUEST FOR RELIGION
By GLENN FRANK

Reprinted by permission of the McClure Newspaper Syndicate. All rights reserved by the publishers.

To the end of time mankind will be seeking to discover the secret and to define the meaning of religion.

A thousand roads will be tramped over in the quest. Some will find satisfaction in the ivory verses of the mystics where the unseen figures of the spirit clutch at meanings undefined and indefinable.

Some will find satisfaction in the high-hearted humdrum of helping humanity after the fashion of the ancient Samaritan to whom bandages and board bills were prayer-rug and rosary.

Some will find satisfaction in the sacramental atmosphere of great cathedrals where, through color and sound and flame, a sense of God and goodness steals insensibly upon the worshipper.

Some will find satisfaction in the barren beauty of a Quaker meeting-house where nothing noisier than an attitude of the heart breaks the harmonious stillness.

Some will find satisfaction in the sawdust aisles of the

factory-built shed that echoes the strident appeal of the evangelist.

It ill becomes us to criticize these many roads of many men, for the meaning of life and destiny may have no single street address.

Some will seek religion in the public life of the state.
Some will seek religion in the private life of the citizen.
Some may seek religion and find only sociology.
Some may seek religion and find only psychology.
To some the end of religion may be social justice.
To some the end of religion may be spiritual peace.

This evening, while these thoughts were coming and going unbidden through my mind, I came upon the following words about religion in Alfred North Whitehead's little volume on "Religion In The Making."

"Religion is the art and the theory of the internal life of man, so far as it depends on the man himself and on what is permanent in the nature of things.

"Religion is what the individual does with his solitariness.

"It runs through three stages, if it evolves to its final satisfaction. It is the transition from God the void to God the enemy, and from God the enemy to God the companion.

"Religion is solitariness; and if you are never solitary, you are never religious. Collective enthusiasms, revivals, institutions, churches, rituals, bibles, codes of behavior, are the trappings of religion, its passing forms; they may be authoritatively ordained, or merely temporary expedients. But the end of religion is beyond all this."

But somewhere and somehow we must contrive to use the internal riches that religion brings for the increase, the enrichment, and the moral unification of the external life that we see and touch and handle.

(Copyright, McClure Newspaper Syndicate, 373 Fourth Avenue, New York.)

John R. Commons

✧

JOHN R. COMMONS, educator, economist and author, was born in Hollandsburg, Ohio, October 13, 1862. He did his undergraduate work at Oberlin College where he received his A.B. degree in 1888. He was director of the Bureau of Economics, 1899–1901. In 1904 he became professor of economics in the University of Wisconsin, a position he has since held. In 1911 he was appointed a member of the Wisconsin Industrial Commission.

With all his other activities, Dr. Commons has been a prolific writer of economic and industrial treatises. Among the best known of his published works are: *The Distribution of Wealth*, 1893; *Social Reform and the Church*, 1894; *Trade Unionism and Labor Problems*, 1905; *Races and Immigrants in America*, 1907; *Labor Legislation*, 1916; and *History of Labor, in the United States*, 1917.

From PROPORTIONAL REPRESENTATION *by John R. Commons, Published by the Macmillan Company, New York, 1907.*

CHAPTER I

THE FAILURE OF LEGISLATIVE ASSEMBLIES

THE American people are fairly content with their executive and judicial departments of government, but they feel that their law-making bodies have painfully failed. This conviction pertains to all grades of legislatures, municipal, State, and Federal. The newspapers speak what the people feel; and judging therefrom, it is popular to denounce aldermen, legislators, and congressmen. When Congress is in session, the business interests are reported to be in agony until it adjourns. The cry that rises towards the end of a legislature's session is humiliating. The *San Francisco Bulletin* is quoted as saying:

"It is not possible to speak in measured terms of the thing that goes by the name of legislature in this State. It has of late years been the vilest deliberative body in the world. The assemblage has become one of bandits instead of law-makers. Everything within its grasp for years has been for sale. The commissions to high office which it confers are the outward and visible signs of felony rather than of careful and wise selection."

Every State in the Union can furnish examples more or less approaching to this. Statements almost as extreme are made regarding Congress. Great corporations and syndicates seeking legislative favors are known to control the acts of both branches. The patriotic ability and even the personal character of members are widely distrusted and denounced.

These outcries are not made only in a spirit of partisanship, but respectable party papers denounce unsparingly legislatures and councils whose majorities are of their own political complexion. The people at large join in the attack. When statements so extreme as that given above are made by reputable papers and citizens, it is not surprising that the people at large have come thoroughly to distrust their law-makers. Charges of corruption and bribery are so abundant as to be taken as a matter of course. The honored historical name of alderman has frequently become a stigma of suspicion and disgrace.

As might be expected, this distrust has shown itself in far-reaching constitutional changes. The powers of State and city legislatures have been clipped and trimmed until they offer no inducements for ambition. The powers of governors, mayors, judges, and administrative boards have been correspondingly increased. The growing popularity of the executive veto is one of the startling facts of the times. President Hayes vetoed more congressional bills than any predecessor, and his record has been excelled by President Cleveland. A city has been known to turn out in mass-meetings, and to illuminate the heavens with bonfires, in honor of a mayor's veto which rescued it from outrages and robberies perpetrated by its own lawfully elected "city fathers." The prevailing reform in municipal government is the transfer of legislative functions, and even legislative discretion, from the city council to the mayor.

. . . Mr. A. H. Green, a few years ago, found "eighty different boards or individuals who could create debt independently of each other." Here was the opportunity of the "boss" and the party machine. Unity must somehow be secured. The "boss," a mere private citizen, gathered into his hands these scattered threads, and centralized the government of the city in himself. He controlled nominations and elections. He appointed and removed officers. He pitted council against mayor, boards against council, subordinates against chiefs, making them all responsible to him. But he was responsible to no one. The latest movement in municipal reform is to legalize the boss in the person of the mayor, to give him sole power to appoint and remove all heads of departments, but to elect him by popular vote and make him responsible to the people. The movement is not yet completed. The council remains a shrivelled and vicious relic. Logically, it should be abolished or reformed.

A similar movement, though later in time, is affecting State legislatures. * * * * The Constitutions of the new States of North and South Dakota, Montana, and Washington, may be considered as stating the thought of the American people at the present time regarding their legislatures. Several administrative boards are created in these new States, all filled by popular election. Among these are commissions to supervise and regulate insurance, railroads, agriculture and labor, prisons, and public lands. These commissions absorb, in various degrees, the powers of legislatures, executives, and judges. They are the nondescript, many-headed agents of the people distrusting the legislature, but not yet ready to confide everything to the governor's autocracy.

* * * * *

These constitutional restrictions, extending to legislatures and municipal councils, have forced another branch of government, the judiciary, to the front. Conscious of popular approval, judges have steadily encroached upon the field of legislative discretion, and reluctantly, it may be, have more and more assumed the right to set aside legislative statutes. This interference, however justifiable the reasons, is fraught with danger to the judiciary. It is thereby, at the expense of its integrity in the field of administration and justice, forced into the political arena, where are the heated questions of political expediency. Popular election of judges, short terms, and partisanship will result. "The executive," says Judge Horace Davis, "all-powerful at the beginning (of colonial history), was reduced to a mere shadow of its former glory, and in these later days is regaining some of its lost power. The legislature, at first weak, afterwards absorbed the powers of the other departments, but is now much reduced again. Throughout all these changes the dignity and power of the judges have steadily increased. . . . Their greatest power, most amazing to Europeans, is the authority to set aside a statute which they hold to be in conflict with the written Constitution. No other courts in the world possess this unique power. . . . The scope of this power is much broadened by the modern tendency to limit legislation. The early Constitutions were very brief, containing usually little more than a bill of rights and a skeleton of the government, leaving all details to the discretion of the legislature. Now all this is changed; the bounds of the different departments are carefully defined, and the power of the legislature is jealously curbed, particularly in the domain of special legislation. It will be seen at a glance that this enlarges the relative power of the courts. It limits the legislature and widens the field of the judiciary at one stroke."

Not only do the judges pretend to override the legislatures, but their exalted position renders them confidently autocratic in other directions. They are learning to dispense with juries, to dangerously widen the scope of injunctions, and to punish for contempt in cases not contemplated in our Constitutions. The legislatures and Congress, which are legally in a position to check these usurpations, are practically helpless from their lack of ability and their loss of popular confidence.

This demoralization of legislative bodies, these tendencies to restrict legislation, must be viewed as a profoundly alarming feature of American politics. Just as the duties of legislation are increasing as never before, in order to meet the vital wants of a complex civilization, the essential organs for performing those duties are felt to be in a state of collapse. The legislature controls the purse, the very life-blood of the city, the State, the nation. It can block every other department. It ought to stand nearest to the lives, the wishes, the wisdom, of the people. It is their necessary organ for creating, guiding, watching, and supporting all the departments of government. Above them all, then, it ought to be eminently *representative*. But it is the least representative of all. Surely, then, for the American people beyond all others, and in a high degree, too, for all peoples who are developing popular government, it is pertinent to inquire carefully into the fundamental nature of these representative institutions, the causes of their failures, and the means, if any can be found, to adapt them to the exigencies of modern times.

Why is it that a legislative assembly, which in our country's infancy summoned to its halls a Madison or a Hamilton to achieve the liberties of the people, has now fallen so low that our public spirited men hesitate to approach it? The municipal council in early times, as now in England and Germany, comprised the stanchest men of the community. The American Congress was once the arena for a Webster, a Clay, a Calhoun, whose debates a nation followed. If it can be shown by what means representative assemblies formerly enrolled the honored leaders of the people, and met precisely the problems of the day, we may be able to see how the social and political conditions of to-day, resulting from changes of the past fifty years, have outgrown those early institutions, and rendered their original fitness a disastrous encumbrance.

Richard T. Ely

☼

THE eminent American economist, writer and lecturer, Richard T. Ely, was born at Ripley, New York, April 13, 1854. He was graduated from Columbia College in 1876. Having won a fellowship in letters granted by his *alma mater*, he spent several years in Germany where he became a pupil of Karl Knies, a foremost representative of the historical school of economics. In 1879 he was awarded the degree of Ph.D. *summa cum laude* by the University of Heidelberg. Shortly after his return from Germany, his work as professor of economics in Johns Hopkins University attracted much attention. Dr. Ely was called to the University of Wisconsin in 1892 and for many years directed the school of economics and political science. His achievements at the University of Wisconsin marked the beginning of a new era in the history of that institution.

In 1885 Dr. Ely was one of the most active of a group of economists who founded the American Economic Association, of which he became president in 1899. Holding the view that economic science should be primarily practical in its aims, Dr. Ely has been active in the sphere of public life and social service. He was at one time (1885-1886) a member of the Baltimore tax commission; at another time (1886-1888) a member of the tax commission of the state of Maryland. In 1904 he founded the American Bureau of Industrial Research. Three years later he became the first president of the American Association of Labor Legislation.

On the eve of the World War, Dr. Ely was lecturing

on economics at the University of London. In 1920 he founded the Institute for Research in Land Economics. Two years later it was incorporated as an independent research and educational institution under the name of "The Institute for Research in Land Economics and Public Utilities." Headquarters remained in Madison until 1925 when an affiliation was brought about with Northwestern University, where Dr. Ely was appointed research professor. The work of the Institute has been admirably directed and developed by Dr. Ely. The year 1930 saw the opening of offices in New York City and the reorganization of the Institute on a new and even more efficient basis.

Among Dr. Ely's published works may be mentioned *Outlines of Economics*, *Monopolies and Trusts*, *Socialism and Social Reform*, *The Evolution of Industrial Society*, *The Past and Present of Political Economy*, *French and German Socialism of Modern Times*, *The Labor Movement in America*, *Property and Contract in their Relations to the Distribution of Wealth*, *Social Aspects of Christianity and Other Essays*, *The Social Laws of Service*, and *Socialism; an Examination of its Nature, its Strength and Weakness*.

This partial list of Dr. Ely's written work speaks eloquently of his application and industry during the years of a life already extended far beyond the scriptural three-score and ten.

From SOCIALISM AND SOCIAL REFORM, *by Richard T. Ely, Ph.D., LL.D. Published by Thomas Y. Crowell & Co., New York and Boston, 1894. Reprinted by permission of the author.*

THE word socialism, which has come into use in the present century, has already acquired a variety of meanings. It seems necessary to any clear thought that we should, first of all, distinguish between socialism in a large but not altogether vague sense, and socialism in a more technical and more precise sense. Socialism in this large sense frequently has reference, in a general way, to the views and aspirations of those who hold that the individual should subordinate himself to society, maintaining that thus alone can the welfare of all be secured. Socialism in this more general sense implies the rejection of the doctrine of selfishness as a sufficient social force and the affirmation of altruism as a principle of social action. Socialism, in this broad sense of the word, means that society is not a mere aggregation of individuals, but a living, growing organism, the laws of which are something different from the laws of individual action. Aristotle was a socialist in this sense of the word, which, it may be remarked, is a true sense of the word; for he maintained that you never could arrive at the whole by a mere addition of the units comprising it, and consequently that the welfare of society could not be secured through exclusive attention to individual claims. The prosperity of the whole, however, he maintained, implied the prosperity of all the individuals which it includes. In other words, this sage of antiquity thought we must proceed in our treatment of social questions from the standpoint of society, and not from that of the individual.

"The state is, by nature," says Aristotle, "clearly prior to the individual and to the family, since the whole is of necessity prior to the part. . . . The proof that the state is a creation of nature, and prior to the individual, is that the individual, when isolated, is not self-sufficing; and therefore he is like a part in relation to the whole. But he who is unable to live in society, or who has no need because he is sufficient for himself, must be either a beast or a god."

The great thinkers in economics and politics in all ages have been socialists in this general sense of the word, and opposed to them has been a small sect of individualists, who reject the conception of the state as an organism, and believe that the standpoint of the individual is sufficient, both in science and in practice. . . .

Socialism is then not restricted necessarily to state activity, but it becomes equivalent to affectionate regard for others in society, and the systematic attempt to improve others. It is used as the opposite of individualism, which then means a selfish and inconsiderate exaltation of the individual.

The second definition of socialism to which reference is made, is that given by Prof. Adolph Wagner, the celebrated professor of political economy in the University of Berlin. Defining socialism in a more general sense as the opposite of individualism, he says:—

"It is, therefore, a principle which regulates social and economic life according to the needs of society as a whole, or which makes provision for the satisfaction of those needs, whereas, individualism is a principle which, in social and economic life, places the individual in the foreground, takes the individual as a starting-point, and makes his interests and wishes the rule for society."

The use of the word socialism in the large sense just described is a legitimate one, for it serves to designate a class of thinkers, and to distinguish them from those who hold very different views. Socialism and individualism are two different philosophical systems. The only objection to the use of the word socialism to designate that social philosophy which is contrasted with individualism in the broadest sense, is that socialism has a narrower meaning, to be described presently, which has become prevalent. Thus, if a writer declares, "I am a socialist!" he is more likely to be classed with Karl Marx than with Aristotle.

The word socialism has, however, other general uses which seem to be altogether wanting in any scientific precision of meaning, and which should therefore be rejected. It is employed to designate in such a vague manner a tendency or attitude of mind, that it lacks all metes and bounds. It has, for example, even been used to designate the thoughts and efforts of those who concern themselves with social affairs. Manifestly, in this sense, it would include a large amount of the individualistic as well as the socialistic philosophy. One writer has called socialism the economic philosophy of the suffering classes. Doubtless he himself would not claim for this statement the character of a scientific definition; for socialism is not the only economic philosophy which has been or may be embraced by those spoken of as the suffering classes. We might likewise call anarchy, or voluntary co-operation, or Mr. Henry George's single tax, the economic philosophy of the suffering classes. The radical improvement of the lot of the propertyless majority has been declared to be the material content of socialism. In addition to the objections already urged to the previous statement, it may be said that it is not necessary to view socialism as a class problem, although it must be admitted that it is so viewed by most social democrats in Germany. Socialism may be advocated by an artist from the artistic standpoint, or by a theologian from a religious standpoint. The true aim of the best socialism, it seems to the writer, is that general social amelioration which proposes to sacrifice no class, but to improve and elevate all classes. It does not necessarily mean the abolition of classes, although under any system of socialism other class distinctions would prevail than those which now obtain.

While each honest and careful definition of socialism tells us something, there is a whole class of definitions which must be simply rejected as dishonest.

For example, when one says that socialism is that system which swallows up individual liberty, subordinating entirely the individual to society, it is plain that the so-called definition is no definition, but a condemnation of that which is to be defined. Then there are certain popular and inaccurate ideas which need not occupy our time. There are those who call any general social upheaval and widespread turning things upside down, socialism, although this upheaval manifestly may be as well anti-socialistic as socialistic. Then there are those—and we meet them very commonly—who call whatever they regard as an exaggeration of the social principle, socialism, especially if it takes the form of state activity. Thus, whether the ordinary man calls the government ownership and management of the telegraph socialism or not, will depend on whether he approves it or not. That kind of governmental activity which is not liked by any particular person is apt to be called by that person socialism. Manifestly we can make no progress in scientific discussion with such vague and unscientific ideas.

The word socialism, as generally employed, has a far narrower meaning than socialism in the broad sense already described. It calls to mind an industrial society which, in its main features, is sufficiently clear and precise. It is not a theory which embraces all departments of social activity, but is confined to the economic department, dealing with others simply as connected with this and influenced by it. This socialism is frequently designated as "scientific socialism." It is with this socialism, which presents a theory of industrial society based upon radical social reconstruction, that the present work deals.

(Note. When the preceding selection was referred to the author, Professor Ely, he wrote that he had found no reason to modify the statements made so long ago; he called attention, however, to the fact that what is given in this quotation is merely descriptive, without criticism either pro or con. He also called attention to the fact that a more critical treatment would be found in Chapter XXXIII in the fifth edition of Ely's "Outlines of Economics" which appeared in April of this year. In this chapter, entitled *Socialism,* the relation of socialism to other movements is pointed out. Those who have an interest in his views will do well to read this very recent discussion in the "Outlines of Economics.")

Joseph Schafer

☼

JOSEPH SCHAFER was born in Muscoda, Wisconsin, December 29, 1867, and spent his boyhood years in southwestern Wisconsin. He was graduated from the University of Wisconsin in 1894; rather late in life according to present day ideas, but indicative of the effort and determination of many young men of that period to acquire a college education, even though its realization were somewhat deferred. For some years thereafter, Dr. Schafer was professor of history in the University of Oregon. He has written a number of books dealing with the history of the Pacific Coast and of Wisconsin. Among these are: *History of the Pacific Northwest*, *The Pacific Slope and Alaska*, *The Acquisition of Oregon Territory*, *The Wisconsin Doomsday Book*, and *Carl Schurz, Militant Liberal*. Dr. Schafer is at the present time superintendent of the State Historical Society of Wisconsin.

From A HISTORY OF THE PACIFIC NORTHWEST *by Joseph Schafer. Published by The Macmillan Company, New York, 1918. By permission of the publishers.*

ORIGIN OF LEWIS AND CLARK EXPEDITION

WHEN Jefferson entered upon his office of President, March 4, 1801, the Mississippi was still the western boundary of the United States. All west of the river was supposed by Americans to belong to Spain, which had been in possession at New Orleans since 1763. As a matter of fact, however, Napoleon had recently forced Spain to give back Louisiana to France, but without publishing to the world the treaty of October, 1800, by which this was accomplished. When the Americans learned, a little later, of the change of ownership of this western territory, and the prospect that France would succeed Spain at the mouth of the Mississippi, great alarm was felt throughout the country. "Perhaps nothing since the Revolutionary War," wrote Jefferson, "has produced more uneasy sensations throughout the body of the nation."

A glance at the condition of the West of that time will explain why this was so. The entire region beyond the Alleghenies was by nature tributary to the Mississippi. It was a fertile land, containing rich valleys, beautiful plains, and far-stretching forests which once teemed with wild game. Daniel Boone called Kentucky "a second Paradise." He and other pioneers at first entered the region as hunters. Afterward they cut a road through the Shenandoah and Cumberland Gap ("the Wilderness Road"), through which they brought their wagons, families, and cattle, to make new homes upon the western waters. The pioneers of Tennessee arrived at about the same time, just before the Revolutionary War, and occupied the high valleys along the headwaters of Tennessee River. From these beginnings settlement had spread rapidly in spite of Indian wars and frontier hardships, until, in the year 1800, Kentucky had a white population of 180,000, and Tennessee 92,000. By that time Ohio had also been settled, partly by Revolutionary soldiers from New England, and already counted 45,000 people. A few settlers were scattered along the rivers of Alabama and Mississippi, and still others lived in the old dilapidated French villages of Illinois, Indiana, and Michigan. We will not be far wrong in placing the total white population on Mississippi waters in 1800 at 325,000.

The prosperity of all these people was absolutely in the hands of the power that controlled the Mississippi. At that time there were no canals joining the eastern and western streams; railroads had never been heard of; and the steamboat, afterward such a wonderful aid in transporting goods and passengers up the rivers of the West, was yet to be invented. Manufactured goods, articles of little bulk and considerable value, were carried across the mountains from the Atlantic seaboard by pack train or wagon, to supply the frugal wants of the frontier settlers. Cattle from the great ranges of Kentucky and Tennessee were driven eastward to market; but all the other produce of farm, mill, and factory, the surplus wheat, corn, pork, flour, and lumber, were carried to the one invariable market at New Orleans.

So long as Americans had the free use of the Mississippi, all was satisfactory. In theory this was one of our unquestioned rights; but the practical fact was different, for the Spaniards owned the land on both banks of the river at its mouth, and our people were dependent upon them for a place to deposit the produce brought down until it could be transferred to ocean vessels. If they, or the French who were about to step into their places, should refuse to continue this right of deposit, or should charge a heavy toll for it, they could sap the very life-blood of the American communities in the entire trans-Allegheny region.

The Spaniards were supposed to be too weak to attempt this with any promise of success; but France had become the dread of Europe, and ranked as the greatest military power of the world. It is not strange that Americans should take alarm at the prospect of having her as a neighbor on the west, especially since this would mean French garrisons planted about New Orleans. The uneasiness of which Jefferson wrote was caused by the fear that France, when once in possession, might undertake to oppress the Americans in order to establish her influence over the western people. Just before the close of the year 1802 the news reached Washington that a Spanish official at New Orleans had actually denied to Americans the right of deposit, which was guaranteed by treaty. This action not only increased the alarm already widely felt but aroused the West to a desire for war in which many eastern people shared.

Jefferson was by nature strongly averse to war, and would sometimes yield a great deal in order to preserve peace. In this case, however, his mind seems to have been made up. We must go to war rather than permit France to take and keep possession of the mouth of the Mississippi. But it would be best, he thought, to delay the armed conflict as long as possible, and meantime he would try to gain the control of the river for the United States by the arts of diplomacy, in the use of which he was a master hand. The plan was to frighten Napoleon with a threat that the United States would join Great Britain in a war against France, and thus induce him, as a condition of peace, to sell us the island and city of New Orleans, together with West Florida. This would give the United States both banks of the Mississippi at its mouth, and insure the control of the river. Jefferson had already instructed Robert R. Livingston, our minister to France, to undertake this purchase of territory from Napoleon; and when the war spirit ran high in Congress, during the winter of 1802-1803, he sent James Monroe to Paris as a special commissioner to assist in carrying out this plan. At the same time Congress took measures to place the country in as good condition as possible to bear the shock of a future war.

It was under these circumstances, when the country was excited over affairs in the West, and fearful of a collision with the overshadowing power of France; when the fate of the Mississippi appeared to be hanging in the balance, and might turn either way; that President Jefferson sent to Congress the now famous message of January 18, 1803, recommending an exploring expedition to the Pacific.

Grant Showerman

☼

GRANT SHOWERMAN needs no introduction to the people of Wisconsin. He was born at Brookfield, Waukesha County, January 9, 1870. He was graduated from the University of Wisconsin in 1896 and received his Ph.D. degree from the same institution four years later. Since 1900 he has been professor of classics in the university that gave him his early training. Dr. Showerman has spent much time in Rome, both as student and as teacher in summer schools, and his experiences there are reflected in some of his books. Among his published works are; *With the Professor*, 1910, *The Indian Stream Republic and Luther Parker*, 1915, *A Country Chronicle*, 1916, *A Country Child*, 1917, *and Eternal Rome*, 1924. *A Country Chronicle* and *A Country Child* are the least academic of his books. They record the author's early experience in a rural environment at a period somewhat removed from pioneer days.

From A COUNTRY CHILD, *by Grant Showerman. Published by The Century Company, New York, 1917. By permission of the publishers.*

WE GO TO LETTIE'S MOTHER'S FUNERAL

WE ARE all sitting in the schoolhouse. Lettie's mother's funeral is today, and we are waiting for them to come. There is something being done to the church, or it would be there instead of in the schoolhouse.

We are sitting in my seat. There isn't any noise except fanning and whispering, when somebody comes in. Tip's aunt comes in and sits down behind us. Tip is with her, and Tip's father. Tip's father has gray whiskers, and always wears a white shirt and a collar. I like the way he talks.

Tip's aunt begins to whisper to my mother. She says: "Poor woman! they say she suffered a great deal. It was a long time too."

My mother turns around a little. She whispers: "Did she know people at the last?"

Tip's aunt says: "They say she just roused up a little about an hour before she passed away, and appeared to reco'nize Harry, but she never said anything."

Tip's aunt sits back in the seat again. Pretty soon she leans forward, and says: "They say the 'Piscopal minister from the Village is comin' to conduct the services." She fans a while. She says: "She belonged to their church, you know." Then she sits back again. She and my mother both fan themselves quite a while. We don't say anything. I feel warm, with my coat and collar and boots on.

At last we hear wheels outside. We can tell they are coming from the house. Then we hear a great many wheels. Then we hear them begin to turn in. We hear them right near. They come crunching over the gravel by the steps.

We all sit still and listen. We can hear men stepping. It takes a long time before we can see them. They come into the entry, and then through the door, and start up the middle aisle. They hardly move. They are going to come by right near us. I dread having the coffin come along.

The Episcopal minister from the Village walks in front. He is dressed in a queer sort of black and white gown, and carries a cross on a stick right in front of him. He looks straight ahead. Then comes the coffin. Lettie and her uncle Harry walk right behind it. Lettie is all covered with a black veil, but we can see her through it. We can see her crying. Her uncle Harry has his arm around her, and he holds his head down. I feel sorry for Lettie.

They set the coffin down on two chairs on the platform where the teacher's desk always is when we have school. The desk is moved off to one side. They have the church organ, and Jennie is sitting behind it. They sing, and the minister reads something. Some of it is a prayer. He reads everything in the same voice. Sometimes it is almost like singing. Our minister never reads prayers, but makes them up.

Grandpa Tyler is managing, the way he always does. At the end, he gets up and says that anyone so desiring can now view the remains. We all get up and go past the coffin. Lettie's mother looks still and white. They don't make much noise going by. I dread it before we go.

When they are all past and we are almost out of the room, Lettie and her uncle Harry get up to look. Lettie stands with her hands folded under her veil. She stoops over and cries harder than ever. She puts her handkerchief up to her eyes, and says: "Oh, my mama! Oh, my dear mama!" Her uncle Harry puts one arm over the coffin, and lays his face down on the glass. His eyes are all red and wet.

My mother gives me a little push. She says: "Come! let's get out. It makes me feel so bad I don't know what to do!" I feel bad, too, but I don't cry. I wonder what Lettie will do without her mother.

The funeral procession isn't so very long. It is a busy time, and some of the men can't get away from their work. My father takes us in the light wagon. Tip's aunt goes with us. Tip and his father go in their buggy, with old Andy. When we go by Lettie's house, I think how empty and still it must be in there. We ride down past the church and our house and the depot, and up to the north burying ground.

Lettie and her uncle Harry feel awfully bad at the grave. I feel as sorry as can be. I wish I could go up to Lettie and tell her. Somehow she seems different, with the black clothes on, and her mother dead. I wonder how it will be when I go up to play with her. I wonder whether she will ever want to play now.

We go out and get into the light wagon. Tip's aunt says: "Poor little motherless girl! I'm just as sorry for her as I can be."

By and by my mother says: "I suppose she'll have to go and live with her aunt now, in Town. Don't you?"

Tip's aunt says: "I s'pose that's how it'll be. At any rate, that's what they talk of."

I sit on the front seat with my father.

Tip and his father are just ahead of us. Tip turns around and looks at me. Pretty soon he says: "Come on up and play, will you?"

I say: "If I can."

We say it without smiling very much.

John Nagle

☼

ALTHOUGH he lived his life in a restricted environment and published a small weekly newspaper to carry his messages to the people, John Nagle was in some respects the most remarkable editorial writer and essayist that Wisconsin has produced. Born in Canada in 1848, he was brought to Manitowoc County when only a few weeks old. There he spent his brief life as educator and newspaper editor. The rural school was his only college, but his early passion for good literature supplied what high school and university might have done for him in another way. His influence on the social and educational life of his county during its formative period cannot be fully appreciated. However, recognition of his ability was not confined to his neighbors. In his later years his editorials written for the *Manitowoc Pilot* were copied and republished from Coast to Coast. He occupied the positions of president of the Wisconsin Teachers' Association and president of the Wisconsin State Press Association. Mr. Nagle died in 1900 at the early age of 52. The few sketches that follow indicate the scope of his work as an essayist.

THE LONE GRAVE

A FEW miles south of Marietta, Georgia, close to the railroad track is a grave. A soldier's body had been found there and buried by railroad hands. Not only was his name unknown, but it was not known on which side he fought. The grave is cared for by railroad employees. It is marked by a simple slab bearing the inscription, "He

Died for the Cause He Thought Was Right." The place is known as "Lone Grave"; it is in sight of Kenesaw Mountain where thousands died, but not even the National Cemetery at Marietta or at Mission Ridge attracts the attention which this lone grave among the hills of northern Georgia does. The train was stopped and the grave was soon surrounded. Then was shown the sympathetic nature of woman, who shares the sorrows of the distressed and mingles her tears with those who have cause to weep. As Mr. Barker arranged his kodak to take a time picture of the grave, a lady stepped forward, and tearing her bouquet of flowers from her breast, placed it on the marble slab which marked the soldier's grave. Her example was followed by others, and the grave was covered with flowers. The solitary grave appealed to them as all "the trappings of woe" could not, and no heartier tributes of respect were ever showered upon the tomb of a monarch than those laid by gentle hands on the grave of the unknown dead who sleeps in a lonely mountain pass in northern Georgia.

HOW ENTHUSIASM DIES

How Enthusiasm Dies, is the subject of an article in a late educational journal. That enthusiasm does die out in the educational field the experience of every one who has done work in the field will bear ample testimony. There are many causes, not the least of which is human nature. Enthusiasm is a fire which feeds on vitality, and cannot be sustained; and then it leads to new things, discoveries which require constant battle for their reception. Parents want their children to make improvements that are visible, and the best teachers will not do this. Everything that takes deep root is slow of growth, but when the time for bearing fruit comes the yield compensates for the delay. America is a country given to rush. To climb to the top is the ambition of everyone, and not to make preparation so that reaching the top is a certainty. Teaching must conform to this demand, and hence there must be false teaching. There can be no enthusiasm in a lie, and many teachers who know better, teach so as to please the people rather than satisfy their own conscience.

RELIGION IS LOVE

RELIGION in its true sense, divorced from malignant persecution of what is deemed error, purified of intolerance, superstition, and pretense of exalted goodness, is love pure and simple. There is no promise of the future that makes it so blessed as the hope that love has an existence which extends beyond the grave. The love of friends is the purest and most exalted element of life, the essence of the soul. It is unshaken by prosperity, it is triumphant over misfortune and makes existence sweet. The mother who mourns a child can have no conception of heaven higher, purer, holier, than a place where she will meet "the loved and lost again."

What in life is worth its survival except it be love? Hope at best is but a wish wedded to faith. But there is solace in the thought that the flower of sweetest fragrance is nourished by the tears which affection sheds, and blooms "where sorrow may not enter." If this life is but a preparation for another, higher and better, then the best and purest attribute of this should be allowed entrance into that realm whose gates of pearl it has opened. Love makes heaven possible and earth pleasant. It is the great heart of the universe, whose pulsations are charity and good will; the life that is immortal, the hope that endureth.

GOOD IN ABSTENTION

THE man who discontinues some expensive and useless habit is benefitted, whether he does so in response to the promptings of his moral nature, or because decreased income suggests retrenchment. Man is always in danger when he can satisfy every wish. If things come easily to him he loses diligence and his character is weakened. There is always good in abstention, whether voluntary or forced.

ABRAHAM LINCOLN

The character of Lincoln broadens with the passage of time. Whether it is that people make him a center for attributes of greatness which every one desires to see in concrete form, or whether the perspective of time enables us to view and judge him better than could be done when his qualities were displaying themselves, is of no consequence. He is one of the nation's idols, and a nation without an idol is a nation without ideals.

Men like Lincoln, who are regarded as he is, elevate the standard of humanity—more in contemplation of the virtues they are credited with having possessed than in what they did. And still men who are in popular estimation invested with the attributes of perfection, were great in life. Death has removed all possibilities of exhibition of human weakness and their character is viewed in the light of their greatness and their frailties are eliminated.

No such man as Washington is popularly supposed to have been could be made of flesh and blood, and the great Lincoln, if he appeared in life before us today, would soon be divested of many of the qualities it gives us pleasure to think of having been his.

The creative faculty of imagination is strong in mature people as well as in children. It lifts the race to higher planes of moral susceptibility. There is no intelligent citizen who will not gather inspiration from viewing the grand figure of Lincoln as it appears to him. All that is best in man finds expression in Lincoln, and no matter how faint the desire to emulate, it stirs to some activity the moral forces in us.

If Lincoln did not understand the great heart of the people, he would not be deemed great himself. He could look through selfishness, contention, and jealousy and perceive the good. He could find

"Books in the running brooks,
 Sermons in stones, and good in everything,"
and this was the foundation of his greatness.

MUSIC THAT IS ETERNAL

There is no person who is not, to some degree, a lover of music, and in all stages of civilization musical instruments of some kind have soothed troubled feelings or aroused passions. But it is a singular fact that those melodies which become most popular have in them something that touches the deeper emotions. A humorous song is short lived. It may amuse, but it leaves none of that indescribable thrill that may properly be called the ecstasy of the soul. A song must have "soul" to be immortal. The plaintive airs of the negroes, as touching in their sadness as they are beautiful in their simplicity, will last as long as melody has the power to please. The words may be, indeed generally are, a meaningless jumble, but the music is of such exquisite beauty, so clearly a product of the heart, that it has the power of touching that organ and making an impression, which, like the memory of the dead, is sweet from its sadness. Men instinctively reverence those airs whose inspiration is from the depth of the soul. Vicious men, and those merry in their cups, will sing humorous songs, but never one of the character under discussion. It would seem sacrilegious, a wanton effort, to injure feelings peculiarly sensitive to impropriety.

The Irish are a people, though of a mercurial nature, subject to fits of despondency. Their airs are the language of the soul and are impregnated with melancholy. There are none sweeter, none more lasting. Scotch airs have also a suggestion of tears in them, and gain immensely by the touch of sorrow. A patriotic song may stir, a lively one may amuse, but there is none that will sink so deeply in the heart as that which is born in sadness.

WOMAN'S AFFECTION

WOMAN clings to life, not because her fear of death is stronger than that of a man, but because she is more affectionate, truer to duty, and less beset by despair. Man's best qualities are revealed by the very activities in which he is engaged, but the depth of a woman's purpose, her strength of feeling and capability for sacrifice, are never fully revealed until some emergency calls them out. There is much that is noble and good hid behind frivolities which belie a woman's nature, and frivolity is readily discarded when a demand is made on those womanly qualities which are much more common than we suppose. A woman's friendship is not easily won, but when it is, its roots find a place in her soul. With capacity for suffering, she has acquired the strength to bear it more uncomplainingly than man.

MOTHER

THERE is no injunction which appeals more strongly to man's affection than that which reads, "Honor thy father and thy mother." When a man thinks of what his mother has endured for him, the affection she has lavished on him, the sacrifices she has made for him, the faith she has in him, he must be worse than a brute if the warm current of his love does not center in her, no matter what her faults.

THE FROST KING

LAST week was a return of the old-fashioned winter when time was young in this land. The snow came down fast and furious, but remained where it fell, and the country roads were smooth, glassy and level, a delight to the traveler. There is between Meeme and Schleswig, Manitowoc County, Wisconsin, a forest, the most extensive in the county, the surface broken with deep ravines and rugged hills. A good road runs through this wood, and a ride over it were worth ten years of humdrum life. At a distance it looked like an immense orchard in blossom, and one could almost fancy the winds were laden with the fragrance of May. Every twig was wreathed with garlands of filmy snow, with a delicate bordering of embroidery gathered from the humid atmosphere by the fairy touch of the Frost King. The evergreens drooped beneath their loads, forming beautiful canopies, fitting bowers for some fair Titania. There was a suggestion of peace in the whole scene, of purity, and an expression of beauty now seldom encountered since "the flowers of the forest" are "a wede away."

THE POWER OF LOVE

THERE is no higher force than love. It has inspired the lovers of humanity in all ages and countries. The love of country has caused the patriot to leave his blood-stained footprints on the sands and snows of a thousand fields. The love of home and family causes the hard hands of the toiler to struggle for the necessaries of life. The love of humanity produced the sacrifices of the Howards. The love of truth sustained the constancy of the martyrs of science and liberty, and causes the privations and sacrifices of the explorer who faces death amid arctic snows and cold and ice. Yes, all the tears that have been shed, all the prayers that have been offered, all the kisses given by the rosy lips of health to the ashen face of death, all the fond hopes expressed amid clouds and mists, have sprung from the great fountain of human affection—love.

MIDSUMMER

THERE is a rare beauty in the woods in midsummer, which

no one can fully appreciate but he whose memory is a storehouse of pleasant recollections gathered in that early period when "life was love." The patches of sky seen through the rents in the green curtain of nature's weaving, flecked with shreds of fleeting clouds, bring to mind the heaven of childhood, which needed not doctrine or philosophy for its revelation. The winds seem to have a softness and fragrance which lull the spirit to rest and thus blot out the harshness of life. Rest, now, has no feature of languor, and the vigorous happy life with which one is surrounded is inspiriting. There is no prescription that can match the woods for efficacy.

THE HIGHEST PLEASURE

IF HEAVEN ever touches earth it is when mortal man finds pleasure in bringing happiness to others; when the spirit of charity is abroad casting out the demon of selfishness from the hearts of men.

Neal Brown

☼

IT IS not often that it is given to one man to excel in many lines of endeavor. To do this he must have a far-reaching vision and superior talents, reinforced by a wide experience.

Neal Brown, lawyer, statesman, business man and writer attracted attention in all these different vocations. He was born in Hebron, Jefferson County, Wisconsin, February 28, 1856. His father was a newspaper man who lived on a farm, and on this farm Neal worked during his boyhood years. His general education was begun and completed, so far as schools were concerned, in the rural schools of the neighborhood, but the home of the elder Brown was well stocked with the best books, which the lad read with avidity, a habit that persisted throughout his life and made Neal Brown one of the best informed men of the state.

At the age of nineteen he began the study of law in the office of L. B. Caswell, at that time a factor in the political life of Wisconsin. In 1880 Brown was graduated from the law department of the University of Wisconsin, and began the practice of law in Wausau which was thenceforth his home. The earlier years of his professional career were devoted almost exclusively to his law practice. He was president of the Wisconsin State Bar Association in 1909. He took an active interest in politics, served in both the state senate and the assembly, and was twice the candidate of the Democratic Party for United States Senator. His latter years were given more largely to the organization of important business projects in Wausau and its vicinity. More as a matter of recreation than profit, he wrote articles dealing with philosophical and literary subjects. His style was singularly clear, precise and masterful. A volume which he published in 1898 entitled *Critical Confessions* can still be read with profit by every lover of English literature. Mr. Brown died at Watkins, New York, September 18, 1917, while on a visit at the home of his sister.

From CRITICAL CONFESSIONS, *by Neal Brown. Published by the Philosopher Press, Wausau, Wisconsin, 1898. Copyrighted by Neal Brown, 1899.*

ANDREW LANG

IN pessimistic mood, one feels that the world of letters has squandered most of its genius, and is traveling toward an intellectual poorhouse. The great poets have certainly departed. Stephenson has gone, and there are but two or three story-tellers left. Fiction has become short and choppy; a matter of fragments, without sustained flights. The few mountain peaks that are left are nodding. The fruits of letters seem over-ripe and ready to fall rotting to the ground. It is a transition time, and perhaps the soil is being fertilized by the rank growths that spring up, for something better to come.

We are seduced from healthy standards by *fin de siecle* tendencies; the color of nature is gone, and we have green carnations and unsubstantial, unreal things. Men are made to seem like shadows walking. We are non-creative. We either imitate, or else we rebel against imitation, and the pendulum swings as far the other way. The result is strange, uncouth, fancies in art and literature, and our romancists make monkeys of men, to borrow a phrase from the vernacular. The commercial autocrats of magazinedom, and certain of the hack writers of newspaperdom set the fashion. With the small arts of puffery they build up small reputations that die in a day. How often the announcement; "a genius is coming, watch for him, he is here,—he has written a great novel, a great poem, or what not." We are put on the *qui vive*, and by and bye when the poor little puffed out product struts upon the stage we find that he belongs to the ephemera. These strains are common. We watch anxiously for the pool to move that we may be healed of these grotesque vagaries of mental disease. We gaze longingly up the road for a rescuer and see but wind-piled columns of choking dust.

We comfort ourselves a little with Kipling; and Besant and Black are still with us, but we sigh to be healed of Hardy's decadence, and of the tastelessness of *The Martian*,—poor withered fruit of DuMaurier's dotage.

We cry out for something in place of this dry rot, this attenuated intellectuality; this vain struggling after startling effects. Our sensibilities are mangled and scarified day by day by the rude contact of a crowd of weird, grotesque, figures who flit their fantastic way across the stage.

We are surrounded by writers of queer distorted verse, drunken with their own turgid, muddy, rhetoric; dancing fauns and satyrs holding revels over social uncleanness like crows over carrion; dreamers of meaningless visions, makers of verse full of incomprehensible gibberish. Are they of healthy human kind who beat time in this rout? Is that young woman who writes tigerish verses of a tigerish passion, all the Sappho we shall have? Must we call a plain case of erotic mania, poetic fervour? Is that jingler of little verselets, that journeyman carver of odd forms of speech, to be our Tennyson? Shall we force ourselves to see deathless harmony in a mere mush of words, simply because it is labeled poetry? Must we give *Jude The Obscure* and *The Martian* a place with *Vanity Fair* and *David Copperfield?* We "have been tolled by holy bell to church, have sat at good men's feasts," and we cannot forget those feasts. If there is nothing else, give us some good stories of bears and tigers, of jungles, of far-off lands where men are breathing free, and where there is good wholesome blood-letting and killing.

Thus the Pessimist.

But we may be comforted in a measure; we have our blessings and must not be unmindful of them. Into this world where everything is worn out and steeped in the ditch-water of dullness, comes an interrogation point of a man,—Andrew Lang. If needs be, he will smash every idol and question every fad. Let the fashions change as they will, here is a man who clings to the verities of truth and mental good health.

He is cool-blooded and temperate when others are furious. He retains his composure amidst the clamours of little coteries of intellectual starvelings frantically admiring each other and bound to coerce all others into a like service. Into this market-place of small wares, Lang comes as the Sealer of Weights and Measures. He hears unmoved the ding-donging of the auction bell, the selling of names. He cannot be hypnotized by the posturings and caperings of literary mountebanks. Over the Kingdom of Fools, he is the upright and just judge, with plenary jurisdiction.

Many idols, some false and some true, have been ranged before this judgment seat. Along with other stucco-work, is poor old Poet Bailey, the solace and comfort of our grandmothers. Look in your *Poets Argosy* or *Gems of Poetry*, and you will unearth among other ancient treasures, "O no, we never mention her," and like lollipops and sweet things from Bailey. I knew Bailey first, through the melancolia of my friend Mr. Richard Swiveller, who turned from the perfidious Sophy to Bailey's soothing charm. I learned Bailey better through Lang, who treated his reputation charitably, bestowing only a spanking,—lightly laid on. In fact Lang thinks Bailey might have been something of a poet, he pleased so many simple folk. In this genial fashion does he judge all small sinners.

But when Lang reads the bead-roll of genius, names that were before heard and forgotten stick like burrs. They stand for something. The dead heroes walk again in new-kindled light. Bunyan, and Montaigne, and Scott, and all great and noble souls gain new nobility and pass unscathed through that wise and kindly judgment. Lang has the grand hailing sign and password of the kinship of genius. He recognized his fellows for what they are across the centuries and the wide seas.

Thus it is that he flashed recognition over to Holmes and Lowell, of all Americans the most like himself. He discovered Kipling in the wilderness of India, and gave him a passport into the World of Letters. And now Kipling has become the man of three continents, with fame enough to fill them all.

Lang is best as a critic and hero-worshipper. He and Nordau are almost the only ones left to police our world of literary nondescripts. Carlyle, that harsh block of Scottish granite, is gone, and humbug and cant may thrive apace. Thackeray, Keeper of a House for the Correction of Snobs, stalks his grim beat no more. Macaulay, who so deftly put Mr. Robert Montgomery in the pillory, is with the dust of the earth. Dr. Holmes, vested with large jurisdiction over vulgar pretenders in these American Colonies, has no further judgments to execute. There are no more. Gallant spirits, loyal to the truth, when shall we look upon your like again? You yet have some security that your work will be carried on, for Lang is your living disciple. You may be sure that some frothy cant will be sponged out; some humbugs will be dosed heroically; some literary reputations will be put in the stocks where we may all have our fling at them. Who shall say that these labors have been in vain? The snobs did not run about at ease while Thackeray was at them. Some of them were killed and some cured.

Carl Russell Fish

☼

CARL RUSSELL FISH, historical writer and university professor, was born at Central Falls, Rhode Island, October 17, 1876. He was granted his A.B. degree from Brown in 1897, A.M. from Harvard in 1898 and Ph. D. in 1900. Dr. Fish came to the University of Wisconsin in 1900 and has since resided in Madison. He has received many marks of recognition, both in his own and in foreign countries. During 1908-09 he was Research Associate in Carnegie Institute. Dr. Fish is a popular lecturer as well as a writer. Some of his published works are: *The Civil Service and the Patronage*, 1904; *Development of American Nationality*, 1913; *American Diplomacy*, 1915; *History of America*, 1925; and the *Rise of the Common Man*.

Fred L. Holmes

✧

FRED L. HOLMES is a native of Wisconsin, born at Waukau, Winnebago County, May 9, 1883. He was graduated from the Omro High School and from the University of Wisconsin in 1906 with the degree of Bachelor of Arts. It was during this student period that Mr. Holmes, in order to finance his education, became a reporter on the *Wisconsin State Journal*. In 1909 he was selected by the late Senator Robert M. La Follette to become business manager of La Follette's *Magazine* and later managing editor, a position which he held until the magazine was discontinued in 1929. In 1906 Mr. Holmes founded the Holmes News Service at Madison, Wisconsin.

It was while working his way through the University that Mr. Holmes attracted attention by historical articles which he contributed to newspapers and magazines. Later he published a volume entitled *Regulation of Railroads and Public Utilities in Wisconsin* which was used for years as a textbook in several universities. Following the war, he published a book entitled *Wisconsin's War Record*, and in 1930 L. C. Page and Company of Boston published his book, *Abraham Lincoln Traveled This Way*. This work showed a close study of Lincoln history and contained a preface by Glenn Frank, President of the University of Wisconsin.

Since he was graduated from the University of Wisconsin in 1906, Mr. Holmes has resided continuously in Madison. He is said to be planning two additional books along travel-biographical lines.

A Log Cabin Enshrined, *By Fred L. Holmes. Extract from Chapter One, "Abraham Lincoln Traveled This Way." Copyright 1930. L. C. Page and Company. Reprinted by special permission.*

IT became necessary to put an end to my dreaming and hasten my wanderings unless I wished to prolong my days of pilgrimage. Instead of a dull, uninteresting country around Hodgenville, as I expected, it is a land of changeful scenery. Valleys and rolling landscapes gratify the eye with vistas of pastoral beauty. I have rarely traveled two miles with keener anticipation than in the trip over the Jackson Highway to the birthplace.

There were moments of trepidation. Would the housing of the humble cabin in a Greek temple on the hill, over the site where it had stood out in the farming country away from the city, dissipate the love for tradition which I had come to associate with the spot? It was my first visit and I longed to have it impressive.

Soon I was at the gates. The road was winding into a little valley and then, from behind the trees, loomed in an afternoon sun the rectangular, granite edifice on a knoll with its long, glistening stone steps fringed with green hedges. At once there came upon me a sense of thankfulness that a patriotic people, under the inspiration of the Rev. Jenkin Lloyd Jones, Richard Lloyd Jones and Robert J. Collier, had voluntarily contributed their $385,000 to a fund to reclaim these hallowed grounds,—"the most signal tribute ever paid by the American people to the Nation's greatest servant."

From the base of the ascent the memorial is a picture of grace and harmony. It stands out alone against the sky above a wide expanse of country. Approaching the Doric-columned entrance, one discerns the bold, chiseled inscription:

HERE
OVER THE LOG CABIN WHERE ABRAHAM
LINCOLN WAS BORN DESTINED TO
PRESERVE THE UNION AND FREE THE
SLAVE
A GRATEFUL PEOPLE HAVE DEDICATED
THIS MEMORIAL TO UNITY, PEACE
AND BROTHERHOOD AMONG THE STATES

About to enter, I read other inscriptions beside the doorway, selected from his memorable speech at Peoria, his address at Cooper Union, and his Second Inaugural. The spirit of his ideals sentineled the threshhold.

The log cabin was now within view and I forgot all else. How humble it seemed; how narrow the doorway; how little the one window near the fireplace; how out of proportion the chimney! There is only one room. It is pitifully small. It measures seventeen feet by twelve, and the whole is constructed of one hundred and forty-three logs.

"And is this really the cabin in which Abraham Lincoln was born on Sunday, February 12, 1809?" I asked. It was the same question that confronts nearly every visitor.

"The history of the building is well authenticated," responded Mr. J. M. Cissel, the caretaker. "It has had a career of many vicissitudes, but it now rests upon the spot where it stood in 1809. After the close of the Civil War it was purchased by George Rodman, whose parents were neighbors of the Lincolns. It was moved several times and used as a school, tenant house and negro quarters. In 1894 it was acquired by A. W. Dennett and shortly thereafter began an exhibition journey to the Nashville Centennial, to Central Park in New York, and to the Buffalo Exposition. The logs were purchased by the Lincoln Farm Association in 1906 and finally returned to this birthplace site, after this memorial had been completed.

"Three presidents have since visited here. The cornerstone was laid by President Roosevelt, February 12, 1909; President Taft attended the dedication, November 9, 1911; and President Wilson accepted the farm as a National Park, September 4, 1916. Thousands of people from all over the world now visit here annually."

"Does the government own the entire original farm of Thomas Lincoln?" I asked.

"Only about a third," he responded. "There are about 100 acres in this National Park. Recent investigations disclose that the farm comprised nearly 350 acres. A part of the land is across the road from the park premises."

I was loath to leave. Walking around the cabin examining its cracks and crevices, its joints and ridge pole, and peering through the chained doorway at the hearth, I was touched with sadness in reflecting upon the obvious poverty of the first owners. It must have been so stinting in the little comforts it afforded.

When I lifted my eyes I found in a filtering light of mellow gold sunshine that the walls of the temple were blazoned with Lincoln tributes from poetry and history. One tablet contained an abbreviation of the autobiography prepared by Mr. Lincoln for Jesse W. Fell at Bloomington, Illinois, in 1859. It was a succinct recital of his life story, classic in its brevity and simplicity. He had been named Abraham, not for a neighbor as often supposed, but for his grandfather, a Kentucky pioneer, who was murdered by an Indian. * * * * * * *

"Don't forget to visit the spring at the bottom of the steps on the right," admonished the caretaker as I was leaving. "Little Abraham drank the water from there."

Down a flight of heavy steps, the spring is in a grotto-like cave high enough for one to stand while drinking. The air was cool. Green patches of moss and scraggling vines have attached themselves to the protruding sandstone and the whole is shaded with trees, dense in their heavy foliage.

Spears of grass on the red clay bank above were withered by continued drouth. It is the most secluded spot on the farm, and its proximity to the cabin undoubtedly accounts for the immediate location of the cabin on the hillside. I drank of its crystalline waters.

Out in the sunlight again the caretaker called my attention to a giant oak but a few rods away.

"That tree is more than a century old," he explained. "Two of us joining hands can scarcely reach around it. I venture that on hot afternoons Lincoln's mother often brought her baby here to rest in its cooling shade."

"The tree is a landmark," interrupted another, who was listening. "For one hundred years it has been a marker in the making of surveys for this immediate locality."

I stood for a while in its shade. Its deep grooved bark is broken into irregular plates; its bushy head is impressive of its individuality and character. The tree has poise and dignity comparable with its age. I felt certain that it had protected the baby Lincoln many warm days during his two years of residence there. Other trees on the farm are of more recent growth but here was one that had an acquaintance with him to whom the world pays reverence. To me it seemed both noble and human.

Part IV

HUMOROUS WRITERS OF WISCONSIN

A MEDIEVAL DISCOVERER

GALILEI, commonly called Galileo, was born at Pisa on the 14th day of February, 1564. He was the man who discovered some of the fundamental principles governing the movements, habits, and personal peculiarities of the earth. He discovered things with marvelous fluency. Born as he was, at a time when the rotary motion of the earth was still in its infancy and astronomy was taught only in a crude way, Galileo started in to make a few discoveries and advance some theories which he loved.

He was the son of a musician and learned to play several instruments himself, but not in such a way as to arouse the jealousy of the great musicians of his day. They came and heard him play a few selections, and then they went home contented with their own music. Galileo played for several years in a band at Pisa, and people who heard him said that his manner of gazing out over the Pisan hills with a far-away look in his eye after playing a selection, while he gently up-ended his alto horn and worked the mud-valve as he poured out about a pint of moist melody that had accumulated in the flues of the instrument, was simply grand.

At the age of twenty Galileo began to discover. His first discoveries were, of course, clumsy and poorly made, but very soon he commenced to turn out neat and durable discoveries that would stand for years.

It was at this time that he noticed the swinging of a lamp in a church, and, observing that the oscillations were of equal duration, he inferred that this principle might be utilized in the exact measurement of time. From this little accident, years after, came the clock, one of the most useful of man's dumb friends. And yet there are people who will read this little incident and still hesitate about going to church.

Galileo also invented the thermometer, the micro-

Edgar Wilson Nye

☼

EDGAR WILSON NYE, better known as "
Nye," spent his boyhood days on a Wisco
farm. He was born in Shirley, Maine in 1850
came to Wisconsin with his parents in 1854. His
humor was noted while he was yet a mere child;
said that his playmates were wont to gather about
while he amused them with funny sayings and hum
yarns. When a young man he went to Wyoming Terr
where he studied law and was admitted to the b
1876. Although he served in the Wyoming legisl
it is not recorded that he was a marked success in po
or in the legal profession. Later he returned to Wisc
and engaged in newspaper work at River Falls. It
well be imagined that serious newspaper work wa
to his taste; in any event he soon entered upon his de
career as a humorous writer. For some time Nye tra
with James Whitcomb Riley, a partnership that in
entertainment wherever the pair appeared. In 1881
his first published volume under the title of *Bill N*
Boomerang. This was followed by *Forty Liars and*
Lies in 1883, *Comic History of the United Sta*
1894, and *Comic History of England* in 1896.
time his health failed and he died at Asheville, N
1896 at the age of 46 years. His humor is often
but never coarse or vulgar.

*The following examples of Bill Nye's humor we
sidered of sufficent merit to be included in "*TH
AND HUMOR OF AMERICA," *edited by Mars
Wilder.*

scope, and the proportional compass. He seemed to invent things not for the money he obtained in that way, but solely for the joy of being first on the ground. He was a man of infinite genius and perseverance. He was also very fair in his treatment of other inventors. Though he did not personally invent the rotary motion of the earth, he heartily endorsed it and said it was a good thing. He also came out in a card in which he said that he believed it to be a good thing, and that he hoped some day to see it applied to other planets.

He was also the inventor of a telescope that had a magnifying power of thirty times. He presented this to the Venetian senate, and it was used in making appropriations for river and harbor improvements.

By telescopic investigation Galileo discovered the presence of microbes in the moon, but was unable to do anything for it. I have spoken of Mr. Galileo, informally calling him by his first name, all the way through this article, for I feel so thoroughly acquainted with him, though there was a striking difference in our ages, that I think I am justified in using his given name while talking of him.

Galileo also sat up nights and visited with Venus through a long telescope which he had made himself from an old bamboo fishing-rod.

But astronomy is a very enervating branch of science. Galileo frequently came down to breakfast with red, heavy eyes, eyes that were swollen full of unshed tears. Still he persevered. Day after day he worked and toiled. Year after year he went on with his task till he had worked out in his own mind the satellites of Jupiter and placed a small tin tag on each one, so that he would know it readily when he saw it again. Then he began to look up Saturn's rings and investigate the freckles on the sun. He did not stop at trifles, but went bravely on till everybody came for miles to look at him and get him to write something funny in their autograph albums. It was not an unusual thing for Galileo to get up in the morning, after a wearisome night with a fretful, new-born star, to find his front yard full of albums. Some of them were little red albums with floral decoration on them, while others were the large plush and alligator albums of the affluent. Some were new and had the price mark still on them, while others were old, foundered albums, with a droop in the back and little flecks of egg and gravy on the title page. All came with a request for Galileo "to write a little, witty, characteristic sentiment in them."

Galileo was the author of the hydrostatic paradox and other sketches. He was a great reader and a fluent penman. One time he was absent from home, lecturing in Venice for the benefit of the United Aggregation of Mutual Admirers, and did not return for two weeks, so when he got back he found the front room full of autograph albums. It is said that he then demonstrated his great fluency and readiness as a thinker and writer. He waded through the entire lot in two days with only two men from West Pisa to assist him. Galileo came out of it fresh and youthful, and all the following night he was closeted with another inventor, a wicker-covered microscope, and a bologna sausage. The investigations were carried on for two weeks, after which Galileo went out to the inebriate asylum and discovered some new styles of reptiles.

Galileo was the author of a little work called "I Discarsi e Dimas-Trazioni Matematiche Intorus a Due Muove Scienze." It was a neat little book of about the medium height, and sold well on the trains, for the Pisan newsboys on the cars were very affable, as they are now, and when they came and leaned an armful of these books on a passenger's leg and poured into his ear a long tale about the wonderful beauty of the work, and then pulled in the name of the book from the rear of the last car, where it had been hanging on behind, the passenger would most always buy it and enough of the name to wrap it up in.

He also discovered the isochronism of the pendulum. He saw that the pendulum at certain seasons of the year looked yellow under the eyes, and that it drooped and did not enter into its work with the old zest. He began to study the case with the aid of his new bamboo telescope and a wicker-covered microscope. As a result, in ten days he had the pendulum on its feet again.

Galileo was inclined to be liberal in his religious views, more especially in the matter of the Scriptures, claiming that there were passages in the Bible which did not literally mean what the translator said they did. This was where Galileo missed it. So long as he discovered stars and isochronisms and such things as that, he succeeded, but when he began to fool with other people's religious beliefs he got into trouble. He was forced to fly from Pisa, we are told by the historian, and we are assured at the same time that Galileo, who had always been far, far ahead of all competitors in other things, was equally successful as a fleer.

Galileo received but sixty scudi per year as his salary while at Pisa, and part of that he took in town orders, worth only sixty cents on the scudi.

THE GRAMMATICAL BOY

SOMETIMES a sad, homesick feeling comes over me, when I compare the prevailing style of anecdote and school literature with the old McGuffey brand, so well known thirty years ago. To-day our juvenile literature, it seems to me, is so transparent, so easy to understand, that I am not surprised to learn that the rising generation shows signs of lawlessness.

Boys to-day do not use the respectful language and

large, luxuriant words that they did when Mr. McGuffey used to stand around and report their conversations for his justly celebrated school reader. It is disagreeable to think of, but it is none the less true, and for one I think we should face the facts.

I ask the careful student of school literature to compare the following selection, which I have written myself with great care, and arranged with special reference to the matter of choice and difficult words, with the flippant and commonplace terms used in the average school book of today.

One day as George Pillgarlic was going to his tasks, and while passing through the wood, he spied a tall man approaching in an opposite direction along the highway.

"Ah!" thought George, in a low, mellow tone of voice, "whom have we here?"

"Good morning, my fine fellow," exclaimed the stranger, pleasantly. "Do you reside in this locality?"

"Indeed I do," retorted George, cheerily, doffing his cap. "In yonder cottage, near the glen, my widowed mother and her thirteen children dwell with me."

"And is your father dead?" exclaimed the man, with a rising inflection.

"Extremely so," murmured the lad, "and, oh, sir, that is why my poor mother is a widow."

"And how did your papa die?" asked the man, as he thoughtfully stood on the other foot a while.

"Alas! sir," said George, as a large hot tear stole down his pale cheek and fell with a loud report on the warty surface of his bare foot, "he was lost at sea in a bitter gale. The good ship foundered two years ago last Christmas tide, and father was foundered at the same time. No one knew of the loss of the ship and that the crew was drowned until the next spring, and then it was too late."

"And what is your age, my fine fellow?" quoth the stranger.

"If I live till next October," said the boy, in a declamatory tone of voice suitable for a Second Reader, "I will be seven years of age."

"And who provides for your mother and her large family of children?" queried the man.

"Indeed, I do, sir," replied George, in a shrill tone. "I toil, oh, so hard, sir, for we are very, very poor, and since my elder sister, Ann, was married and brought her husband home to live with us, I have to toil more assiduously than heretofore."

"And by what means do you obtain a livelihood?" exclaimed the man, in slowly measured and grammatical words.

"By digging wells, kind sir," replied George, picking up a tired ant as he spoke and stroking it on the back. "I have a good education, and so I am able to dig wells as well as a man. I do this day-times and take in washing at night. In this way I am enabled barely to maintain our family in a precarious manner; but, oh, sir, should my other sisters marry, I fear that some of my brothers-in-law would have to suffer."

"And do you not fear the deadly fire-damp?" asked the stranger in an earnest tone.

"Not by a damp sight," answered George, with a low gurgling laugh, for he was a great wag.

"You are indeed a brave lad," exclaimed the stranger, as he repressed a smile. "And do you not at times become very weary and wish for other ways of passing your time?"

"Indeed, I do, sir," said the lad. "I would fain run and romp and be gay like other boys, but I must engage in constant manual exercise, or we will have no bread to eat, and I have not seen a pie since papa perished in the moist and moaning sea."

"And what if I were to tell you that your papa did not perish at sea, but was saved from a humid grave?" asked the stranger in pleasing tones.

"Ah, sir," exclaimed George, in a genteel manner,

again doffing his cap, "I am too polite to tell you what I would say, and besides, sir, you are much larger than I am."

"But, my brave lad," said the man in low musical tones, "do you not know me, Georgie? Oh, George!"

"I must say," replied George, "that you have the advantage of me. Whilst I may have met you before, I cannot at this moment place you, sir."

"My son! oh, my son!" murmured the man, at the same time taking a large strawberry mark out of his valise and showing it to the lad. "Do you not recognize your parent on your father's side? When our good ship went to the bottom, all perished save me. I swam several miles through the billows, and at last, utterly exhausted, gave up all hope of life. Suddenly I stepped on something hard. It was the United States.

"And now, my brave boy," exclaimed the man with great glee, "see what I have brought for you." It was but the work of a moment to unclasp from a shawl-strap which he held in his hand and present to George's astonished gaze a large forty-cent watermelon, which until now had been concealed by the shawl-strap.

* * * * *

From BILL NYE *and* BOOMERANG, *Belford, Clarke & Co., Publishers,* 1884.

THE RELENTLESS GARDEN HOSE

IT is now the proper time for the cross-eyed woman to fool with the garden hose. I have faced death in almost every form and I do not know what fear is, but when a woman with one eye gazing into the zodiac and the other peering into the middle of next week and wearing one of those large floppy sun bonnets, picks up the nozzle of the garden hose and turns on the full force of the institution, I fly wildly to the Mountains of Hepsidam.

Water won't hurt anyone of course if care is used not to forget and drink any of it, but it is the horrible suspense and uncertainty about facing the nozzle of a garden hose in the hands of a cross-eyed woman that unnerves me and paralyzes me.

Instantaneous death is nothing to me. I am as cool and collected where leaden rain and iron hail are thickest, as I would be in my own office writing the obituary of the man who steals my jokes. But I hate to be drowned slowly in my good clothes and on dry land and have my dying gaze rest on a woman whose ravishing beauty would drive a narrow-gauge mule into convulsions and make him hate himself to death.

AN ANTI-MORMON TOWN

A MORMON missionary turned himself loose in Rawlins the other night and attempted to proselyte the good people into getting another invoice of wives to assist in taking off the chill of the approaching winter; but there was a feeling in the audience that the man who represented the church of the Latter Day Saints was a little off in addressing them, so they went to a dealer in old and rare antiquities and purchased some eggs that had a smell which is peculiar to eggs that have yielded to the infirmities of age.

The Rawlins people raised the windows on the sides of the building and broke eleven and one-half dozen out of a possible twelve dozen of these eggs, which had been coined in the year of the great crash. It was the year when so many hens were not feeling well.

They broke them against the brass collar button of the orator, and they ran down in graceful little brooklets and rivulets and squiblets and driblets over his white lawn tie and boiled shirt.

Rawlins is not strictly a Mormon town, and the lecturer who took some clothes through in a valise the other day bound for Evanston, where he could get them washed, was arrested by a New York detective who was sure he had at last caught the man who had Stewart's body.

George W. Peck

ALTHOUGH born in Henderson, N. Y., in 1840, George W. Peck was distinctly a Wisconsin product. His parents came to Wisconsin in 1843 and settled in Walworth County. Young Peck learned the printer's trade in Whitewater; thus launching himself into his life work. For some years he shifted his field of activity at frequent intervals. We find him connected with the *Jefferson County Republican*, the *Ripon Representative* and the *La Crosse Democrat*, in which latter venture he was associated with "Brick" Pomeroy. Up to the time he was elected Governor of Wisconsin, Mr. Peck was continuously in newspaper work with the exception of three years—from 1863 to 1866, when he served in the Union army.

Mr. Peck finally located in Milwaukee and there established *Peck's Sun* which soon became widely known as a humorous publication. The "Bad Boy" series caught the popular fancy and Peck became a household name. The democratic leaders capitalized his wide acquaintance with the reading public and elected him mayor of Milwaukee in 1890. About this time the parochial school question became a bitter political issue. The Democratic party stood for non-interference; Mr. Peck was their candidate for governor and was elected after a spirited campaign. In this exalted position he served two terms after which he resumed his residence in Milwaukee. He died April 16, 1916.

Peck did not rank with Bill Nye as a humorist. His work was less widely known and lacked the delicate touch of irony through which Nye attempted to show Americans some of their idiosyncrasies.

From PECK'S SUNSHINE, *By George W. Peck*

BOUNCED FROM CHURCH FOR DANCING

THE Presbyterian synod at Erie, Pa., has turned a lawyer named Donaldson out of the church. The charge against him was not that he was a lawyer, as might be supposed, but that he had danced a quadrille. It does not seem to us as though there could be anything more harmless than dancing a cold-blooded quadrille. It is a simple walk around and is not even exercise. Of course a man can, if he chooses, get in extra steps enough to keep his feet warm, but we contend that no quadrille, where they only touch hands, go down in the middle, and alamand left, can work upon a man's religion enough to cause him to backslide.

If it was this new "waltz quadrille" that Donaldson indulged in, where there is intermittant hugging, and where the head gets to whirling, and a man has to hang on to his partner quite considerable, to keep from falling all over himself, and where she looks up fondly into his eyes and as though telling him to squeeze just as hard as it seemed necessary for his convenience, we should not wonder so much at the synod hauling him over the coals for cruelty to himself, but a cold quadrille has no deviltry in it.

We presume the wicked and perverse Mr. Donaldson will join another church that allows dancing judiciously administered, and may yet get to heaven ahead of the Presbyterian synod, and he may be elected to some high position there, as Arthur was here, after the synod of Hayes and Sherman had bounced him from the Custom House for dancing the great spoils walk around.

It is often the case here, and we do not know why it

may not be in heaven, that the ones that are turned over and shook up, and the dust knocked out of them, and their metaphorical coat tail filled with boots, find that the whirligig of time has placed them above the parties who smote them, and we can readily believe that if Donaldson gets a first-class position of power, above the skies, he will make it decidedly warm for his persecutors when they come up to the desk with their grip sacks and register and ask for a room with a bath and a fire escape. He will be apt to look up at the key rack and tell them everything is full, but they can find pretty fair accommodations at the other house, down at Hot Springs, on the European plan, by Mr. Devil, formerly of Chicago.

UNSCREWING THE TOP OF A FRUIT JAR

THERE is one thing that there should be a law passed about, and that is these glass fruit jars, with a top that screws on. It should be made a criminal offense, punishable with death or banishment to Chicago, for a person to manufacture a fruit jar, for preserving fruit, with a top that screws on. Those jars look nice when the fruit is put in them, and the housewife feels as though she was repaid for all her perspiration over a hot stove, as she looks at the glass jars of different berries, on the shelf in the cellar.

The trouble does not begin until she has company, and decides to tap a little of her choice fruit. After the supper is well under way, she sends for a jar, and tells the servant to unscrew the top and pour the fruit into a dish. The girl brings it into the kitchen and proceeds to unscrew the top. She works gently at first, then gets mad, wrenches at it, sprains her wrist, and begins to cry, with her nose on the underside of her apron, and skins her nose on the dried pancake batter that is hidden in the folds of the apron.

Then the little housewife takes hold of the fruit can,

smilingly, and says she will show the girl how to take off the top. She sits down on the wood-box, takes the glass jar between her knees, runs out her tongue, and twists. But the cover does not twist. The cover seems to feel as though it was placed there to keep guard over that fruit, and it is as immovable as the Egyptian pyramids. The little lady works until she is red in the face, and until her crimps all come down, and then she sets it away to wait for the old man to come home. He comes in tired, disgusted, and mad as a hornet, and when the case is laid before him, he goes out in the kitchen, pulls off his coat and takes the jar.

He remarks that he is at a loss to know what women are made for anyway. He says they are all right to sit around and do crochet work, but when strategy, brains, and muscle are required, then they can't get along without a man. He tries to unscrew the cover, and his thumb slips off and knocks the skin off the knuckle. He breathes a silent prayer and calls for the kerosene can, and pours a little oil into the crevice and lets it soak, and then he tries again, and swears audibly.

Then he calls for a tack hammer, and taps the cover gently on one side, the glass jar breaks, and the juice runs down his trousers leg, on the table and all around. Enough of the fruit is saved for supper, and the old man goes up the back stairs to tie his thumb up in a rag, and change his pants.

All come to the table smiling, as though nothing had happened, and the housewife don't allow any of the family to have any sauce for fear they will get broken glass in their stomachs, but the "company" is provided for generously, and all would be well only for a remark of a little boy who, who when asked if he would have some more of the sauce, says he "don't want no strawberries pickled in kerosene." The smiling little hostess steals a smell of the sauce, while they are discussing politics, and believes she does smell kerosene, and she looks at the old man kind of spunky, when he glances at the rag on his thumb and asks if there is no liniment in the house.

The preserving of fruit in glass jars is broken up in that house, and four dozen jars are down cellar to lay upon the lady's mind till she gets a chance to send some of them to a charity picnic. The glass jar fruit can business is played out unless a scheme can be invented to get the top off.

Marcus Mills Pomeroy

☼

MARCUS M. POMEROY, popularly known as "Brick Pomeroy," was born in Elmira, N. Y., December 25, 1833. After serving his apprenticeship in a printing establishment he came to Horicon, Wisconsin, in 1857 where he conducted a paper known as *The Argus*. At successive periods he was editor of the *Daily News* in Milwaukee and of the *Union Democrat* in La Crosse. He returned to New York after the Civil War where he engaged in journalistic work. Pomeroy was widely known in his day as a popular humorist; at the present time his work is all but forgotten. Best known of his books are "Gold Dust," "Brick Dust" and "Perpetual Money." He died in Brooklyn, N. Y., May 30, 1896.

APPENDIX

While this work does not attempt to cover writers of text books, technical works, or the occasional book written by lesser authors, a partial list of such writers is here given. Many of the writers in this list have produced work of exceptional merit. Even this appended list is far from complete because of inability to assemble all deserving names.

CHARLES R. VAN HISE, Madison. (*Technical works in geology*)

E. A. BIRGE, Madison. (*Technical works covering biological subjects*)

T. C. CHAMBERLAIN, Madison. (*Technical works in the field of geology*)

CHARLES E. BROWN, Madison. (*Works on Indian antiquities*)

H. E. COLE, Baraboo. (*Antiquities and early Wisconsin history*)

A. O. BARTON, Madison. (*Winning of Wisconsin, and other works*)

WILLIAM DAWSON, Milwaukee. (*Poems*)

WALTER HEWITT, Oshkosh. (*Text books*)

MATHILDE G. SCHLEY, Milwaukee. (*German language works*)

H. W. ECHARDT, Oshkosh. (*Accounting in the Lumber Industry*)

H. R. HOLAND, Ephraim. (*Old Peninsula Days*)

GEORGE B. MERRICK, (*Old Times on the Upper Mississippi*)

GEORGE L. TEEPLE, Whitewater. (*Short Stories*)

CHARLES K. LUSH, Milwaukee. (*The Federal Judge, The Autocrats, etc.*)

ELMORE E. PEAKE, Lake Geneva. (*Several works of fiction*)

GEORGE W. PECKHAM, Milwaukee. (*Magazine articles*)

CHARLES A. KEELER, Milwaukee. (*Poems and bird books*)

HENRY E. LEGLER, Milwaukee. (*Historical sketches and magazine articles*)

ALGIE E. SIMONS, Milwaukee. (*Socialist publications*)

ALBERT H. SANFORD, La Crosse. (*Text books and historical sketches*)

ELLIOTT FLOWER, Madison. (*Works of fiction*)

CHARLES KENDALL ADAMS, Madison. (*History and biography*)

WILLIAM FRANCIS ALLEN, Madison. (*Essays*)

JOHN BASCOM, Madison. (*Essays*)

CONSUL W. BUTTERFIELD, (*Historical works*)

JAMES F. A. PYRE, Madison. (*Works on literature*)

HORATIO WINSLOW, Madison. (*Poems*)

MYRA GOODWIN PLANTZ, Appleton. (*Poems*)

JOHN HICKS, Oshkosh, (*The Man from Oshkosh*)

RALPH G. PLUMB, Manitowoc. (*Badger Politics*)

MARY GRANT O'SHERIDAN, (*Poems*)

RICHARD LLOYD JONES, (*Essays*)

MRS. JOHN KINZIE, (*Waubun*)